ELIS

Irish Callgirl

CH00684389

Anna Rajmon
Based On A True Story
+18

Table of Contents

Dedication

This book owes its existence to the amazing people around me who always keep their hearts full and their eyes open. A big thank you to all the kind-hearted souls who inspire us to do better daily!

About the Author

Anna, originally from the Czech Republic, has experienced a life full of challenging moments. Despite her education and achieving high professional positions, she eventually found herself in an unexpected situation where she decided to enter the world of prostitution to provide for her daughter. This dramatic turn in her life led her to write a book that could inspire people worldwide with her story. She aims to illuminate a world many are curious about, but few truly understand. Through her story, she also seeks to caution girls who are considering entering the world of escorting and to highlight the shameful behaviour and dangers associated with this lifestyle. Anna hopes that her book will bring awareness and change and that it can help those who find themselves in similar situations to the one she experienced.

Author s Note

Many writers add an intelligent sentence or paragraph at the beginning of their book. Some try to immortalise their words or contextualise by stating that their mind stands behind every line. I have been contemplating my own attempt at such clever remarks for a long time.

In the end, I came to the conclusion that no philosophical motivational quota can capture what I tried to achieve by writing this book. First of all, it is essential to realise that this is a real story. Not just a story that happened but rather one that is still unfolding.

Many people are blind and deaf to the problems that do not concern them personally, or those they like to pretend do not concern them.

But are you sure it does not concern you? How many secrets hide behind a seemingly carefree facade? How well do you know your loved ones? How many of them pay for sexual services? It could be your husband, friend, brother, your best friend's fiancé, Brian from next door or the guy you went on a date with yesterday.

Who provides sexual services? Is it your daughter, who claims to be studying abroad, your fiancée, who started working nights as a waitress, your wife or your girlfriend who travels abroad too often and comes home every fourteen days? How many girls sell their bodies in the buildings you pass on your way to work? How many girls are often forced behind closed doors to do such things? How many women are attacked and sexually abused in this context every day, even just a few meters from you, and you do not know about it?

I'm not trying to convince you that something like this applies to everyone around you, but it is important to realise that it could apply to them, and one day, it could directly affect you. Those women are not just numbers; they are human beings who suffer, and many of them do not want to be where they are. Please, do not be deaf and blind to the suffering of others.

For girls who are considering a career as a prostitute and may believe that they would only do this job temporarily, this 'career 'is not temporary, but forever! Many spend "temporarily" forty years of their lives in this industry. Others who managed to escape face the consequences of their decision for a lifetime, and the pain they carry accompanies them every step. The parts of you that it takes away, you will never be able to replace! We all long for "shiny" things, but is it really worth it? Success has many forms, but paid sex will never lead you to it. Maybe other paths are more complicated, but they are worth it more!

Introduction

When I was a little girl, I lived in a beautiful town, and a river flowed beneath our house. As children, we loved playing in the unpredictable flow and discovering its secrets.

When it was calm, everything was easy; we built dams, waded in the water up to our knees, jumped from rock to rock, and enjoyed everything that this small natural oasis offered us. Sometimes, I played there alone for hours, and other times, my dad took me there to swim on hot summer days. I came from a low-income family and grew up in a land without any sea; I had never seen it, and to me, as a child, it was my biggest dream. Other girls wanted ponies, but I longed to gaze at the seemingly endless water from a sandy beach. Well, everyone has their priorities.

During a walk along the river, I held my dad's hand, and the farther we went, the more impatient I became; asking, "Are we going to the sea soon? Is the sea just around that bend?" a high-pitched, annoying, childlike voice whispered. Patiently, my dad tried to explain that we would have to walk for many days to reach the sea, but it was as if I didn't hear him, and I eagerly asked questions about only that one topic. I knew where I wanted to go and where I was heading, and the geographic layout couldn't stop me. I never lost hope, and every day, I walked a little further along the river, hoping that one day I would get there, that one day I would overcome all obstacles and face the high waves with my feet sinking into the wet sand, with the reflection of the setting sun in my eyes beyond the horizon. I didn't dwell on the complexities that might come my way, the language barrier, or the fact that I might be all alone there. When I closed my eyes, all I saw was that goal; I never pondered how I would achieve it.

Walking along the river long enough sounded like a sufficient plan in my head. There are so many changes as you grow up; you start to notice the journey, and reaching the destination often becomes impossible. "You listen to that ugly voice in your head that makes you doubt yourself. You can't handle it, you're too weak," and so over time, you choose a path that you don't necessarily desire, but it's easier and more acceptable. Fear overwhelms you, and that fearless child you once were is gone.

I've fulfilled my childhood dream many times, standing by the sea, the salty water whipping my face, witnessing countless sunsets beyond the horizon, yet something was missing from that child I once was. I wanted to find within myself that smiling, annoying blonde girl who loved jumping in puddles and was afraid of nothing.

The river beneath our house is still the same, and so is the sun that shines in my eyes by it, the same sun I saw in foreign lands, but my perspective has changed. I look at the stones I used to jump on only from a distance; they are still the same. They haven't grown, but my mind is no longer as open to adventure. My brain whispers terrible things to me, banal logical considerations that were not there before: "Your foot will slip, you'll fall and drown," and as I extend my foot, the thoughts become darker and darker, "fractured leg, skull, arms, internal bleeding, cardiac arrest, shock, drowning…" and I obediently retract my foot and continue walking.

As children, we have dreams, desires, and goals, and no obstacles exist; we can fly if we want to. Adulthood limits us; we only fly in dreams, and even then, we wake up in the morning shaken with horror, wondering what the hell happened. Then we check if we have all our limbs whilst wiping sweat from our foreheads and convincing ourselves that "nothing like that ever happened." If I could go back and be that tiny, innocent soul again, I would do so many things differently, but going back is impossible, and I have to live with what I have. I've taken countless missteps and experienced much, but all my decisions have led me to where I am and allowed me to be the person I am. This book is my way of giving you a small glimpse into my story. I'll show you many mistakes I've made, some out of fear, a fear which comes with a backpack on its back into our lives at a certain age, settles in, and becomes a part of you without giving you time to think. It becomes your best friend, always there for you in moments when you least need it. Some mistakes were out of stupidity, others out of desperation, and the rest for incomprehensible reasons that are still a mystery to me. I've never been good at planning; I stuck to plan 'A' and hoped that everything would somehow work out. Who needs plan 'B' when you can have a life full of intriguing twists and surprises? For someone who seeks adrenaline, I definitely recommend strictly sticking to plan 'A' under all circumstances and hoping that it will work out eventually. It's good to know your options and limits and accept life experiences that teach you where your boundaries lie. It took me a while to accept what I've been through; I'm still unsure if I managed to absorb everything that happened. My personal demons haunt me in nightmares at night, and in everyday life situations, my friend 'fear 'appears to remind me of the traces of the past. The past disrupts my presence and ability to concentrate.

When someone talks to me, often an image of something negative that happened appears before my eyes, and their words slowly vanish into the air. It's quite challenging to concentrate on a story about flower gardening when someone is beating you with a belt and choking you in your vivid memories. On the other hand, there are positives; I'm learning to be a master of pretence. Most of the time, I'm able to remember the last two sentences a person said and continue from there, so the person doesn't even notice that they've been monologuing almost the entire time. The whole world of prostitution is a twisted business, and it changed me in incredible ways. I can't pretend it didn't happen; for almost four years, I was a puppet of greedy women and a toy for men who don't consider sexual workers as human beings but merely as objects for satisfaction. Every day was a fight for survival, a life in fear that was reinforced by the agency that desired nothing but hefty earnings. Can you imagine being raped, beaten, lying on a bed in tears, and simply swallowing the suffering that happened to you and standing in a humiliating outfit by the door smiling at your next 'owner, 'who decided to rent your body for the next few dozen minutes? I wouldn't wish it upon anyone to experience. I didn't run away from any of it; now, it haunts me, and forgetting seems impossible. It's like a walk in Jurassic Park; you're on alert, waiting for the shadows of the past to devour you alive. I drew energy from sunrises when I walked into the quiet Irish streets and felt the scent of a few hours of false freedom. Sometimes I went to church, helped people I met, bought breakfast for the homeless, fully aware that it could be worse, and my situation isn't that bad compared to others. Helping someone who truly needed it helped me reconcile with myself. It flooded my heart with comfort and tranquillity, a strange sense of joy from brightening someone's day, even if just for a moment. Sometimes, it's essential to know that the whole world is not against you, and even small miracles happen. Often, a single smile from a stranger is enough to give you courage and show you that the world can be as good as it is bad.

In my words, you may occasionally notice a hint of sarcasm; I have this superpower of trivialising the complexity of situations when they are emotionally challenging for me. After all, we all love it when someone tells us the truth with a bit of exaggeration. I left a fair part of my soul in Ireland, and now I'm trying to reclaim it, hoping I might succeed one day. Maybe I'll never be that little fearless girl again, but hopefully, one day, I'll muster the courage to jump on those rocks by our river and at least get a little closer to the brave little girl I once was. Allow me to further introduce you to my story and to bring you closer to the world most of you may have distorted ideas about. The intention of this book is not to harm anyone but to shed yet more light on the world we live in. Despite the fact that most of the stories in the book fall into my worst experiences, many men visit girls for understandable reasons, mainly because they feel lonely. Many of them treated me with respect and kindness, and there were nice individuals among them. In describing some events, I had to delve deep into the past, re-read messages I had written down, and searched for information. I listened to various voice recordings I made shortly after painful events. This book took over three long years to write, and during the process of documenting my experiences, I had to face anxiety and panic attacks several times. It wasn't uncommon for me to get up from the computer, walk around the room, and take deep breaths. Memories wouldn't let me focus; cold sweat covered my back, tears filled my eyes, and my hands shook. My throat tightened, breathing became difficult, and my chest felt heavy, as if someone had placed a massive boulder on me. Experiences I usually don't think about and try to forget were revived so that you could read about them today and see how difficult such a life can be. Every day, I fight again with all my might. It's not the trauma that defines us but how we choose to face it and how we decide to move forward. I'll probably never come to terms with the pain I carry within me, but not succumbing to it and focusing on the positive things life offers every day; I consider at least limited success. During my time in this business, I've gone through three names, and Elis was the one I used in Ireland. Girls often have fictional names primarily to protect their privacy and to separate this 'profession 'from their private lives. I pondered for a long time whether to publish this book under my real name, but I concluded that sooner or later, my true identity would be revealed. Elis, in a way kept me protected and separated the world of prostitution from my private life, but I never managed to split it entirely. What is done is done, and despite burying my past along with Elis long time ago, I still have to live with that part of me and who I was. So, despite the fact that the decision to admit my real name wasn't easy, mainly because I wanted to protect my loved ones, I realised that it's important to acknowledge who we were and move forward with the best version of ourselves. Ultimately, our past always catches up with us, but our future self can face it with our heads up!

I'd like to think that my story serves informatively but perhaps also as a warning to many who may be affected by it. During my time in this business, I encountered many questions about my profession. These questions were mostly repetitive, but the principle remained the same. Everyone was interested in the structure, the stories I would rather forget; what kind of girls perform this 'job 'without the fake smile?

A small taste of a world covered in shame and prejudice is encapsulated in this book. I tried to write everything as honestly and accurately as I remember it. Individual names are changed for obvious reasons, nonetheless, I attempt to offer a detailed description not only of situations but also of places and of people so that the reader can touch my past and taste a small portion of the world that is closer to us than we think.

Chapter One: Love and Other Missteps

Wouldn't it be great if newborn babies were given a "life manual" right after birth? Imagine how much easier our lives would be if we had such a treasure. This manual would provide options for all life situations, with countless solutions listed under each scenario. It would be a real lifesaver! Unfortunately, no one ever gave me such a thing!

So, like every ordinary mortal, I make mistakes that positively or negatively influence my life. If such a manual existed, the first page would indeed contain life advice such as: "Never trust men" or "Everyone lies". Now, I sound like that guy from the TV series House, but that limping weirdo had aspects of truth. Starting today, my life began to be much more interesting.

Well, I could not complain about the diversity of life events so far. However, today, something happened that probably influenced me forever. It was simply a stunning morning, with a tropical heatwave in Dublin that raised the temperature up to around 20 degrees, and my partner woke me up with the sentence: "It's a boy, a boy; I've been trying to wake you up for ages…"

Subsequently, I saw pictures of a creature that I knew nothing about, but I knew that from now on, this little boy would change my life beyond recognition. You guessed right; it definitely wasn't my child, but my partner had become a father in the past twelve hours.

Gentlemen, there is no better sentence with which you can wake up your girlfriend; I recommend trying it at home. After swallowing the pill of bitterness and endless hours of feigned excitement, I spent some time lying on the bathroom floor in a fetal position, devoting myself to my tears. How did this happen? I keep asking myself this question repeatedly, constantly replaying the situation in my head, but I still don't know the answer. If I haven't bored you to death yet, I should go back to the beginning of this story; I just don't know where to start. Perhaps your roots predetermine the choice of life partners; maybe up there stands a tall bearded man, puffing on a pipe, holding a list, and sending babies into the world, and this man writes a note for each child. If that's the case, my paper probably said something like "creator of life's mistakes" or "whatever can go wrong in your life, it will."

Well, I could start telling you about how I was born, grew up, miraculously made it to this day, or just cut to the essential moments of my life, which are the ten thousand things I messed up. To truly understand the impulsiveness of my nonsensical decisions and life mistakes, you must get to know me a little bit. I come from a loving family in a small town in the Czech Republic. Sometimes, my parents loved alcohol more than their children, but I can't complain about a lack of love. Despite the modest income, we had each other, or at least occasionally. Such a childhood toughens you up; you learn to cook, stoke the fire in the stoves, shower in icy water, shoot a gun, or change your brother's diaper. Basically, you can do a little of everything, and you think you have a good foundation for life. I quickly understood that life is a cocktail full of good things, but occasionally, someone throws in something disgusting.

The key to success is to mix this cocktail so well that it has a balanced taste and never leaves only just a bitter aftertaste and also to pour in enough vodka to make everything look more favourable. I lived like an average child; if we skip everything, that is not anyone's business; at fourteen, I found my first summer job. I started working at the church, a beautiful place full of history, compelling people to ponder the depths of life.

At this age, you think about depths of all sorts quite often, so it's no wonder I fell for a local priest as much as a teenage girl can fall for a middle-aged man. I spent days and evenings there just to be close to him. I wished he would love me as much as he was in love with God, but as you can probably guess, that didn't happen. He was perhaps the first and last man in my life who promised me nothing and, therefore, did not disappoint me. However, he was also the first realisation that you can't always have what you want, and unrequited love hurts. I then started to take an interest in boys in my age group who had not decided to sacrifice their genitals for a life in a decaying historical building. Full of expectations, I entered a relationship with a boy two years older than me. You know how it is, the first love that never ends, love that lasts forever? That was it, the first mutual love, and then I was off, a year-long relationship full of pain and happiness. The first experience when my partner told me he had been unfaithful, but with hindsight, I must say, compared to my subsequent discoveries, this guy had character. I remember it like it was yesterday: after a beautiful love-making session in an abandoned cabin somewhere in the woods. Well, teenagers don't have much choice when it comes to love locations. He leaned over to me, kissed me, and said, "Sweetheart, I have to tell you something; I slept with my ex a few days ago." To say something like that to your girlfriend requires courage, balls, and the expectation that you'll get punched into them. Well, that punch ended my relationship with someone who felt the need to share something that was promised only to me. Do you notice the word 'EX'? Yes, exactly, it's something from the past, something you once decided to leave lying somewhere and definitely shouldn't be picked up and dragged into the present. It's like throwing out everything you don't need, but then you start missing the old milk carton, so you go to the dump looking for your old, gross, mouldy, empty piece of trash.

Once it's thrown away, let someone else take it to recycling! After this breakup, I felt like a knight who had won the war; of course, I was totally above it all, and my armour was a ton of ice cream, chocolate, and dozens of `tissue boxes emptied at the speed of light. So, I moved past the pain and suffering that my first relationship brought me. And how do you best learn from your own mistakes? By making even bigger, better and more significant mistakes. One beautiful evening, an event took place that reliably attracted every alcoholic in the region. Everyone pretended to be more important than the others, hiding behind titles, evening gowns, and fake smiles as they celebrated the birthday of one of the local business people. I happened to be there entirely by accident. Do you remember the priest from the church? That old scar of mine asked me if I could help him with the preparation of this auspicious party, and I agreed. Why should I not have agreed, too? I was just over sixteen, a young, single teenager who knew she would have access to

3

alcohol in the evening and no one would be offended. I had no idea what I had agreed to. That event was very boring for my former self; I couldn't understand the conversations of the people around me, so I went to sit in the inner garden. I was convinced I would finish my drink and leave, but as many of you know, this statement is not a guarantee of anything, and the direct translation of "finish the drink and leave" means "watch the football and have another six beers." However, I, as a friendly, young, and responsible girl would definitely have stuck to my resolutions if 'he 'had not appeared there. This guy, let's call him Peter, sat next to me. Given that we shared the same feelings about this celebration and both of us were practically there by mistake, we came to the conclusion that we should exclusively maintain our conversation together. That guy completely charmed me; he was witty, kind, appeared intelligent, and that suit looked so good on him! At that moment, I had absolutely no idea that he would be my future - now ex-husband, that he would be the father of my child, or that he would give me many new captivating experiences and a million reasons to leave him. When you meet someone new, there should always be a short video about them, something like a quick preview of that person's life. Can you imagine that? You press "play", and you know everything! It would be ideal if, for a reasonable fee, this video also included a sequel called: "What happens if I stay with this person?"

Think about your ex-partners and ask yourself if that wouldn't make your life easier in several aspects. Activating the video would be voluntary, although, for some beings, it would be completely unnecessary. Regardless of how much the world sometimes warns us, we simply bulldoze through that advice headlong because why not just try it and enjoy life to the fullest extent possible? As I have already mentioned, everyone lies!

"I know what's best for me", and then comes the armour in the form of ice cream, chocolate, alcohol, napkins and romantic movies. Anyway, there was no video about Peter, and so I found myself in the presence of a charismatic individual inclined towards silly jokes without any warning. Oh, those beginnings, you constantly believe that this is it, what you have been looking for all this time, and never, never, honestly think that anything could happen to make you change your mind, at least until you see the truth.

When I met Peter, it never crossed my mind that anything between us could change or go wrong, but as it usually happens, things started to appear that showed me that he might not be the one I had imagined for a lifetime. Several months after we met, it turned out that my father had cancer and he had to go to the hospital for a longer period. I was studying then, and every family member was having a hard time dealing with this situation. I always had a pleasant relationship with my father, so this misfortune probably affected me much more than the other members of my family. At the same time, I was experiencing teenage infatuation and omnipresent puberty. One beautiful Friday afternoon, when I came home from school, I told my mom I would sleep at Peter's place. I didn't ask for permission; I took it for granted, she had to accept it. However, she did not reconcile with the situation at all. I was strictly forbidden to go anywhere; I was supposed to stay home, study, and not do anything inappropriate, forbidden, or natural for my age.

If I had listened to her back then, everything in my life would probably be different today, but I am my father's daughter and thus inherited only the finest qualities. I was stubborn, arrogant and didn't let anything be forbidden. After attempting to negotiate with my mother, which is, was, and always will be impossible to win, I started packing my things, saying that I had the full right to do so.

My mother ended this heated situation by saying, "If you leave, don't return."

This was serious; it required thinking, taking appropriate steps and maybe discussing it with Peter. However, my stubbornness knew no bounds, so I packed what I could, replied to my mother: "Anything is better than living under the same roof with such a hag," and ran away. I was deeply offended! I remember sitting outside with Peter on a bench, explaining to him the detailed seriousness of the situation by saying,

"Do you understand that, the cow kicked me out?"

The continuation of this diplomatic conversation went on in a similar tone until Peter accepted the fact that I will be living with him. I was surprised when the first stop of our long journey started at his father's apartment, and for a long time, I couldn't understand why I ended up there. Despite Peter being over twenty years old, his father was eighty years old, his apartment smelled awful, and his father's war stories at that time were about as interesting to me as math at school. The paradox is that today, I would like to hear those stories, but unfortunately, there is no opportunity for that anymore. For some reason, Peter left me in that den for over two hours, saying he needed to take care of something. Of course, I tried to be polite because it was his father, but that visit drained all my energy. Don't get me wrong, I deeply admire older people, but at that time, I was sixteen years old and my brain functioned as naturally as it does for a girl at that age. When Peter picked me up, I went to his place, and since then, we lived happily ever after. Ha ha, no! The happy ending did not happen! We got used to living together; during my studies, I visited my father in the hospital daily and tried to play the role of a model girlfriend. I cooked, cleaned, did laundry and of course we had a lot, a lot, really a lot of sex. Well, I was a woman, as I should be, although very young. As for my cooking, at that time, I was still learning, and most of my dishes ended with an additional step: pour into the toilet while stirring continuously. However, my knight in shining armour started misbehaving somewhat, and I suspect it wasn't due to my culinary skills. Almost every evening, he wasn't at home, never sent a text, never answered his phone, was never there for me when I needed him. Damn, now I realise that history repeats itself, but more about that later. About six months into our relationship, we had afternoon coffee with his best friend. I didn't particularly like that guy, but he was his best friend, and I wanted him to like me. It had been six months since Peter and I had been together, so it was an appropriate time to ask where I stood, so I posed the question: "What do you actually think about me?" The answer was surprising: "You're nice, but it annoyed me a bit when Peter left my sister because of you."

"Uh, what? Excuse me? Sorry, how because of me, what's going on here?" Suddenly, my mind was flooded with an excessive number of questions. I did not know about any sister then, let alone replacing someone. This led to a fascinating conversation, which reaffirmed my belief that the male species is a kind in which more than the necessary amount of trust should not be placed to maintain a relationship. However, alarm bells rang in my head, and I wanted to know more, so I asked. In the end, I found out that the day when I had to stick around at his father's place, Peter had his hands full because he was in the process of evicting his girlfriend from the apartment. And those evenings when he wasn't with me, and I was at home alone, closed off and crying, those nights he was with her. That hurt and broke my heart in half. I should have gathered myself and left, gone back home, and left it all behind, but as you might have guessed, I didn't. My ability for naive stupidity, which I have allowed myself to keep to this day, knows no bounds. Unfortunately, God gifted me with some strange inclination to believe that things will change and to seek out the good in people, even despite how badly they mess up.

You simply take a small hammer to crush all the pain within you, lock it up in an iron box, and then throw away the key. So, I was offended and unpleasant for a few days, but then I tried to patch things up with the hope that it would get better. Well, wasn't I naive girl?

People don't change, especially not because of something they've done, but you forgive and pretend like nothing happened. Yes, of course, he was nice for a while, but honestly, no one wants a nice guy for just a few days. If that were the case, there would have long been a rental service for guys. It would be called "Rent the Good One" or something similar. You would go there, set your criteria, and then choose something with good performance and a nice exterior. You would peek under the hood, make sure it doesn't have a severe exhaust gas issue, which I personally consider essential, and ensure that it doesn't guzzle too much fuel. As a final step, you would find out how much mileage it has and rent it for the weekend because you want a pleasant ride and to relax. But have you ever seen something like that? No! Exactly! So we, women, have to make do with catching males about whom we know nothing and hope that it will be the right one without having any information on its technical condition or previous owners. If we return from my romantic musings back to Peter, he didn't change; in fact, it was even worse. He started drinking heavily, was hardly ever at home, and my youthful naivety prohibited me from accepting the fact that a happy relationship doesn't look like this. How can you best convince yourself that you are in the wrong relationship? Well, of course, you get pregnant! Nausea from the smell of goulash and a one-week menstrual delay indicates that something sinister is happening in your belly, and for a change, it's not related to intestinal problems. The pregnancy test was the only appropriate solution, even though Peter was against me peeing on the stick of truth. Two minutes of endless waiting followed, which seemed like an eternity, and then the test revealed the reality of what was happening in my belly.

A little person was growing there! For some women, it's a miracle they've been waiting for for years, but for a seventeen-year-old girl, studying and in a not entirely fulfilled relationship, it was a nightmare. I must say that Peter accepted this fact very well despite my expectations. No, I'm just kidding! In fact, he didn't speak to me for three days. I didn't know what to think; I didn't know how to tell my parents; I didn't know anything. My vision of what I definitively wanted from life did not involve being a mother at the age of eighteen. Peter was talking a lot about an abortion and I was considering that it probably wasn't such a bad idea, although I wasn't very inclined towards it. In that situation, it seemed like a very convenient solution. Unfortunately, or fortunately, I can say that Czech legislation is not inclined for children to decide for themselves, so I was forced to discuss this fact with my mother. My mother is a very kind person, but sometimes she's headstrong, and she sees abortion as murder. In many aspects, I would agree with her, but not in my case. She commented on my decision with

9

the sentence, "You will give birth to that child even if I have to raise it myself!" Any attempts to change her mind were unsuccessful, so I found out who was in charge!

My mother looks a bit like a bear, a strong, fearless, determined woman capable of tearing a cow apart with her bare hands. Defying such a person goes against all laws of nature. Peter celebrated his excitement over the new addition every night until morning, and I was at home alone, drowning in mixed emotions. Typical female logic mainly consists of if a man doesn't want to speak to you, you just keep sending creepy messages and calling him until he changes his mind and perspective on the situation. However, this decision of mine had the opposite effect and reinforced his need to quell his frustration with alcohol. With a growing belly and an incapable alcoholic by my side, I had no idea what would follow; everything seemed far too challenging, and my desire for companionship led me to get a dog. This decision didn't receive much support from Peter, but this little dog is now a part of my family and ultimately the only guy in the world who has never let me down and never broken a promise to me. Unlike a man, he'll always be excited to see me, even if I lock him in the car boot for hours. My dog never implies in the morning that I look ugly; on the contrary, he always enthusiastically licks my entire face when I wake up. When I take him for a walk, he never protests; he prefers a stroll over sitting with a beer on the couch watching a match. He's actually ideal for my life, but I consider him more of my second child than a partner of my dreams. Anyway, ladies, if you want to know the recipe for happiness and your partner is an incapable sloth, get a dog. He's the most faithful guy in my life.

Especially since I had him neutered, he hardly even looks at a female dog anymore. Maybe I should practice this with partners too, cut their balls off and hope for a better tomorrow. After some time, the anger would dissipate, and although this solution may seem mildly morbid, its results would be guaranteed. Anyway, Peter's testicles were never removed, and he changed before my eyes, just definitely not for the better if anything, the opposite. I was in tears every evening, standing by the window, watching my beloved seek solace in a half-litre of beer and worry more about maintaining his buzz rather than me. He started becoming aggressive towards everyone and everything around him, mostly towards me and the dog. With a pregnant belly, depending on a man who had transformed into someone else in recent months, still home alone and full of fear about the future, I was prone to depression. I couldn't take care of myself, couldn't envision being with the child at my parents. Thus, I remained in the apartment, weeping, hoping everything would change. Arguments were a daily occurrence; Peter grew increasingly aggressive, and one evening, it escalated into an ugly physical conflict. Peter returned home from the pub earlier, and I remember being happy, thinking something had changed, that we would finally be together and happy. However, that was a mistake, indeed! Barely had I settled into the chair when the usual cycle of painful reproaches began:

"I support you; you do nothing but study and take care of the dog. How do you think I feel?"

"You've ruined my life completely! Now, let's look at your reaction! How do you deal with problems? Of course, you cry"

Over time, you stop hearing all those words and just hear the sound of shouting. I understood that it was a difficult situation for him; I tried to handle it the best I could in my state. However, my dog perceived the shouting very well and wanted to protect me every time the father of my child tried to attack me. Peter always took him and threw him against the wall. Many times, I thought he was dead, and I was more afraid for him than for myself. I always started screaming and crying; in that situation, I needed to do something, but the feeling of helplessness was so strong it cannot be described. That fateful evening, when the dog ended up against the wall, I wanted to run to him, but before I could, I was stopped by a hand and thrown to the ground. He took my head in his hands and started hitting it against the concrete floor in the kitchen, which was covered with a thin layer of PVC, and kicked me a few times. I cried on the floor, holding my stomach; everything hurt. In the meantime, he was saying something, but I didn't hear the words. After that situation, I knew nothing could be the same as before, that nothing would ever be the same again. Similar experiences were more common until childbirth, and I had stopped believing that anything would change between us. The period of childbirth is one of the most beautiful and, at the same time, worst memories for me. I was overdue by a few days, and since my doctor didn't seem to like the sound of the baby's heartbeat, she sent me to the hospital for a check-up. I didn't leave the hospital after that; the doctors put a bracelet on my wrist, labelled me as "temporary hospital property," and turned me into a prisoner within the hospital walls and white coats. I called Peter to tell him what had happened, and surprisingly, he answered the phone; he sounded very kind and seemed to understand everything. The doctors decided to expedite the birth and gave me suspicious pills to survive for three days. It was a three-day long labour, where I could experience what contractions feel like and how I would feel on that fateful day. You see, when you weigh over a hundred kilograms; everything hurts; you can hardly walk, and someone puts their hand into you every day with the stupid look of a paedophile and says, 'not yet, mommy, 'so the only thing you think about is taking a pill that can cause even more pain. Yes, I wouldn't say I liked those pills, and what I hated even more was Peter's behaviour during this period. It was like a roller coaster with him; once, he supported me and stood by me, and then he scolded me for every little thing. Since the male ego knows no bounds, he needed to be present at everything, absolutely everything. Every morning at eight o'clock sharp, I got the aforementioned "happiness pill." Still, I had to devise a cunning strategy with the doctor to pretend that my body received this treatment in the afternoon when Peter could be at the hospital. That doctor was very nice, but she also wasn't happy for me and my relationship. If something didn't happen according to what my dear half imagined, it was bad and everything had consequences. One beautiful evening at seven o'clock, the extraordinary pains reappeared, but they escalated, and I knew it was happening. Unfortunately, none of the staff took me seriously after three days of endless attempts to induce something that definitely wasn't coming out of me.

The head nurse, with a syringe in hand, decided it was just pains from all those hormones and that if she injected this incredibly long needle into my backside, I'd feel better and might even get some sleep. But there wasn't any sleep that night. I walked around the room, took about ten showers, and couldn't wait for the morning check-up when someone would finally realise that the baby wanted to be on dry land for the last few hours, and swimming in the amniotic fluid was getting boring. The check-up revealed that I was dilated to three centimetres, and we needed to rupture the amniotic sac. Like the biggest badass, I sat in the chair, ready for the big moment, until the doctor pulled out scissors, which, probably yesterday, some giant used to trim his nails. My courage vanished without a goodbye, leaving me alone with the woman in the white coat and that monstrous steel tool. I would have peed myself at that moment and pretended that my water broke just to avoid having someone stick a meter-long pair of scissors into my vagina. I jumped out of the chair and told that murderous blonde that she definitely wouldn't be sticking that into me. She smiled and said, "But please, you won't even feel it."

It was tough to believe, but in my head, there was definitely an image that either the baby or I would feel it. After twenty minutes of arguing about why I didn't want this thing inside me, this Czech "Kill Bill" convinced me that I had to go through with it. In agony, I sat in the chair, turned my head to the other side, and with my eyes closed, I awaited brutal and sharp pain. Suddenly, all I heard was: "Done, we got it!" and I reassured myself that I probably wasn't the first one surprised by this equipment. When we arrived at the delivery room, the thought crossed my mind that Czech hospitals need a complete overhaul. It's an enjoyable environment where you have a room in which you see a frightening iron bed and a small bathroom. The room is lined with white tiles, reminiscent of a horror movie about a psychiatric hospital from the 1980s. There are doors to another room in the room because how could you properly enjoy this if you weren't screaming with some other lady suffering from pain, from whom a little person was emerging? When Peter arrived, we joked about it together, and I thought the birth was relatively easy. Since I was exhausted from a lack of sleep, I indulged in interrupted sleep from contraction to contraction for the first few hours of labour. After a few hours, the pains intensified, and I was surprised that Peter was still where he should be. The birth reached a stage where I couldn't lie down, I couldn't even walk anymore, I didn't know what to do. I remember desperately needing to pee, but damn, I couldn't do that either. I shuffled around the room at a snail's pace towards the shower to relieve the pain and then back to the room. After a while, some guy decided to lay me on the bed and shove his whole hand into me. They probably felt that it was not painful enough for me, and at that moment, exactly, the phase came when I screamed louder than the lady from the next room and regretted not letting them inject me with all the drugs they offered. Giving birth without analgesics is nonsense; if I ever have to go through this experience again, I swear I will come to the delivery room armed with all available medications! At this stage of childbirth, everything bothered me. First, I wanted slippers because the floor was too cold, but shortly after, I kicked them off. Then I wanted the lights off, but it was too dark, so it was necessary to turn them back on. The light switch in my room changed positions so often that it could almost file a criminal complaint for abuse. Women who claim that childbirth is the most beautiful thing in a woman's life are lying or were under the influence of powerful drugs and the assertion that someone would experience an orgasm during childbirth I also want to refute. In my opinion, it's not possible, and if it is, then be damn careful with such a woman because she evidently revels in pain and probably has sadomasochistic tendencies she didn't tell you about. After about eight hours of torture in the delivery room, where I fainted on the floor in pools of blood, they finally took me to the surgery room. I swear, if someone had told me at that moment to stab someone and the pain would disappear, I would have lovingly killed everyone present in that small room. Before going to the surgery room, they informed me that the pain actually led nowhere, and to improve the situation, they would cut open my abdomen and take out that little angel from there. At that moment, doctors gave me almost every available medication; interestingly, suddenly, it worked. Glucose to keep me from falling asleep, something to stop contractions, and many other drugs that I must say made me feel alive again. After a few minutes, they decided to inject a long needle into my back, which I bravely accepted. I started screaming and crying, begged the nurse to hold my hand, and tried to convince all the doctors that I wanted general anaesthesia. Well, it was a magnificent endeavour for all involved. While the doctor finally managed to persuade me to let the anaesthesiologist do his job kindly, I was seated, let something be injected into my back, the application of which I didn't even feel in the end, and was laid on a cold operating room table. The last thing I remember was the doctor with a green syringe, whom I cursed enough for him to inject something into my vein to make me fall asleep and stop talking. I don't know how long I slept, but a wild scream awakened me and then I realised it was my scream. I was out of it with everything you can find in a hospital, and despite that, I still felt pain. The doctor gave me another green injection, and then I woke up in the intensive care unit, where I lay on a soft bed, couldn't feel my legs, and knew very well that my whole backside was sticking out. When my brain functions returned to normal, the first question was whether the child was a boy or a girl. The next question was where Peter was because regardless of what an asshole he was, he helped me through every minute of this excruciating process. I can't imagine anyone beside me who could have handled it better, and I honestly admire all the women who went through it without psychological support. Of course, I looked around the room because I wanted to find my little girl. Yes, it was true. I had a daughter, an amazing, beautiful daughter, whom I carried in my belly for over forty weeks, slowly giving birth to her for a day, and no one had shown her to me yet. As I looked around the room, I saw only two ladies in the same impoverished state as I was. Suddenly, a nurse entered, holding a baby in her hands, and I knew certainty that this little angel belonged to me. She put her in my arms, I looked at her tiny, drooling face, and I was sure it was worth it. In that fateful moment, I promised her that I will protect her and do everything for her in the

16

world. All that pain seemed to disappear; I didn't perceive anything else; the whole world faded away, and there were just the two of us and no one else. This little magical being completely stole my heart and although she wasn't planned, she was wanted a million per cent! This is love at first sight; you see that crumpled red creature, and you fall in love. Your heart beats at an enormous speed which could be the echoing from the glucose, and you know that this bond cannot be broken by anyone or anything in the world. When I didn't have her with me, I felt inhuman pain; my belly hurt so much that I couldn't walk. Just imagine, you shuffle around the room, you're hunched over so much that your head is almost at your knees, your butt sticks out, and you try to prove to yourself that you'll make it to the toilet in the next thirty minutes. In this special post-operative room, you're also tormented by hunger; I hadn't eaten anything for two days, and then I received broth from a cube. At that moment, a bowl full of broth from a cube was crowned as the food of the gods. I'm not a person who can go without food, and after two days, I would have eaten anything or anyone! After going through the third day, when I managed to eat a whole banana and shower without assistance, the doctors moved me to a standard room. I think that shower convinced them that I was capable of moving up a level, and as a bonus, instead of two roommates, I got only one. The only condition was to go to the room alone through half of the maternity ward, and I was sure I could make it three hundred meters in the next twenty-four hours. After a short struggle, I did it, and I won. I was in a new room without a guard, but I still had the head nurse with a syringe, who regularly visited me. The hospital is probably one of the most horrifying places in the world for me precisely because I hate injections. During my stay in this building, my body received so many of them that I could easily pretend to be a sieve. My little princess moved with me to the room, and from that moment on, it was impossible to sleep. From now on, she ruled, and she showed us both who wears the trousers in this relationship, even though, in her case it was more a nappy trousers. Who would have thought that such a tiny bundle could create so much fuss; her communication was not in line with mine, and for some time, it was all about guessing what this little one wanted. Peter was at the hospital with me every day, at least for a while, but I wasn't sure why he was going there; I didn't trust him. I didn't know if we were playing happy family or if he was trying to ease his conscience. One thing couldn't be denied about this guy: from the moment that little bundle decided to come into the world, Peter did his utmost, and despite everything he had done to me in life, I started to believe again that something would change, and I fell in love again. One day, when I was lying on the hospital bed, and he was sitting next to me, out of nowhere, he started talking about marriage. Immediately, I thought he was joking or emotionally unstable after all this. But as they say, love conquers all, so I tried to take it as a new beginning, mainly because of the little one. I have one fantastic quality for which there is a unique term in the Czech language, and that is that I am simply 'flushable, 'like a toilet. Basically, this means that no matter how much harm someone does to you, your brain cannot connect it with pain for longer than necessary. In a way, I'm glad for this trait; despite sometimes overreacting to certain stimuli, I can calm down very quickly and logically filter the whole thing into a form that doesn't hurt me. Sometimes, it takes minutes, sometimes hours, and in the worst situations, days to weeks, but I always get used to it, accept it, and either store it deep inside me or let it go and wave goodbye. With this trait, I tried to forget all the bad things in my temporary relationship and try again. However, as the saying goes, when you forgive and give a person who once hurt you a new chance, it's like giving them a new bullet for their gun because they missed the first time. From this follows that Peter literally knocked me down again, but we'll get to that later; now we really need to go through the part about the idyllic family. Don't worry, it's not that long. I spent a few more days in the hospital; bruises from injections were everywhere, and without energy and sleep, two days before Christmas, I moved home. In all that chaos and stress, Peter brought my clothes and shoes from the hospital, so I left that strange building in December in slippers and his jacket. If I had a coffee cup in my hand, someone would definitely throw some coins in it. My walking ability had progressed to the level of a 'heavily sick turtle', so to get to the car took me what seemed like an eternity.

Czech winter is a fascinating time; it's either raining, there's a strong wind, and it's freezing, or it's snowing, there's a strong wind, and it's freezing. When I left the hospital, I experienced the first weather option, which is quite typical for December. So imagine a tiny blonde girl, barely dressed, looking like a homeless person, leaving the hospital grounds at minus ten degrees, walking at the speed of a ninety-year-old. Personally, if I met someone like that, I would think they were one of those street junkies someone shot in the belly because they owed money for some powder that takes you to another dimension. I definitely needed a shower and clean clothes. On the way home, my belly hurt; every bump on the road caused me suffering, and I cursed the Czech road workers. No one thinks about people post-surgery. Finally, after some time, we arrived home. When I opened the door, it was evident that Peter had tried to make everything nice and clean. The only thing he didn't clean up was a black bag in the kitchen the size of a dinosaur. It was a bag full of beer cans and bottles of alcohol. I immediately remembered him telling me in the hospital that he no longer drinks, that all this had changed.

"Maybe he was celebrating the baby's birth with friends", I told myself and I didn't dwell on it further, but that was a huge mistake. Do you remember the first rule of the 'manual'? Never trust guys! The paradox of society is that honesty and good manners have long ceased to be considered common qualities but virtues. The apartment looked like a Christmas idyll; it was raining outside like from a shower-head and there was no Christmas tree because there simply wasn't one, and someone probably also raided the fridge. Well, at least the coffee was there. Someone might argue that coffee while breastfeeding isn't healthy, but coffee makes me happy, keeps me alive and I consider that a strong enough argument. The reason behind the absence of Christmas decorations was that nobody knew when I would be discharged from the hospital, which I believed was a fair enough justification. We prepared for our first Christmas as a family of three; the only one missing was my dog, whom I temporarily placed with my parents. I was thrilled; Christmas in isolation, everywhere smelled almost like disinfectant. I slept for a maximum of three hours a day, and with my split belly, I couldn't even put on my panties by myself. Several days after giving birth, I had a dream that my little angel stopped breathing. This example is fascinating in showing how the human body can react because, during the day, I couldn't even go to the toilet without someone's help, but after waking up from this nightmare, I ran straight to the crib. After realising that everything was okay, it took me about three seconds to fall to the ground in pain. I thought I had torn my belly; tears flowed, and the last traces of adrenaline washed out of my body. I crawled into bed, intending to continue my precious sleep, but the little screamer didn't like that at all and decided to convince me that sleep wasn't crucial for me. After feeding and putting the baby to bed, I crawled to the toilet, where I fell asleep, leaning against the wall. I dare say it was probably the worst place I've ever managed to fall asleep.

During the six weeks after childbirth, Peter was an incredible support; I never thought he could be so amazing. One evening, we were sitting together on the balcony; I was enjoying my coffee, him his cigarette, and out of nowhere, he asked me if I wanted to marry him. I didn't expect it to be a formal proposal, so I said yes and expected my 'YES! 'to end this conversation, but to my surprise, it continued. This guy probably meant it seriously with me, and the idea of marriage impressed me quite a bit; everything looked very rosy, and Peter seemed like every woman's dream man, at least for the last few weeks. The first weeks were really demanding; nights full of crying and screaming drove me crazy; I slept standing up or during ordinary activities. I was absolutely exhausted, and besides taking care of the baby, I was trying to finish my studies through distance learning. It was one of the most challenging periods of my life; I looked like a zombie crossed with Uncle Fester. I was fully aware of what was happening; I was young and ambitious, and suddenly, there was a baby at home who needed me. Due to the pregnancy, which also wasn't a walk in the park, I didn't emotionally bond with my daughter as I should have, at least not at the beginning. I started seeing a psychologist who didn't tell me anything I didn't already know: I was just exhausted, young, and felt like I couldn't handle it. I had a hysterical baby at home who cried eighteen hours a day, and in the meantime, I tried to study. I don't want to discuss the period of tranquillisers combined with anxiety and depressive states. All I can say is that I was weak and exhausted. As my condition began to improve, Peter went abroad for work, and my parents primarily helped me with my daughter; if I hadn't had them at that time, I would have gone crazy. As parents, they didn't stand out in many ways, but as grandparents, they were terrific. I ran from breastfeeding to books and desperately tried to finish school, occasionally get some sleep, and be a good mom. Two days before Peter was supposed to return from abroad, he called me and asked how I felt. I joked about the medications and said I was actually okay. He asked me if I wanted to get married on Saturday, and I, stupidly excited, exclaimed, 'Yes!' Finding out about my own wedding five days before it happens is a challenge, and I, as a strong woman on antidepressants, proudly accepted this challenge. I'm unsure if I was sane enough for such a decision, but it happened. It's like a girl's dream when the prince on a white horse comes for you, and then you walk down the aisle in a beautiful white dress with a train, entering into the marital union, which with a ninety per cent chance will end in divorce.

Happy pills -

the feeling of never ending joy

Side effects:

Struggling with the motional rollercoaster

Blissfully ignorant

Wild and impulsive choices

Bursting with sheer joy!

Embrace the magic of fairy tales!

I was thrilled, even though it was rushed;

I knew I loved him, and I told myself that nothing in the world could tear us apart.

This is exactly what the naive idea of a nineteen-year-old girl desperately trying to have a perfect family life looks like. But life isn't perfect, and making hasty decisions while taking Xanax is definitely not something I would recommend.

There's a really high chance you'll do something idiotic, but I'm an expert on stupidity, so I jumped into it headfirst. The wedding was far from a fairytale; I got married in an old church, I found a dress in a hurry, and my body uncontrollably enlarged. With this comprehensive equipment of a proper Slavic woman, I had a huge problem fitting into my wedding dress. In the rush, we forgot about music, the organ, the toast; at least someone managed to drag the priest into the church. One downside of a church wedding is that half of the people get bored to death, and the other half freezes to death, even though it's over thirty degrees outside. We kneeled, stood up, said something, and kept stupidly smiling at each other; well, it was beautiful! It was a wedding full of love, naivety, and sensory infatuation, so in the end, it was like something out of a romantic movie. I was immensely surprised that I managed to persuade my dad to this event, who was a massive opponent of social events and especially church ceremonies. He was in an unbuttoned shirt the whole time and almost had to wrap his legs in foil so they wouldn't catch fire when he entered the church grounds, but he was there. He was the only one who cried at the end of this farce and the only one who hugged me and said from the bottom of his heart, 'Just be happy, little girl'. This memory is as precious to me as salt! It's said that everything changes after a wedding, and that's what happened to us! It didn't take long, and everything returned to the old ways, again the disappearing at night, arguments, screaming, crying, and helplessness. Yes, old Peter came back home to me! My mental health certainly didn't improve with the arrival of old Peter, but unfortunately, my feelings towards him didn't change either, which I still can't explain to this day. At that time, I didn't have friends; there was no one to whom I could turn, to whom I could confide. I felt lonely and drowned in my own feelings of self-pity and Peter's daily reproaches. I was utterly broken; in fact, I felt dead inside. The only happiness for me was my daughter, to whom I couldn't give as much sincere love as she needed, and of course, my dog, whom I almost defended every day from Peter's attacks after he stood up for me. It was getting worse and worse; he was away for long hours, I didn't know where he went, and I was home alone all day, taking care of the little one, the school, and the dog, and my only interests were cooking, walks, and books. Every evening or morning, when he returned from the pub, he found a new reason to attack me and leave me lying, crying on the floor or arguing with me and leaving. It hurt me, it broke the dog, and what hurt the most was that my daughter had to hear or see all of it. Such periods were always concluded by a short, promising phase of "I don't want to lose you." I used to like these periods; Peter was home after work, we had dinner, planned vacations and enjoyed our time together, and then suddenly, out of nowhere, as if he flipped a switch, it was all back to square one. I talked about the whole situation with one of my brothers, and he himself told me that we needed to find something to help me with that, so he sent me to a mothers 'club to make friends. However, this so-called mothers 'club definitely didn't impress me positively. Not only did I find it very difficult to fit in because I was the youngest mother in the local hyena circle, but honestly, I wasn't interested in open discussions about baby poop, breastfeeding, vomiting, childbirth, or pregnancy. This club was divided into two parts: the first group consisted of mothers probably from better social backgrounds, mostly over thirty, and the child had its entire future planned even before it was born. These women knew precisely which brands were in vogue now, and besides dirty nappies, they could only talk about how to squeeze money out of their husbands or which hairdresser was the best in the region. So they were automatically put into a box labelled "cows"! The second part of this club consisted of mothers who tied their children in tie-dyed scarves and were staunch advocates of breastfeeding until the child's eighteenth birthday, failure to do so was a serious sin for which we would be ruthlessly judged.

Everything was made of organic materials; they acknowledged nothing but organic food, and a razor was the evil that no one could force them to come into contact with, which was quite evident. I liked the concept of a mothers 'club, but I didn't fit into either group. So what do you do when you don't fit in somewhere? You create an opportunity to fit in somewhere or do it as I did and make your own club for parents with children. I've never put as much energy and enthusiasm into anything as I did into this project. It was supposed to be a place where anyone who has a child, anyone who wants to unwind, anyone who doesn't want to pay exorbitantly for entry into a room where you'll find ten women who look like grizzly bears and another ten who are trying to resemble Barbie dolls could come. It was supposed to be my little sanctuary and shelter from the world and especially shelter from Peter. I don't know where I got this energy, but I managed it. Finding free space for a completely non-profit project was hard work, but eventually, we succeeded! The next part was to get toys, carpets, actually anything that could be useful, and for that, I used everything from social media to ordinary flyers. Within a week, I had toys that could equip a whole children's home. It wasn't difficult to find participants for such a club either; a few of them changed during the entire period of operation, but the 'strongest' ones stayed. We talked, made friends, went on trips with the children, roasted sausages, played games, exercised; basically everything you can think of. We were open to possibilities, and three times a week, we created a perfect meeting for everyone. In this place, I finally started looking for friends; I felt like I wasn't so lonely, and it made me immensely happy to watch my daughter and how glad she was around her peers. In this club, I found my first friend in a long time; let's call her Marta. She was a great, young woman from Slovakia had a newborn girl and at home the same jerk as I did. I liked her; despite all the hardships of life, she always smiled and saw happiness in her daughter. One day, we decided to go out, just her and me, without the children; it was the first time in three years that I was somewhere, and it was terrific. Peter was looking after our princess, and I could enjoy a fantastic, youthful life for about thirty minutes. I ordered a beer, we talked about liberating topics like dirty nappies and the best baby food on the market, and then my phone started ringing; well, of course, it was Peter. He told me he was going to the shop with his dad, and I should immediately return home and watch our daughter. I absolutely didn't want to; damn it, I was out for the first time in three years, so I naturally started to resist. It's like a natural reflex that, after three years, I had left my cage and didn't want to winkle back into it under any circumstances. Looking back, resisting was a mistake. I told him he could take the little one to the store with him; absolutely nothing prevented him from doing so. After all, he could watch her for once since I've been taking care of everything for so long. He started yelling at me that the child was crying and that if I didn't return home immediately, he would leave her there and let me handle it however I wanted. Such a nice guy he was. He completely knocked me off my feet, and you can't even imagine the frustration in such a moment. I didn't have to explain the delicacy of the situation to Marta too much; she perfectly understood what had just happened. After a diplomatic assessment of the circumstances, we unanimously agreed that my husband was an idiot. I decided it would be better to follow his advice and return home. At that moment, however, I had no idea what awaited me at home and how this day would turn my life upside down.

Chapter Two:
Fight Or Run Away

Upon unlocking the door, I was greeted by the utterly frantic cries of my six-month-old princess at the time. Immediately, I rushed to the bedroom from where the screams emanated, and in the crib, I found my tearful, bald treasure, her face as red as a tomato. I quickly picked her up and began to comfort her, realising at that moment that she was completely alone at home. Yes, that jerk left her there because I didn't arrive on time! After that little rascal finally stopped crying, I noticed something utterly shocking! Under her right eye, she had a huge red mark; I didn't have to think long to realise that her loving father had slapped her, thrown her into the crib, and then disappeared who knows where. I didn't know what to do, but my first reaction was to call Peter and find out what was happening there. I still didn't want to believe it, hoping it had some logical explanation and that it wasn't as bad as it seemed. But you know what? It was even worse than it looked! Peter, of course, cheerfully ignored all my attempts at any contact which suited him, so I gave up and subsequently took a photo of the red mark on her face and sent it to Marta for evaluation. Unlike my husband, she was ready to react immediately with her phone in hand, providing me with professional advice. After about a two-hour conversation full of advice, anger, and unkind words, I finally realised that it couldn't go on like this, that I had to grab my little girl and disappear. But I had no idea where to go or what to do. I urgently needed help to solve this, and I knew I couldn't handle it overnight, especially not alone. When Peter arrived home, he behaved as if nothing had happened, pretending to be a good father who had gone shopping and come home to take care of his girls. I remember following him and asking him what happened, why he hit her and how it was possible that she was home alone. He looked at me, smiled, and calmly told me that he simply couldn't handle that terrible screaming and that it was extremely frustrating the way the baby communicated. So, ladies and gentlemen, my daughter got slapped because she couldn't fluently express her needs and feelings at the age of six months. Moreover, the way he answered me was completely lax;

it was exactly the kind of response you get when you go to tell the shopkeeper that you accidentally knocked over a bottle of milk from the shelf. With a stupid smile on your face, you apologise only because you were caught in the act or because that older man at the end of the aisle might scold you. The man I lived with had no sense of guilt and didn't realise what he had done; in fact, he didn't give a damn! Nothing helped; it didn't matter if I screamed, cried, or tried to communicate normally; there was no reaction, just nothing. I might as well have talked to a wall; it would be the same! The next evening, during her bath, I discovered that our daughter had three long scratches on her back, and when I saw that, I burst into tears. It's an unbelievable feeling of despair when you know that the little innocent being only has you, and you are there to protect her, and I failed! It couldn't go on like this; it terrified me more than monsters under the bed! Considering that in the Czech Republic, maternity leave typically lasts three years, it was absolutely unthinkable to stay here for another two and a half years and wait to find a job. I had to resolve this situation as soon as possible! Marta provided me with the contact of a social worker who had once helped her a lot, and I desperately needed to be shown the way. The first and last meeting occurred at our home without my husband's knowledge. I couldn't tell him this; I feared the consequences would be fatal. I described the situation in great detail to this lady and expected advice, or rather, I hoped for a document with detailed points one to ten, containing an absolutely detailed explanation of where to go, what to do and how to solve this. I received no advice or documents; instead, I received a summons for questioning from the Criminal Police of the Czech Republic. Today, I understand that the lady didn't want to harm me; she was doing her job and protecting my interests and my child's interests, but at that time, it made my life much more complicated. Unfortunately, I still believe that state institutions should choose somewhat different procedures. If someone asks you for help and you call the police on them, you'll make their already colourful life even less boring. You can manage to keep a social worker hidden, but try hiding the cops, that's a whole different level. If you manage to do that, you're a real badass, and I take my hat off to you! I wasn't a badass, and I couldn't hide this. My husband was determined that he wouldn't pay for his sins, and all that was left for him was to convince me that I agreed with this decision and fully supported him. Unfortunately, he eventually succeeded, and I lied because of him. To this day, I don't know how he managed it, but today, I'm glad I did it because my daughter loves that guy. He's a different person now, but back then, he definitely deserved someone to show him that every action has its reaction. Our marriage was like a roller coaster; it was good for a while, and then it turned sour, and I didn't love this person anymore; in fact, I didn't even recognise him. I remember how repulsive he was to me; I couldn't sleep next to him, I couldn't live with him, he disgusted me! In this very challenging time for me, my brother and his girlfriend decided to move to Ireland for better prospects. Her family lived there, so they had an excellent opportunity to make a big life move and disappear. In the last few days before their departure, my brother stayed with us, and we were such a happy family. One evening, I sat with him in the kitchen; we chatted and played with the little one, and then my husband came home; he was so drunk that he could barely speak. He staggered into the kitchen and started yelling at me, accusing me of everything he had done for me over the years and what a small, ungrateful beast I was, and that I almost got him arrested. Well, I told you it would have a sequel, and honestly, even then, I knew it. I expected the worst, so I immediately handed the little one to my brother, stood up, and tried to calm down the screaming monster, but I couldn't. He grabbed me by the hair and pulled me tightly to him to prove his superiority and strength. Tears streamed from my eyes, and all I could say was, "If you touch me, I'll call the police..." At that moment, he grabbed a knife from the kitchen counter and started waving it at me; I was scared, terribly scared! I heard my brother shouting at him, but I couldn't hear the words. My brother took his niece to the next room and in the meantime, I tried to keep the knife away from me as far as possible, at least until someone came to help me. To this day, I have a beautiful scar on my finger from that struggle, and every time I look at it, it reminds me of how strong I was when I decided to leave. It couldn't go on like this; I was afraid of what would happen next when he came home drunk and angry. After successfully completing my high school exams, I found a part-time job during maternity leave at a large store as a cashier; I needed to save some money and escape from that unhappy relationship. Eventually, I had to cancel the mother's club because there was simply no time left for it with work, taking care of the home, my daughter, and a drunken husband. Later, I decided to get my driver's license and start studying at university. Let's be honest: I wanted to get away from him so badly that I took on a bit too much, but at that time, I realised that I, in a way, liked stress, and it kept me constantly on edge. My need to become independent grew, and the final straw was an event when my husband admitted to me that he slept with a local alcoholic woman the day after our wedding. I think no one has the right to do this; infidelity is excruciating for both parties. Moreover, you'll probably earn a VIP ticket to hell and extra torture in the afterlife. Despite all this, I still believe that women are pretty simple creatures, well, if they're not complete bitches. I know many men won't agree with this statement and will argue that women are the most complicated things in the world, but gentlemen, let's be honest, it's not a walk in the paradise with you, either! If a woman is normal, happy, and doesn't have a jerk at home who hurts her, she'll never go to anyone else. I didn't even go when I was being hurt, but even if I had decided to try somewhere else, I don't believe anyone has the right to judge me. If she's not normal, the situation is somewhat more complicated, but in that case, you have at home what you choose yourself. After all that happened and how many things piled up on me, it was natural that I worked on an escape plan. This affair of his with the local notorious woman wasn't the first and certainly not the last infidelity on his part. Still, this story tortured me like the most experienced mafia boss! This lady was over 50, drank at the local pub every evening until morning, and pleased every local drunkard. To top it off, she dressed like a fifteen-year-old prostitute, accentuated by a short leather skirt, high heels, a deep neckline, and a black wig. If you've ever seen how transgenders do their makeup, you can perfectly imagine her face and the way she dressed. These individuals, heavily laden with makeup, try to conceal masculine features and strive to appear as feminine as possible. Still, unfortunately, this often means they misjudge the extent of what is acceptable. This lady had a similar approach, but instead of hiding masculine features, she desperately tried to mask signs of ageing. Honestly, I hope she wasn't a man. Several days after I found out about this, I was sitting at the checkout at work, and suddenly, she appeared there, unloading items onto the belt and smiling at me like sunshine. How could she even look at me? Doesn't that woman have even a little shame? I swallowed a very vivid vision of wanting to stand up and smack her head against one of the shelves, but as a proper lady, I naturally maintained decorum, at least for the necessary time. That is until she spoke to me. She looked at me and, with her stupid smile, said, "What's wrong? Why are you so sad?" And I responded with absolute calmness, "And wouldn't you be sad if some local whore seduced your husband?" After my response, the smile vanished from her face, and I struggled to maintain a composed demeanour; it took me a lot of energy not to spit in her face. As soon as she left, I had to escape to the warehouse; I couldn't pretend any longer. I sat there on the floor, hugging my knees, which touched my chin and cried. I knew my husband was a jerk, but this was so humiliating! Anyway, as they say, every cloud has a silver lining, and this gave me the strength to fight for myself and my daughter. I gathered all my pride, and that very evening, I searched for information on universities and looked for anything that would help me leave. As soon as I was accepted, I was obsessed with learning. I had immense motivation, and I knew I could do it. I remember reading textbooks and taking notes between customers when I was sitting at the checkout; I smiled at how eager and ambitious I was! One day, my boss approached me and offered me something that couldn't be refused; he told me that if I was interested, there was a vacancy for an assistant manager position. Being the right hand of my superior, that offer impressed me immensely; it meant a lot to me. It meant that someone noticed my qualities and appreciated my efforts, but it also meant taking on a full-time position instead of part-time and getting more money in less time. I told myself I could handle it; after all, it was one of the first steps towards a better future. Before I knew it, I was dealing with much bigger problems than just missing change in the cash register. On weekends, I was practically there from morning to evening, opening in the morning and closing at night. In addition to office work, I had to be able to do a bit of everything; we were short-staffed, and more than once, someone didn't show up for work. I was a jack-of-all-trades, and most importantly, I was exhausted! I had to take my daughter to work several times because my husband either couldn't or didn't want to take care of her. The little brat loved it there; sometimes, when I had time off, she begged me to take her there, but honestly, I had different ideas about how to spend my days off. I tried to give her as much attention as possible and balance everything else. We argued at home daily; sometimes, I came to work with a new bruise or other injury. Some men, for some reason, can't bear it when their wife tries to have a better future and not be dependent on a man who doesn't even deserve her, but none of that made me give up. That guy, whom I saw every day at home, reminded me that everything I was doing made sense! I met a large number of people every day, and as it usually happens, I once met someone who caught my eye. In my lifelong story, he plays a negligible role, but at that moment, it was convenient to meet this guy. He lived nearby; he practically came to that shop every day, and we chatted casually several times. One day he asked me for my phone number and if I would like to go somewhere with him. I didn't lie to him; I told him straight away that I was married and not looking for any fun; after all, it wasn't difficult to notice that I still had a ring on my finger. Of course, I also admitted that my relationship had been unhappy for a long time. We arranged our first meeting, and then we went to a café together twice and I knew I would have to come clean at home. Despite it not being sexual, I was attracted to that guy, and I felt good with him. I would be a naive fool to think that sooner or later, something wouldn't happen between us. However, I didn't want a lover, so before anything happened, I knew I had to end my failing relationship. How cruel, right? For my husband, it wasn't good timing; he was having one of his ambitious periods, but I knew it was just temporary again, and as quickly as it came, it would disappear. In the evening, we sat at the kitchen table, and I told him that all this had to end and that I couldn't go on. He was sorry. I remember he cried, but we both knew that nothing could save this anymore. I didn't want to lie; I gently explained to him that I was seeing someone, but I don't think he ever believed me that I wasn't cheating on him. As two adults and reasonable people who were aware that not everything lasts forever, we argued in such a way that our neighbours could sit comfortably in their living room, eat popcorn, and wonder how this drama would end. After a stressful argument, we eventually agreed that I would stay there until I found another place to live and somehow, we both hoped we wouldn't kill each other in the meantime. I had to take out a small loan for housing; otherwise, I would never have been able to leave from there. But such a loan isn't just handed out, especially if you've never applied for one before.

No bank wants to take that risk and be the first lender, so this task was quite challenging. It took me about two months to obtain the money and move out. And during those two endlessly long months, I had the opportunity to get to know my husband even better. Because if you don't figure out who you're living with for five years, a breakup will open your eyes! One beautiful afternoon, I faced a sight I'd been trying to erase for years. What's the likelihood that someone you live with turns out to be homosexual? The probability is about as high as winning the lottery, without even buying a ticket. I hit the jackpot immediately. Remember my husband's best friend and, coincidentally, the brother of his ex-partner? If not, let me lovingly remind you. I don't remember what the weather was like, but let's pretend it was a beautiful, sunny day. I went out for a walk with my little one, and if I had known what awaited me when we got back home, we would have stayed outside longer. I held the little one in my arms, went upstairs, slowly opened the apartment door, and a few meters away, my husband was kneeling on the floor, chewing on his best friend's genitals. This completely shook me, but I had a child in my hand; I couldn't even say anything, not that I had anything to say at that moment. So I took the little one away, and we went outside to extend our time outdoors. An unlimited number of thoughts raced through my head and my brain was driving me crazy, but I can't say it hurt me; I didn't love him anymore, we weren't together and I had someone else. However, I was with that person for a while, so it's clear that I was interested in whether this was happening throughout our relationship. Suddenly, all the other things started to make sense, and a huge puzzle started to form in my head. On one of our first dates, he looked at a guy and asked me if I liked him. At that time, I took it as a typical jealous question until he told me he really liked him. If you don't realise that your partner might have a taste for men when he says something like that, then you're probably naive. I was trusting even when he ordered a box of sex toys and asked me to shove those twenty-centimetre latex "tools" up his ass. So what? I wanted to be a tolerant, extremely cool girlfriend who was made for the 21st-century world, and the fact that he liked something a little different wasn't a problem at all. But then, when you see him sucking off his best friend, you realise that you've had the problem all along! I don't remember if we talked about it; actually, there probably wasn't much I could say. After a few days my loan was finally approved, so I could start focusing on finding a new apartment. I don't think it was a huge amount; honestly, I didn't even want significant finance, I didn't need much; I bought furniture second-hand and for a year, I was without a television, but it was worth it. After all, I didn't need a TV; my daughter and the dog were enough for me. That guy I was dating at the time helped me find housing through his connections; it was a lovely, big apartment and importantly, it was affordable. I transformed it to my liking, and over time, we made it into a beautiful home.

I was with that gentleman for a few months, so I didn't even bother creating a fake name for him. My brother always called him the "microwave repairman"; interpret that as you wish. To this day, I believe he appeared in my life for one reason only: to help me leave

Peter. He broke up with me via text message, saying he wasn't ready to be a dad, not even in practice, so he fulfilled his purpose and disappeared.

By the way, I never forced him to do anything like that; of course, he knew about my daughter, but I was not going to hide her from him, given the situation I was in. That's where my brief acquaintance ended, and I was single again. At that time, we were hiring new employees at work, and a girl who I interviewed applied to us. I didn't like her; she looked like a weird Barbie with such long nails that during the entire interview, I couldn't think of anything else but how it was physically possible for her to wipe her butt. If we didn't have vacancies, I would never have hired her, but at that moment, there wasn't much of a choice. I have to give this girl a name; at that time, I didn't know it, but somehow, she turned out to be my best friend. Let's call her Emma; it's a short, descriptive name, and most importantly, it was the first thing that came to mind. I didn't have to spend much time with her; Emma was studying and had found a part-time job with us, just starting to live with her boyfriend and needing every penny. This girl could drive me crazy in an incredible way; every day, she was late because she followed the rule "better late than ugly" and never felt guilty. On one September day, I had to go to Prague for training, and coincidentally, Emma was attending training too. So we decided to go together and somehow survive it, and what initially looked like misery turned into a pleasant trip to the city. I fondly remember it, except for the training; that was terrible boredom. It started with me having to pick her up at six in the morning, but it wouldn't be Emma if she wasn't late. I waited there for forty minutes, and she came only when I had decided to go alone. I was damn angry the whole way, and after we argued, there was thunderous silence in the car. Emma and I stayed in the same room and we started to get to know each other much better, laughed a lot, and during walks on Charles Bridge, we found out that we actually had a lot in common. When we drove home from Prague, we were already inseparable, but at work, I was still the boss, so I sometimes had to pretend to almost whip her so that the other employees wouldn't strike. Her tardiness annoyed everyone, and for me, it was difficult to separate work life from personal life, especially since I had my first friend after an extremely long time.

34

Sometimes, I scolded her; mostly, it was a perfect acting performance; no one suspected anything, and everyone was satisfied. So that's how a real friendship was born, and to this day, she's like a sister to me. Anyway, I started spending a lot of time with her and her boyfriend, Mark; we were inseparable. My daughter adored these two beings, and we did almost everything together. Mark was amazing; he would do anything for that girl, and she loved him too. They were like a couple cut out of a romantic movie. When I looked at them, I had a perfect idea of what my future relationship would look like. After some time, when you're still alone, you start to miss love, and my fear of dying alone in a small apartment with seven cats became more and more a potential. One evening, Emma and I went out; honestly, I wanted to say that we went hunting, but it's not easy with a taken girl, unless she's a promiscuous creature. So please, calm down your raging hormones, and instead of two attractive blondes in totally sexy outfits, imagine two nuns covered from head to toe. Anyway, that evening, I confided in her about how lonely I sometimes felt, well, not that it was so difficult to figure out. It was completely visible, and if I spread my legs, it was highly likely that loud squeaking and creaking would be heard, like when you open old doors and a few spiderwebs fall out of my pants. Emma had a completely innovative solution, which, after eight drinks, seemed like a perfect choice. At her advice, I downloaded a dating app, and that same evening, we looked at pictures of guys from the area and approached the least disgusting and suspicious individuals. If I had created my profile myself, my description of what I was looking for would have been absolutely easy. It would have been something like: "Looking for a man, not picky. Just don't be an asshole!"

Given that the description was written by my closest person, who drank a dangerously large amount of alcohol, the criteria for choosing a partner were written in long, detailed sentences. This detailed description lured out a forty-year-old man who claimed to be thirty and tried to pick me up in a shiny leased car. We had only one date together; the sympathy didn't seem mutual. This guy was like a walking advertisement for a midlife crisis, and in the end, he didn't want anything to do with me because I was supposedly too clever for him. I found out the truth later that with my one hundred seventy centimetres and fifty-eight kilos, I was too fat for him. What can I say? Some people just like women, and some people like to grind their penis on bones. After some time, another guy contacted me, saying that if I was interested, he would love to introduce me to a friend. I was a little horrified, but I kind of liked him from his stories, so I was curious about what kind of person he would be. I gave him my phone number, and somehow, we started communicating; he wrote quite nicely and was funny. It didn't occur to me at the time that he was a perverted and chauvinistic idiot. After a few days, we arranged a meeting, and I must say, I was really looking forward to it. It was another blind date, but I had a good feeling about this guy.

Chapter Three: Mr. Mysterious

Our first date was supposed to take place at a local reservoir; I arrived there first and waited for the arrival of the mysterious gentleman. After some time, he showed up with a slight delay. He wasn't particularly interesting; he was a young, slender guy in a T-shirt and jeans. He looked a bit like the main character from the movie 'Megamind', except he wasn't blue, but despite the poor first impression, something about him still caught my attention. I've always had a weakness for intelligent and mysterious men, and he embodied both. His sense of humour was unconventional; I never knew when he was serious or just messing around, keeping my mind constantly alert. It wasn't perfect, but considering the bleakness surrounding me, I didn't want to dismiss it immediately. Unfortunately, I wish I had. Desperately craving someone who would love me, on this journey of searching for love, I thought this unremarkable guy could be the one. The first date was decent, so we arranged another meeting, although it wasn't particularly memorable, considering I can't even remember it. Over time, it seemed like a perfect synchronisation; he was a family-oriented, young, intelligent entrepreneur with an original sense of humour. His cooking skills were pathetic, as befits a guy, and he could even burn water for coffee. After a few months of dating, I introduced him to my daughter, whom he had only known from my stories, and they immediately charmed each other. He might have loved her more than me and constantly talked about how he longed for his own child. And as it often happens, without planning it, a miracle occurred, and instead of one heart in my body, there were two beating hearts. One beautiful day, I peed on that fateful plastic stick again, and it was all over. We hadn't been together long enough to start a family, but on the other hand, I felt good with him and from a logical point of view, he seemed like a suitable candidate for the father of my child. That day, I arranged a meeting with him at my favourite Japanese restaurant. Such news must be conveyed with a significant dose of enthusiasm, combined with an acceptable level of care. It was a big moment; I had to prepare the announcement perfectly. I rehearsed my monologue for hours in front of the mirror, anticipating almost all possible reactions as I waited for the hour when he was supposed to pick me up. Finally, he arrived, took me to the agreed place, and in that pleasant setting of the rising sun, I splattered soup on his face within a few minutes. Yes, he was another careless scammer in my life, with a terrifying need to manipulate the opposite sex. As soon as I told him that his offspring was growing in my belly, I was informed that he had a pregnant wife at home and that he was not in a situation where he could do anything about my condition or support me in any way. I began to collapse under the influence of emotions, crying and screaming at him. With an utterly icy gaze, he looked at me and said, and said a completely pointless phrase, "Jesus, calm down!". It's useless because it has never once in the entire history of humanity led to someone actually calming down. After listening to his long, nonsensical talk about his reasons for unknowingly making me his mistress, I poured hot water with vegetable content and several unidentified ingredients into his face. With this decision, I earned a ban from the place with the best food in town and cut off another man who thought with his genitals. The mysterious gentleman followed me home and tried to convince me that the situation wasn't as catastrophic as it seemed, but his words were hardly believable. I'm afraid it couldn't get worse. I was pregnant with a guy who sprayed his sperm everywhere like a garden hose, a year of life wasted, and the whole idea of a sweet future irreversibly down the drain. A broken heart in pregnancy cannot be healed with alcohol, so I reached for the old good classics in the form of chocolate, romantic movies, and tissues.

A broken heart is like broken ribs; no one sees it, but it hurts with every breath, and that pain literally crushed me from the inside. After the first ultrasound, I sent him photos of that little worm developing inside me, but he barely replied to my messages. After discussing my collapsed life with Emma and being aware of what it's like to be a single mother trying her best, there was nothing left but to convince myself that abortion was the most suitable solution to the situation.

This was a very tough and painful decision for me, but under the circumstances, there was no other way. After this experience, I firmly decided to put an end to dating and rather stay alone. Honestly, the more men I met, the more I understood serial killers.

After a few weeks, I tried to mend my broken heart with a sewing kit and stuff it into the chastity belt so that nobody would get to it for a nice long while. After this delicate operation, my chaotic life began to return to normal. Studies, work, and my daughter were the only things I focused on. Sometimes, I felt like I had taken on too much. Still, it was a fantastic feeling to know that I was doing my best for us—however, none of what I did guaranteed an extraordinary financial situation. I struggled with money and often had to ask my parents for a little financial help.

It was always very embarrassing for me. My parents never had excessive financial resources, yet when they knew I needed help, they gave me what little they had. In this regard, they never turned their backs on me, and I always appreciated that immensely.

After many long, peaceful, and occasionally lonely months, Mr. Mysterious contacted me again. When I saw his name on the display, I felt like buying him a toaster and placing him and the toaster into the bathtub together. I tried to push this thought out of my head while gathering the courage to open that notification staring at me from my phone. I expected everything, but the reason for his message surprised me. He offered me a position in the administration leadership for his company. The salary was much more pleasant than I could see on my current pay-check and benefits like a company car or an eight-hour workday instead of thirteen hours appealed to me. After all, I had been through, it would have been insane to start working with him, but my financial situation was dire, and the time I spent with my princess was minimal. So, after careful consideration of all the pros and cons, I decided to accept the offer for existential reasons. I wanted to stick to the rule, "You don't step into the same river twice," but it wouldn't be me and the second time I didn't just step into the same river, I bathed in it.

This was a considerable risk; the thought of seeing Mr Mysterious in the office every day seemed like a nightmare, especially since I immensely enjoyed my job, and I had absolutely no idea how to explain my departure. I'm not one of those bold individuals who doesn't care what others think of them. My former colleagues were mostly envious female vipers who definitely wouldn't understand that I was going for something better.

It required devising a perfect plan, but every time I started thinking about it, I was on the verge of collapse. As a result of long deliberation over an acceptable lie, resolving the whole situation took me far too long. As someone who wanted to make everyone happy, I made myself unhappy. I informed my superior that I was changing jobs, but I was forced to adhere to the notice period. Mr. Mysterious wanted me to start immediately, and I couldn't risk someone else being offered the position. Subsequently, I reached a compromise with everyone, and I hoped to survive the next few months in good health. The compromise looked like this: a work regime at 320% deployment, and I became the main candidate for an available bed in the mental hospital. I worked for Mr. Mysterious from Monday to Friday every day, and on weekends and after work, I went to my former job. While I tried to learn all the new things coming my way at my new job, I taught everything I was already a master at to a new colleague who was supposed to take over my position. After weeks of stress with maximum sleep deficit, I could entirely focus on my new job. The beginnings were very demanding, but over time, I learned to leave my emotions at home and only see Mr. Mysterious as my superior. All the girls I met at work helped me a lot with this part, especially when they came to spread their legs to that chauvinistic pig. Despite letting his penis think for him, he was quite funny, and over time, I fell in love with the job at this company. I felt important, and that drove me forward. Several times, I took work home, didn't sleep at night, and did everything to make the company work as best as possible.

The offer of an eight-hour workday wasn't entirely accurate, but I chose it myself and loved it. My colleagues became friends, and most of the time, we spent weekends together or at least one evening a week. We joked about our clients, grilled, went to the mountains, played with old cars, or enjoyed free fall in motocross. And when things got really tough, we sterilised our emotions together with alcohol. Don't worry, it wasn't that often, and I still devoted most of my time to my little angel. She was the main reason why I changed jobs, but sometimes, you just have to switch off. I was balancing between work and family, and for the first time in ages, I felt thrilled despite still struggling with my financial situation. Well, you know how they say, when everything is going too well, something inevitably has to go wrong. It had been a year and a half since I was alone; I was happy but lonely, and fate decided to pull another ace from its sleeve.

41

I have just entered "ugliest male names" into the internet search engine to name this ace without resorting to vulgarity. The internet offered me the name "Narcissus," As soon as I saw it, my eyes lit up. I apologise to all bearers of this name. It fits this scoundrel perfectly. This name speaks volumes, so ladies and gentlemen, allow me to introduce Narcissus, a Slovak guy who, together with Mr. Mysterious, turned my life upside down. As I reflect on it, most of my life's mistakes were my own doing, but since it's always better to blame someone else, let's talk about my next life mistake. My romantic decisions and life have been so fascinating that I feel like a character straight out of one of Taylor Swift's hit songs. I guess most women experience that feeling at some point in their lives.

I met Narcissus at work; he was our client, and I was supposed to be available to him all day as part of customer service. Most of the time, our conversations revolved around work, but later, our discussions became much more open. I was impressed by the Slovak language; his accent made my panties drop to my ankles, and it was hard to resist that chemistry. His visually attractive face and athlete's body completely mesmerised me. Moreover, he seemed intelligent, slightly dominant and had a refined sense of humour. It was challenging to focus on anything; millions of hormones were coursing through my veins, and everything reminded me that my sex life practically didn't exist. I always prided myself on knowing exactly what I expected from a man, and an asymmetrical face definitely didn't fit my criteria. It was the first time someone got me based on looks rather than personality. And that was a big mistake! Ladies, we need to realise that the superpower of looking good in photos is not a guarantee of a quality life! He lived and worked in the Netherlands and didn't spend much time in the Czech Republic or Slovakia, which put me off. I didn't just want a lover; I wasn't a one-night stand kind of girl; I longed for love, and that was probably my biggest weakness. He stayed in the Czech Republic for a few days, and we saw each other daily. He was a romantic; he took me to the movies, to observation decks to watch the stars, and for long walks around the lakes. Every minute with him was as if nothing else in the world existed. It wasn't love; it was just sensory infatuation with a hint of lust, so I expected that when he got into my pants, he would disappear. One

42

fateful evening, his last night before leaving for home, it happened and it was far from anything romantic. The act of love took place in the back seats of his car after a day-long trip. I mention this fact for an idea of comfort and hygiene. He wasn't concerned at all whether my vagina was sweaty and smelled like a fat truck driver; he was only interested in how quickly he could shove that erect piece of meat into me. Charming! As soon as it began, it ended; this impressive performance lasted about three minutes, and I deserved some award for my acting.

To my surprise, after that miserable sexual experience, he didn't start ignoring me; on the contrary, he used words of love and longing messages, and I felt like a crazy teenager. It began to escalate, and it culminated on the day when he cried to me on the phone that he couldn't handle the separation anymore, found a job in Slovakia for the same company he used to work for already, just to be closer to me, and begged me if he could stay with me over the weekend on his way to his new beginning. I didn't know what to say. In a way, I was impressed. So I arranged with my parents that they would spend the weekend with their granddaughter, and on Friday, Narcissus arrived exactly as promised. Two days turned into a week, then two, and it slowly dawned on me that I wouldn't be able to get rid of this person. I wasn't thrilled about it, but I was glad I wasn't alone, and besides, he helped me pay the bills. Don't get me wrong, but after the divorce, my husband left me with high debts. I was paying off my loan, which I took when I was running away from him, and together with rent, food, and gasoline, I had almost nothing left from my pay-check. I still worked for Mr. Mysterious, and Narcissus had a new job every week. It didn't take long for me to realise that he wasn't as intelligent or charming as I thought, but for the first few months, he disguised it perfectly, and it took me a while to realise certain things. He got along with my friends; Emma approved of him, my little princess liked him, and I thought maybe, over time, my feelings towards him would turn into love, which I didn't feel for him yet. One day, he asked me if I could sign a contract in my name for him; he needed a functional phone and a plan, unfortunately, I was stupid and kind enough to complied. A few weeks later, it was a car loan; I resisted a bit, but in the end, it wasn't that difficult to convince me. I was told that for Slovak citizens, there is a limit in my country, and he stays here only because of me because he loves me. It is necessary to reiterate that my naivety knows no bounds, and manipulating me was relatively easy, so with a snap of a finger, my name was used on two contractual agreements. It was clear to me that it wouldn't be easy to leave this relationship. The idyll ended; he had me under his thumb, and he was well aware of it. Suddenly, a strong and healthy woman turned into a puppet, and I was treated accordingly. We constantly argued; he brought drugs home, and I didn't want such things near my daughter. He was capable of attacking me because of the discharge in my underwear, thinking it was semen. If any of you have had a similar experience with your partner, I advise you to get rid of him before it's too late! I thought this time it would work out, but once again, it turned out that this relationship was just another mistake, from which I only had lessons learned in the end, and I am glad that nothing else remained after that person. He held me by the throat several times and tortured me mentally, physical attacks were not uncommon either. I was afraid of him, scared; I didn't know what kind of person he was; he could turn absolutely any word against me, argue over trivial matters, and attack me for no reason. I was emotionally at rock bottom, broken, and completely messed up. All the problems I had at home were reflected in me, and everyone could see that something was wrong with me. I was forbidden to bring work home, participate in recreational activities with colleagues, and much more. It couldn't go on like this, but I was tied down, and the moment I cut him off, he would stop paying the financial obligations that were in my name. It was absolutely out of the question for me to afford to pay anything extra; I was barely making ends meet as it was. Eventually, he decided to leave; of course, he kept the car with the promise that he would keep paying for it. Secretly, I hoped that a bus would hit him somewhere. I made a contract to protect myself at least a little, but he refused to sign it, saying that if I didn't trust him, I could pay for everything myself. After he left, I received threatening messages for several months; he rang my doorbell in the evening, and sometimes I was even afraid to go home. Once, I even went to the police; I needed to know what I could do, but I was only told that until something happened to me, they didn't have the authority to intervene in any way. Apparently, helping and protecting is just a saying. Once more we find ourselves facing the thrilling challenge of state institutions! I tried my best to keep my personal problems from affecting my work, but in the end, I probably wasn't as strong and independent a woman as I thought. I made mistake after mistake; I was swimming in debt, and eventually, a month before Christmas, I was fired with the explanation that the entire office would be automated and I was no longer needed. I cried my eyes out, and I knew I had brought it upon myself to some extent, but fortunately not entirely, as overall staff levels were being reduced. Finding a job around Christmas was not easy; it seemed almost impossible. I went from interview to interview, trying to impress, but there was always someone better, more educated, or sexually more attractive. The internet was flooded with offers like: "Do you speak six world languages fluently, have at least twenty years of experience in the field, are you ambitious, a young individual with six university degrees?"

I could barely speak English, and I didn't finish the university degree because of Narcissus; moreover, in my current situation, I needed a decent salary. For the first few months, I believed in myself; I had a lot to offer, but over time, my confidence dwindled, and it disappeared somewhere. It was replaced with reminders of unpaid bills, and wherever I looked, I owed money: daycare, rent, loans, and even stupid internet. I couldn't move from the spot, and you wouldn't believe how a lack of finances cuts you off from everything and everyone. I was devastated; I would stick to the rule "what doesn't kill you makes you drink", but I didn't even have money for the cheapest wine; I couldn't even buy food. My stress level reached its maximum, and when you're entirely at rock bottom, unable to find a job, and your ex threatens you, and your daughter cries because she has nothing to eat, you'll do anything to solve it. The stage where I picked myself up and promised to do everything to be happy again came right after the period of self-pity when I collapsed, sitting in the corner of the room, contemplating suicide. My child was my lifeline; no matter how dark my thoughts were, she was my light at the end of the tunnel, always. Maternal love is powerful, and I knew I would sacrifice my life for her to breathe. The crazy and hopeless situation threw me into the search engine, and from standard job positions, I moved on to those you don't have to send your resume to, job offers in erotic services. Going through all those repulsions would be much easier for me with a bottle of alcohol, but if I had money for alcohol, I would never stoop to something like that.

Chapter Four:
How To Kill The Soul

And here begins the story I want to tell you. All those romantic relationships and bad decisions led me here. If I were in your place, I probably would have long ago turned my attention to this chapter, but for me personally, none of what was supposed to happen made sense without those fateful kicks. After a long search and gathering all my strength, I responded to one of the ads. It was a forty-year-old man looking for a young woman for casual meetings. The financial reward he offered matched my previous salary, and I thought to myself that I could survive it.

I absolutely didn't know what to expect from it. We were exchanging messages for a while, and then the first meeting took place. A forty-year-old smoker who looked about twenty years older, with a belly like a woman at the end of pregnancy, and he seemed very uneducated due to his way of expressing himself. After a brief conversation, which I couldn't really concentrate on, he put money on the table and announced that I was his for a month. I had absolutely no idea what I was agreeing to, but the thought of having sex with such a creature was repulsive in itself. I knew I could survive it; I just tried to convince myself that I had to. He leaned in to kiss me, his breath smelled like an ashtray, and I had to pretend that I didn't mind. The touch of his rough hands on my soft skin drove me crazy, and every minute felt endlessly long. Every moment I felt his body on mine brought on an overwhelming urge to vomit, and with every command, tears filled my eyes, and I prayed for the suffering to end. When I heard his rapid breath and suspicious sounds, I thought either he had finished or had a heart attack, but either way, it was a considerable relief because it meant it was over, and my torment at least momentarily ceased. He rolled onto his side, panting loudly like a runner after ten kilometres, and I thought the worst was behind me, without knowing what else awaited me.

When someone pays you, it's as if you've lost the right to be human. Someone else almost owns you, tells you when to see him, when to breathe, what to do, and you slowly lose your freedom and the right to be human. I expected it to be just a few meetings a month, but what came was horrifying. He constantly messaged and called me; when I didn't answer the phone, threatening messages started to come, and I was warned that if I didn't start communicating with him, he would take the money back. At night, I had to record erotic videos according to his fantasies while my daughter slept in the next room. It was awful but far from the worst. On our third meeting, he brought a medium-sized leather bag, and what was inside terrified me. He started pulling out one thing after another from the bag with a sweet smile, and I just sat there with an incredulous, disgusted expression, wanting to escape from my own apartment. First, it was white lingerie, then an anal plug, handcuffs, a collar, a leash, a whip, and other erotic accessories. Each item raised a million questions and mixed feelings in me. I was informed about what the gentleman likes, which took away all my words, and it was followed by thunderous silence. I had been humiliated countless times in my life, but this person took away my dignity, crumpled it, threw it into that leather bag, and even spat on it.

Because there's no better feeling in the world than crawling in white lingerie on your knees, having a silicone penis-shaped thing stuck in your ass, a collar around your neck, and a leash held by someone you find disgusting. I was commanded to call him "sir" and ask for things I absolutely didn't want, followed by torturous sex that more resembled rape. Every cell in my body screamed, "STOP!" but I couldn't do anything, defend myself; I just prayed for it to stop. Although it hadn't even been a month, this couldn't continue. I was afraid to say that it was impossible anymore, but every contact with him bothered me. When I received his message, my heart stopped and I was covered in a hot sweat. Getting rid of him wasn't easy, but in the end, I managed it, although he tried to cause problems in my life for a while. It wasn't like a breakup; it was more like exorcising a demon! I had to figure out what to do next, so I visited websites with offers of this kind of "profession" again, but this time, I decided to try a club in Prague. Throughout this time, of course, I attended interviews and responded to regular job offers, but the result was always the same. Unfortunately, around

Christmas, there weren't many job opportunities available, and the harder I tried, the worse it got.

I arranged a meeting and travelled to Prague. I found myself in front of an old building with a neon-lit entrance, like I was in Las Vegas. I descended the stairs and was greeted by a red light, feeling nervous and a little afraid of what awaited me. After the experience with the disgusting smoker, I hoped nothing as dreadful would happen again. My eyes adjusted, and the first thing I saw was a bar on the left side of the enormous room, with leather couches scattered around the walls and a small stage with a pole in the middle. Half-naked girls sat on the couches, and the red light considerably enhanced their faces. It was a clever thing; in the dressing room, they all looked like old junkies, but under the glow of that red miracle, they were beautiful models without any flaws. An older lady, who called herself Judith, greeted me and welcomed guests to the club, keeping an eye on the girls present. She was a friendly, well-groomed woman of a certain age, smiling at me and trying to make me feel as comfortable as possible. She slowly showed me around the club and explained the rules while trying to extract information from me about whether I had any experience in this field.

After the tour, I was asked if I wanted to stay overnight and "work." I'll keep using quotes around that word throughout my story because I never saw it as real work. I told her I would stay; I needed the money. Anyone who hasn't been in such a situation can barely imagine what financial hardship will make you do, especially when you're responsible for more than just yourself. After a moment of deliberation, I joined the scantily clad ladies and sat on an empty couch. The girls weren't friendly; they scowled and marked their territory in every possible way. If they could, they would surely snarl and proudly pee on the couch. When any man entered the room, they swooped down on him like hungry vultures, giving him a false sense of importance and attractiveness. One would shout, "Where are you from, handsome?" while another would caress his body and beg him to buy her a drink, and the third would ask him if he would go to a room with her. If a man splurged enough on drinks, the girls profited, and so ultimately, drinking the night away was financially rewarded, similar to persuading two random men to have sex.

I sat in the corner, observing all the madness unfolding before my eyes in the glow of red spotlights. I watched the fake smiles; people behaved like animals, and the companions present fought for the favour of the men and their fat wallets. Later, I learned that it was one of the rules: when a male entered the room, the girls were ordered to keep him company and try to get him to a room. This part was never my forte; I always sat alone on the couch and did nothing. It might have seemed like I was giving them the impression of taking the first step, a false pretence that they had to dazzle me to make something out of it, but the truth was, I prayed to be invisible.

Every night was like one big party. Girls in erotic costumes sniffed meth in the bathroom, the music was so loud you couldn't hear your own thoughts, alcohol flowed freely, and amidst it all, a beautiful woman gracefully danced around the pole, and the horny males couldn't take their eyes off her. None of them knew she was a mother of two children, barely sleeping, working in a hair salon during the day, and dancing at the pole at night to provide for what was closest to her heart. Even if they knew, they wouldn't care; all they were interested in was her body and their satisfaction. I never drank in the club, and I didn't even touch drugs. I drove there by car, and my priority was to stay sober so I could spend my days with my child. It worked like this for a while. In the evening, I dropped my sweetheart off at her grandparents 'and drove to Prague, a two-hour drive from my parents 'place. Somehow, I survived the night; I threw up twice on my way to the car. Alive and incredibly tired, I tried to reach my parents, take my smiley to the kindergarten, then go home, get some sleep, pick up my daughter from kindergarten, spend the afternoon with her, drop her off at her grandparents, and go to Prague. At that time, it wasn't just my problems I had to deal with; financially, I was supporting my brother, who lived in Ireland. He had a work injury and couldn't walk on one leg, and finding another job was challenging for him. We all have bills to pay, and for me, my family always came first. I didn't want to throw him or anyone else overboard, but it was difficult trying to take care of everyone and everything, especially when I was suffering the most. Nobody except my brother knew about it, but one day, my nerves snapped, and I told my parents about it, or rather, I screamed at them. I couldn't handle more accusations and insults; I was tired and utterly disgusted with myself in the worst way possible. Moreover, the carousel of lies was too much; I bottled everything up and didn't know how to deal with it. I overreacted when my mom came to me and started blaming me, saying that my daughter needs a home that she spends more time with them than with her own mom, and I got a lecture about what a lousy mother I am. I couldn't handle the pressure. I burst into tears, and after a while of arguing, I blurted out: "I don't work at the bar; I lied to you. I failed, and I had no other option; I'm a prostitute at night!" There was pain and helplessness in every word; tears were streaming down my face, my body was shaking, and I felt ashamed of what I did, embarrassed that I said it, but at the same time, I felt relief. That bubble of lies was destroying me; it was holding me back, and now it was out there.

Dad looked at me, crying. I saw the disappointment in his eyes, but he hugged me as tightly as only a father can hug his daughter; I felt love and support. My mom, from a distance, said in a very arrogant tone, "Well, I knew it…"

That's my mom; when you have her nearby, you can throw away all the books and disconnect from the Wi-Fi because she's like a walking encyclopaedia. She thinks she knows everything, she's been everywhere, and anything you can imagine has already happened to her, at least in her head, but if you want to get along with her, always agreeing and never opposing is a straightforward recipe for peace. We never talked about it again, but looking into my parents 'eyes was almost impossible; they felt guilty because they couldn't do anything to help me, and I felt like I had disappointed them as a daughter. Let's go back to my first night in that place of sin. Imagine an innocent girl with no idea how she ended up in such a place, her palms sweating nervously, afraid of everything that could happen in the next few hours. A girl sat next to me, a blonde of a healthy-looking size started chatting with me. I don't remember what we talked about, and I don't even remember her face, but I'll never forget when our conversation was interrupted by a man who decided to sit down on our ugly leather couch.

A bald, unattractive guy from Finland, middle-aged, with glasses and a beer belly, leaned towards us and mumbled something in English. I didn't speak the language, but the lady beside me seemed confident and responded fluently. After a while, she leaned towards me and said, "This guy wants you." I automatically responded, "Well, I don't want him!" "He wants you like a piece of meat for one-time use," or at least that's how it sounded to me. In this world, I was new, and I still didn't fully realise that I didn't have the right to say "no," which was subsequently explained to me. The ugly man grabbed my hand and, like a war victim that night, led me to the bar, where he planned to pay for the rental of my body. Disgusting! Didn't he realise I was scared, trembling, and didn't want him? Maybe he did, but perhaps he didn't care too much. At the bar, he paid and dragged me down the stairs to one of the rooms, which he rented for thirty minutes together with me. There were specific rules; one of them was that they didn't buy love, only sex, so we had to adjust accordingly. Everything was very mechanical, and every move of mine had to aim towards his climax. I sat on the bed, unable to utter a word. The bald man seemed to have more experience in this regard than I did, and without even looking at me, he undressed and confidently squeezed his hefty bum into the shower. After a few minutes, his corpulent body with water droplets moved to the bed beside me. He lay on his back, waiting for what he had paid for. I reached for the basket full of condoms on the nightstand, my vision blurred by tears, and tried to think of something else as I attempted to put protection on his penis. I took that small, repulsive member into my mouth, the latex was scratching my throat, making me want to vomit. I felt hands in my hair, gripping my head from both sides, treating me like a toy as he moved up and down, pleasuring himself with loud sounds of ecstasy. When oral gratification was no longer enough for him, he grabbed me firmly by the hair and pulled me towards him. I couldn't open my eyes to look at him; I just felt his breath on my face. Without a single word or shred of pity, he threw my body onto the bed, turned me onto my stomach, grabbed me by the waist with one hand, lifted me, and made me arch my back while using his other hand to push my head into the pillow. He penetrated me from behind, and I couldn't even move; I was paralysed, feeling a sharp pain shooting through every inch of my body. The torturous encounter ended with his sighs, revealing his climax. He pulled off his little tool from me, patted my back heroically, and, with a perverse smile, removed the condom filled with semen, tossing it into the bin behind him. I rolled onto my back and watched him slowly dress; neither of us said anything. He was a content individual who had just emptied his balls, and I was a confused and terrified girl who just wanted to be in a safe place. When he finally closed the door behind him, I started cleaning the room. The disgust towards myself was so immense I cried uncontrollably and wondered how long I could keep doing this. As I climbed upstairs, Judith ran to me, shouting from a distance, "So, how did it go?" With tear-filled eyes, I tried to act bravely, and my response was, "Well, I guess I have lower moral standards than I thought."

Judith started laughing and walked away. I still think she was mocking me because, in the eyes of others, prostitutes don't have any moral standards, do they? In many respects, I would agree, but there are exceptions among sex workers; it's just hard to distinguish who is who. Everyone will tell you a touching and heartbreaking story about how they ended up in this "profession," but the question is when it's a well-crafted lie and when it's a true story.

This club was full of such stories:

The dark-haired girl addicted to methamphetamine, who called herself Stacy, complained that she had to close her beauty salon and had no other source of income. Still, maybe no one wanted to pay for services from a perpetually dosed girl with sharp scissors. I would be afraid to let someone uncontrollably shaking, with white crud around their lips, and speaking incoherently, cut my hair too. Adriana, a thirty-year-old coquette whose curves resembled those of a fourteen-year-old girl, could earn more in one night than all the other girls together. She wore high-platform shoes and a schoolgirl outfit. During the day, she worked as an accountant, and in the evening, she copulated with the half of Prague. Under the glow of red lights, she appeared as a beautiful young girl, and she enjoyed it. At home, she had a boyfriend who lovingly supported her in this. Why did she do it? This girl loved money, expensive clothes, luxurious cars, the best cosmetics—things that an accountant's salary wouldn't provide. Pregnant Maggie, a forty-year-old brunette, who had three children at home and was married to a lawyer. She described herself as a happy wife and mother, and her husband had no idea what she did at night; she told him she worked as a waitress. She had an ugly complex; she didn't want to rely on her man's money, so she decided to earn her own. I see nothing wrong with that except how she chose to achieve her independence. You wouldn't believe how many perverts want to bang a pregnant milf, and she lovingly spread her legs for six guys every night to prove she could take care of herself. In the morning, she returned to her children, kissed her husband, and was an excellent little wifey until the evening when she stumbled back to the club and made happy several more perverse males. I'm curious about her husband's reaction when he finds out one day. During my time providing sexual services, I met several young women in the same situation. Their husbands didn't know but eventually found out. I don't know how a guy could not notice something like that, but if you find out, your heart must be shattered. Sadly, many of these women don't even realise that their "job" isn't compatible with their relationship.

Several companions were of different nationalities, so I never had the chance to find out what led these girls astray, except for one.

Her name was Christina, a Ukrainian with fluent Czech, a sweet, innocent blonde with the face of an angel. Her mom passed away when she was a child, and she moved with her dad to Prague. She studied and worked as a cook, dreaming of opening her own restaurant, but fate turned her plans upside down. Her dad got sick, and without insurance, treatment in the Czech Republic is financially draining, just like anywhere else in the world. She didn't want to lose another family member and decided to sacrifice herself to save her father's life. She was in love, and before deciding on this "venture", she was engaged. But her morality didn't allow her to lie or cheat on that person. She told him about her plans and broke up with him. She was the girl I was closest to. When someone paid for her company, she experienced the same agony as I did, so we were there for each other. I can't wrap my head around how someone can want to pay for sex with someone they know nothing about, and I wonder if knowing that the woman is suffering would change anything. Every subsequent night for me was as

54

painful as the first, but it was easier with Christina. It was nice to have someone in a world where you're just a piece of meat for sale.

When I had been in the club for about a week, a group of Russian guys appeared who were eager for fun. The girls attended to them with due attention, and I sat in my favourite corner of the couch, pretending to be invisible. Unfortunately, I wasn't invisible enough, and one of them noticed me, arrogantly pointing at me without bothering to come over or talk to me. One of the girls who was currently enjoying their company stood up and approached me with graceful steps. As she slowly approached, I knew what would follow, and deep down, I prepared myself for the fact that for the next few dozen minutes, I would become a commodity. She looked into my eyes, smiled, and said, "Clearly, they desire you, so run away." This sentence always pierced through me like a knife blade.

It doesn't mean, "You're an attractive woman, and the gentleman would like to get to know you better." Games of courtship are irrelevant in this field; they simply come and choose their prey, and there's no option to protest. I stood up, put on my fake smile, and before I knew it, the Russian male was already paying for his desire at the bar. He was a walking testament to arrogance, disdainful of me and everything I embodied in that place, and he behaved accordingly towards me. We entered one of the rooms. He closed the door behind him, and before I knew it, he grabbed me by the hair and pulled me towards him. From the expression on his face, I expected him to spit on me; he was so disgustingly domineering.

He unbuttoned his trousers, pulled out his 'pride', and with all his might, pushed me down onto my knees; barely had I put on the condom when I already had his penis in my mouth. He held me by the hair and thrust into my throat in such a way that I was choking, tears streaming down my face, every movement was pure agony. He pulled me up by the hair and threw me onto the bed, with every command adding the address "Ty suka," which added a 'charming touch' to the whole situation. Sex in this place isn't the tender lovemaking you know or can imagine; it's just another form of violence, violence you actually agree to or are forced to consent to. With this man, scratches and slaps were not uncommon; he took me rough while choking me so that I couldn't breathe. I gasped for breath and tried to remove his hand from my throat. He let go of me, saying, "What, doesn't the little whore like it?". It was followed by his fingers forcefully penetrating my anus, against which I vehemently protested. It hurt like hell, but he couldn't care less and sadistically yelled at me, "I paid for this, and I want anal. Do it!". I gasped for breath and tried to remove his hand from my throat; he let go of me, saying, "What's wrong, bitch, don't you like it?" If I could say that I didn't want something, it was anal sex, and so I said it. He reacted with shouting, slapped me, and violently tried to force me into it. Fortunately, someone heard him, and before he could succeed, security rushed in and escorted him out. I remained motionless on the bed; I didn't even know for how long. The bartender brought me a shot of whiskey and tried to console me. This is something I wouldn't wish upon anyone, and no girl who decides to work in the sex industry for any reason deserves such treatment. Unfortunately, during my time in this "job", I encountered a few more of these violent bastards, and I remember them all. It hits you so deeply and profoundly that you can never get it out of your head. Over time, your brain creates a certain kind of protection and makes you forget about all those men, but you'll never forget those who hurt you the most. I would have returned the favour to them in the same measure; I would have prepared a mobile table with medieval torture tools, tied them to the bed, and let any feminist who was interested unleash their wrath upon them. Unfortunately, for a reasonably logical reason, it's illegal, so the idea isn't feasible, but it certainly helps me quiet the pain that still lingers within me. After some time, I met Matthew. Matthew was a typical middle-aged bald jerk who wore suits, drank top-shelf liquor, and utterly despised anything that identified as a woman. It's genuinely paradoxical that many men who frequent these services actually hate women and hold them in contempt from the bottom of their souls. Matthew was very well-off, had warm relationships with the club owners, and thought he could get away with anything. His crazy ideas knew no bounds; he behaved as if he owned the world and, worse as if he owned all the girls. One beautiful afternoon, he brought a wooden coffin and placed it in one of the rooms, forcing the companions to get into it or have sex with him in it. It's morbid and twisted to have such desires; thankfully, this story happened a few weeks before I came to the club, so I didn't have to participate in this sexual fantasy, and I only know it from hearsay. The club owners constantly had to find new girls for him; none of them wanted anything to do with him after a while. For his low self-esteem and relatively small penis, it made him feel good to humiliate others, especially women. One day, the bartender from the club called me, asking me to come to Prague, even though I wasn't supposed to be there until the following evening. "There's a crucial client here named Matthew, and if you were to get along with him, you could mainly see him only and you wouldn't have to work in the club as often," she said. After all I've been through at that place, the idea of spending time with just one person actually appealed to me, and in total ignorance of who it was, I headed to the scene. All I received was his list of requirements that I was supposed to meet, but I didn't quite match most of the points. It was called "Matthew's Ten Commandments," and the way it was written could tell you a lot about the person. To my surprise, I found out that by some oversight, I deleted every single conversation from that time, except for one with the bartender, who arranged these meetings with him.

I found his list of needs, which he described as follows:

1. *Not dead, aged 18-29.*

2. *Must be slender with a normal-sized buttocks.*

3. *Must wear dresses; trousers are for men, no retro, and no tattoos.*

4. *I'm punctual and don't like waiting.*

5. *I smoke all the time and everywhere; she doesn't have to be an active smoker.*

6. *Alcohol served in small doses is essential; a teetotaller won't have fun.*

7. *Fun is in communication, so she should have something in her head.*

8. *The fun part takes a long time, and I'm in no hurry.*

9. *I'm not an astronaut; oral with a condom is disgusting!*

10. *The fun ends with my satisfaction, and that's why I'm there.*

When I met him, he sat in one of the rooms, smoking, and looked at me, saying, "Well, sweetheart, you're definitely not a model." It touched me, but I was warned in advance not to take his words too personally. He had an incredible ability to offend you with what hurt you the most and crush your confidence in such a way that only few people can do. If it was a girl with crooked teeth, he compared her to a witch; a girl with a postpartum belly or stretch marks constantly heard about how disgusting it is, she looks like a jelly and that she was repulsive. His favourite phrase was that a woman over thirty is practically dead and its like expired goods that no one wants. He was no king of beauty; he actually looked like Shrek and Obelix had a child, an average belly "sluggish" middle-aged guy who smelled of cigarettes and Scotch. When I first saw him, he criticised everything from my hair to my dressing style, and at that moment, I knew this was going to be tough. Unfortunately, I was still in a situation where I couldn't afford to make decisions as I wished. Still, I had to do what was necessary, so I agreed to continue to see this bald, domineering troll for as long as needed. Over time, I learned to ignore his absurd remarks, and beneath that shell, he was profoundly hurt and dissatisfied. He couldn't swallow the fact that I didn't drink; it was unacceptable to him, but I was driving, so I had to be extremely careful. Sometimes, I arrived a bit earlier and had a drink with him so I could leave in the morning with the certainty of being sober. He took me to a strange wellness centre owned by his friend nicknamed "Hedgehog"; it was a beautiful place, with four luxury rooms downstairs with a hot tub, and upstairs was a bar where his friend usually served.

MATTHEW

Usually, it was just him and me there, which felt a bit strange, but later, I found out that the purpose of this place was not for wellness stays; it was just a cover. Wealthy gentlemen knew this place well; they ran there with their mistresses or escort services; in fact, it served as a better "brothel" for a large clientele. Evenings spent chatting at the bar, where I had to agree with his bundle of absurdities, were agonisingly long. During one night, he could smoke countless cigarettes and drink a whole bottle of Scotch; by morning, he could barely descend the stairs to the room where my traumatic sexual experience took place, after which I usually could look forward to an early departure home. Due to the amount of alcohol and probably other factors, his manhood didn't work too well, and taking care of his satisfaction was tedious and exhausting; moreover, the omnipresent smell of tobacco and alcohol prolonged these torments infinitely. When it finally happened by some miracle, he had an erection and later even ejaculated, he usually fell asleep, and I had to sit and wait obediently until the man woke up. As part of the agreement, I would drive back to the club with him in the morning, and he would decide when I could leave. Usually, it happened right away when we arrived, but sometimes he forced me to stay and spend more long hours with him while he danced around the pole and played Czech songs from the eighties, and I was practically dying of exhaustion in the meantime. Once, when I was driving back home from Prague, I fell asleep at the wheel and scraped the car against the guardrails. Luckily, nothing worse happened, but I couldn't continue like this anymore. How did I end up here, and why was my life such a wreck? I was ashamed of myself! I had disgusting sex with complete strangers; sometimes, there were two men in one evening, and other times, I was forced to sell my body to six men in one night.

The remaining evenings were spent with that alcoholic. I cried, I vomited, and nobody had any idea how exhausting it was! In the meantime, I tried to be a good mother, daughter, and sister. Nobody saw how stressed out I was; I couldn't sleep, I couldn't eat, I suffered from depression, I couldn't find a job, and to make matters worse, I received threats from Narcissus. I thought this was rock bottom, and it couldn't get any worse, but little did I know that it could be much, much worse. I had to come up with something else. The plan was to save as much money as possible in the shortest time possible, pay off the debts, and be content with my "boring" life, surrounded by my amazing family. If I paid off everything that was driving me crazy, I wouldn't be stressed out every day. If I were alone, I would never have made such a decision, but I was responsible for two lives, and I would breathe for my daughter if it was necessary! It was time for another evening with my friend Google, and I was searching for an answer to get out of this mess. I didn't need to degrade myself to pay ordinary bills; I didn't need to sell my body to pay for gas to Prague; I didn't need to go through all this for money that I could have earned in a regular job, which I couldn't find. Have you ever tried looking for a job around Christmas, January, or February? It's almost impossible! Google spat out more job offers in the adult industry, but this time, it was in different countries. Germany was the closest, but if you've seen just a snippet of German porn, you know perfectly well that the sexual practices of German perverts are only for the strong-hearted. Poland offered me the same as the Czech Republic. In Switzerland, prostitution is legal at the highest level; you have to register and pay taxes. Paying taxes wouldn't bother me, but having my name associated with this profession for life was something I really didn't want. Then, I came across a Czech agency that mediated work in the adult industry in Ireland.

The ad read as follows:

"Hello ladies; we would like to offer you Tours in Ireland. We provide effective advertising, accommodation, transportation, and a team of trained people who will care for you and are available to you due to their professional conduct and experience. You can earn €4,000 per week with us. We will help inexperienced girls and explain everything. Our motto is correctness, discretion, and reliability. If you are interested in our offer, don't hesitate to contact us."

I found this advertisement on the internet while I was writing these pages; it's still the same one I responded to, and currently, it has 98,980 applicants. It was published by a lady who calls herself Susan, who would later become my "boss" or perhaps a pimp might be a more appropriate term. With despair in my eyes, I decided to contact this dubious person who was supposed to help me put my life back together. I received a response on January 15, 2020, and now I know that it was a bunch of lies. If I could go back in time, I probably wouldn't have replied to her back then.

This is the exact response I received at that time:

"Hello; this concerns city tours in Ireland; the minimum stay for ladies is seven working days, with the option to extend as needed. We always try to accommodate the Tour dates 100%. Ladies work in verified, discreet hotels such as Clayton, Radisson Blue, Hilton, etc. Working hours are from 10:00 am to 11:00 pm. Prices are 30 minutes for €100, 45 minutes for €150, and 60 minutes for €200, with additional surcharges going to you, of course. If a lady wishes, she can also work out calls, but only to verified hotels. Costs such as accommodation, flights, and earnings are split 60% to 40%, with 60% for you, and the same percentage is also used to cover expenses. Ladies have a non-stop operator on their phone throughout their stay to assist them, especially if they have limited knowledge of English. If you are interested in our offer or have any questions, we can arrange a personal meeting or a phone call."

Then we called each other. I remember hiding in the bathroom at my parents 'house and being as quiet as a mouse. Susan provided me with all the information I needed to know before my first trip. She told me roughly how much money I would need and sent me the phone number of a photographer in Prague who photographed all the girls for this agency.

Photographing, advertising, it's disgustingly absurd when you realise that human bodies are photographed and offered on escort websites and horny perverts just browse through and choose one of the many girls. It's like choosing perfume or ordering food, and it sends chills down my spine when I realise how bizarre it is. While I did this "work", I found it difficult to open those websites, so I only visited them when it was necessary. I still "worked" nights at the club while trying to figure out how to proceed without raising suspicions about what I was about to do. It required more lies, and I couldn't tell anyone about it, not even Emma. Due to my ambitions, education, and previous position, everyone considered me an intelligent girl, and the last thing I wanted was for people around me to have prejudices. My family and friends were always the most valuable to me, and I loved them with all my heart. As the departure date approached, I decided to give up my apartment;

Emma and her boyfriend were looking for a place to live, which supported my decision. Although I planned to leave for only a few months, there was no reason to pay rent and utilities when I couldn't afford it.

Plus, I had to move my life to another country and entrust it to a woman who didn't even tell me her real name. That's either absolute trust or total stupidity and desperation!

Emma and Mark started moving into my apartment, and it was a truly challenging time for me. Prague, the club, being mom, moving, Ireland—I was so scared, and I couldn't confide in anyone. It hurt me the most to be without my little girl, but she had spent the last few weeks with a zombie mom, and I knew I couldn't delay it any longer. In the interest of preserving health and good relationships, at that time, I found it more than reasonable to leave and resolve our lives once and for all. I always did everything for her; she was my light at the end of the tunnel, and I was determined to do everything to get our life back!

I know thousands of people would say I had a choice, that I could have done it differently, that they would have found another option and resolved the situation. Maybe they would have seen it, and it would have been great, but believe me, if you have common sense and you are in the situation I found myself in, you don't leave your child, and you don't go to another country where eight men daily will lie down on you if you have a choice. Looking back on that situation now, with the benefit of hindsight, I would have to make the exact same decision, I still don't know of any other way out at that time. It's easy to judge someone when you've never been in their shoes, don't know all the details, or know what that person has been through.

Not every single mother is to blame for her situation; not every prostitute wants to do the "job" she does, and not every unemployed person is too lazy to find a job. We are surrounded by a system, order, and rules that can make our lives easier or complicate them. Life doesn't ask; it throws sticks in our way, unpleasant things happen, and sometimes, we are forced by circumstance to make decisions we would never make otherwise. Like moving your daughter to your parent's house, taking her away from all her friends and unenrolling her from kindergarten because your aging parents wouldn't be able to drive her fifty kilometres to the city every day. Or after a night spent at the club, coming home and sleeping on a mattress placed a meter and a half above the ground on small cabinets because your friends are moving into your apartment.

If there was a choice, I would choose differently, but we choose based on experiences and knowledge, and maybe in ten years, I'll see a solution that I didn't see at the time. But back then, I sacrificed myself for a better future, and it was one of the hardest decisions of my life! I spent many of my last evenings in Prague with Matthew; he was in love with me, or at least that's what everyone said. Towards the end, he became much more open with me and shared things from his private life. When I told him about my escape plan, he hugged me, and it wasn't the slimy embrace where he desperately tried to put his hand on my butt. It was a friendly and supportive hug. I was glad I could finally see something good in that person.

Of course, I couldn't tell him the whole truth; he thought I was flying to Ireland to be with my brother and I would have a regular job there. I told him the same lie as everyone else, but my shame was too great to be able to reveal my true intentions. I never told him anything, and I didn't expect anything from him, so it surprised me even more when he brought me money in an envelope to give me a more pleasant start. It was a thousand euro; I immediately sent half to my brother, who was still at home with a work injury and had no money, and I used the other half to pay for the flight and the photos that Susan wanted from me. The money I earned at the club until then, I left it to my parents so they would have enough for food and other necessities. I planned to leave them my treasure and wanted to ensure she would be well taken care of. I was preparing to make one of the hardest decisions of my life, but at that moment, it seemed like the only option, and sometimes, we have to deny ourselves to be able to protect those we love.

Sometimes, fear is powerful, and when we're afraid, we don't always make the best decisions.

I said goodbye to my family; I hugged my little princess so tightly that I almost squashed her, and the next day was D-Day. As I drove to

64

the airport, I cried like a little girl; I still kept thinking there must be another way, another possibility, but I couldn't find any other solution. My mind was immersed in longing, and I was sure I would miss everyone terribly. Leaving your own child is like tearing your soul in two halves; you bleed incessantly, and there's no way to soothe that pain. It was one of the greatest pains I've ever experienced, and at that moment, I didn't even realise how long I would have to deal with this kind of suffering.

My inexperience also took their toll, and I couldn't even imagine what I was getting into. The club was different from "working" in hotels; my knowledge of English was worse than basic, and if you've ever heard an Irish accent, it's something that can hardly be considered English. Native speakers have trouble understanding them, so you can imagine what it was like for me, a woman raised in Slavic traditions. I had visited my brother in Ireland several times, mostly on weekend trips when I still worked for Mr. Mysterious. So, it wasn't such an unfamiliar country for me, but the current reason for this visit definitely didn't make my trip a pleasant one, quite the opposite. I was anxious and stressed throughout the entire flight; the unknown frightened me. Perhaps the only positive thing about this trip was that I had someone from my family on that island, but considering what I went there to do, it could hardly be regarded as a positive thing. They say money doesn't solve problems, but I still think mine could have been definitely solved at that time. I just needed one minor financial miracle, but it didn't happen, so I had to plunge into the unknown and hope for the best. Throughout the journey, I kept asking myself endless questions about what it would be like and when I would return home.

Chapter Five: How To Lose The Freedom

I met my brother right after landing at the airport; he came to pick me up on crutches as he was still dealing with the aftermath of his injury. After an agreement with Susan, I could spend two days with him on arrival, and then I had to start my "shift".

The first thing you notice after arriving in Ireland during the winter months is the brutal cold. Damn, I'm from a region where it can occasionally drop to minus twenty degrees, but this was a kind of cold I wasn't prepared for. When the wind blew, I could feel my cheeks starting to crack.

My brother took me to his place in a small town about an hour away from Dublin, and I was looking forward to embracing the warmth. Those two days were amazing; I enjoyed every moment. After all, I hadn't been stress-free for a while, but unfortunately, it was just a "demo version" of happiness. After two days, I had to leave, and the first on the list was a hotel in a town called Dundalk. I don't understand why they sent me here first; it was a cruel decision.

This town doesn't have the best reputation, mainly because of the people who live there. You can find everything from drug dealers to farmers who think soap is a dirty word.

I borrowed money for the hotel, which I couldn't afford after all the expenses. I was supposed to meet a girl in front of the hotel who would provide me with money for accommodation.

I met the girl, she handed me about five hundred euros in cash, and I went to check in. It wasn't suspicious at all when a young girl with a giant suitcase arrives to stay at a hotel for three days, doesn't speak any English, and can pay for accommodation and a deposit in cash.

Looking back, it's almost admirable that it didn't seem suspicious to anyone in ninety per cent of cases. I had to download the Telegram app, which was the platform Susan and her henchwomen used to communicate with me. Even during the journey to the hotel, I received one message after another. This pimping agency was characterised mainly by the fact that none of its members could provide all the information in one message. It was as if they all underwent a four-day torturous course on how to drive you crazy in ten steps. From morning till night, every day, every minute, all you could hear was the sound of incoming messages. You didn't have a moment of peace; you couldn't ignore it or even turn off your phone. After a few weeks, I started to become highly allergic to it! Honestly, if you're one of those people who write a message of six words in eight messages, with two of them consisting only of nonsensical emojis, frankly, having a phone should be illegal for you. You're likely a very unpopular individual among your friends, and behind your back, they're planning to steal your electronic devices. Throughout the whole time, from the moment I opened my eyes in the morning until I crawled into the hotel room, my phone was beeping as if the end of the world was coming. The worst part was probably not that I received notifications but why those notifications were coming. I expected that after several hours of travelling, I would have the chance to eat, unpack, and prepare quietly, but that wasn't an option. Time meant money, and for this agency, money was everything. The more money you earned, the more popular you were. That day, I had an operator named Alex; of course, that wasn't her real name, but since every member of this twisted team had a made-up name, it didn't make sense for me to waste time and creativity trying to conceal their names. For greater authenticity, I'll use the names given to me since I had started "working" with them.

Alex wasn't evil, but she was under as much pressure as the other operators from Susan and Jane, who were like the main bosses. Operators had to "keep the numbers within the tables" at all costs, often the highest.

The work of an operator was by no means easy. Most of those who did it were on maternity leave or had "worked" in prostitution themselves in the past, so after thirty years of selling their bodies, suddenly, they found that they couldn't fit into the job market anymore. Instead of completing their education or trying to build a career, they decided to stay in the field.

The operator's job involves a lot of tasks. Each of them had at least five phones that had to be on from morning till night. One phone equalled one profile of a girl on escort websites.

The phones rang incessantly, and they had to answer every call and pretend to be the girl the man was interested in. Then, they had to arrange a meeting with the horny caller, bring him to the apartment or hotel, check with the girl if she was ready, and send the man to her. Throughout, the operator had to stay in touch with the girl, even after the man had arrived, to find out how long he would stay and when she could schedule the next meeting. It wasn't uncommon for a girl to have to handle eight to ten men in a row; as long as the phone was ringing, nobody cared if you could handle it physically or mentally. I cried and begged so many times that I was no longer able to continue; my body trembled, and I could barely walk, but nobody cared. On top of that, the operator had to be available to the girls who were moving to another city, find public transportation for them, and for the less intelligent ladies, even guide them to the stops or practically be with them all day. They also communicated in group chats with their bosses and informed them about how the girls were doing and how much they had earned. Practically, from the morning, when they opened their eyes, until evening, they were locked up in their apartment with their phones, usually four or five days a week, with hardly a chance to even go to the bathroom, and under tremendous pressure, they participated in the atrocities that were happening, all for a monthly salary of about a thousand to fifteen hundred euros. Some operators enjoyed their work, and others did it only because they had to. Throughout the time I worked under this agency, I only came across three operators who were disgusted by the whole affair and were able to show emotions. Unfortunately, a woman who has emotions instead of sharp elbows doesn't belong in this world, so it's no wonder they all left the agency and found a job where they didn't have to deal with the torturous processes of sexual deviance. After checking in, Alex asked me to check my ad and see if I really offer all the services listed there. When most people hear the word ad, they think of a woman washing her hair with a miraculous shampoo or yoghurts at the lowest prices in the shop at the end of town.

This was an ad for selling meat, human meat. When you opened the website, you saw photos of girls of all kinds; aroused males could choose a blonde or a brunette, short or tall, curvy or slim, depending on their fantasies and tastes. The ad included several photos of the girl from all possible angles, mostly involving two hours of Photoshop work, and rarely did the man meet the same girl he saw in the pictures. To avoid disappointment and a decrease in erection, there were reviews; yes, each ad contained several reviews where men who had already visited the girl could vividly describe their experience and recommend her to other slimy males. Who actually has the right to judge something like this? Some fat, smelly uncle just comes along and publicly judges whether another person is attractive and sexually capable. In my opinion, something like this is particularly repulsive, mainly because it involves advertising human beings. However, for this agency and most girls, reviews were as valuable as the Holy Grail; the more positive reviews, the more men came, which equated to higher earnings. Disgusted by this whole strategy and angry, I convinced myself to open my ad to check that I wouldn't do anything more than absolutely necessary. Most of the words contained in this ad were utterly new to me at the time, such as: "OWO, CUM, french kissing, hard-sport, foot fetish, role play, love dancing, shared shower etc." It might excite someone, but when you imagine offering something like that to unknown men, it turns your stomach upside down.

After discovering this misinformation, I immediately contacted Alex. I assured her that I wouldn't do any of it, after which I was told to contact Jane, who was in charge of the advertisement.

Jane, the princess of the whole agency, was my second boss under Susan's leadership.

When she was younger, she used to travel around Europe with Susan and were in the same situation as me, except that these two enjoyed it. They wanted the attention, like most of the girls who do this job, and gladly sold their bodies. Well, I don't know about Susan, but Jane always spoke positively about this profession and liked to boast about her past. There's nothing more beautiful in the world than being proud that you've screwed with half of Europe.

Jane didn't have much understanding, and me as a newcomer in this world, I had to believe and listen to what she said. I told her that I disagreed with the services listed on the website and detested the idea of semen in my mouth or providing unprotected oral sex. Jane had an answer for everything; at that time, I didn't know her, but today, I know exactly what kind of person she is. She would go over dead bodies to achieve her needs, lie and pretend like a pro, she could present everything in a way that you would believe her. In short, I was reminded of the mess I was in. How much I owed them for the hotel, how much the flight cost me, and the photos they needed, also a little emotional blackmail was added: "Think of your daughter; you'll do it for her so that you can be back with her soon. You know, Ireland is small; those guys all know each other, and they'll tell each other everything. If someone leaves unsatisfied, no one will come to you, and you'll be done. You know why you're here, right? You'll manage this for a while, a few months, and you'll be back home with your little girl, don't worry!"

She made you feel like she understood you and that you were essential to her; she had no competition in manipulating others and always got what she wanted. After our long conversation, I managed to convince her to remove things like anal sex or peeing on people, which I was unable to do. She instilled in me a fear that if I didn't fulfil everything the men wanted, I would end up in an even bigger mess than I already was. Honestly, I never forgave her for this, and I don't think I'll ever be able to forget. If karma hasn't caught up with her yet, I hope it will do one day. Considering that plan 'A' failed, this was plan 'B' and plan 'C' didn't exist; I felt so powerless that I followed all orders. I just wanted to earn enough to pay off my debts and leave for home as soon as possible. On the first day, I earned seven hundred euro and satisfied seven men, each staying with me for half an hour. That evening, my body hurt like with the flu; my muscles were stiff, and I just wanted to go to bed. The sad part was that although they promised earnings of around four thousand euros a week, that wasn't true at all. I was left with sixty per cent of that, from which I had to pay for food, transportation, condoms, and cosmetics myself. They would contribute forty per cent for accommodation and advertising, which, considering hotel prices, was a negligible contribution. I still owed them some money, so even after the first day, I was in financial debt. As I mentioned, my first day at the hotel in Dundalk was terrible; one man left, and I had about five minutes to touch up my makeup, clean the room, shower, and dress, and I had to rush to the peephole to look out for the next idiot heading towards my room. The first guy I met about an hour after arriving at the hotel was a sixty-year-old Irishman with a terrible rural accent. If I could go back now, I would kick him out, but at that time, I remembered Jane's words and had to convince myself that I could handle it.

The man was a local farmer, an utterly disgusting person, smelled of tobacco and cigarette smoke, hadn't showered for at least a week, and at that time, with my broken English, I tried to persuade him to get into the bathroom. It seemed like he didn't even know the meaning of the word "bathroom," when he shoved two fifty-euro notes, he became convinced that I belonged to him and tried to force me into a service that appeared on my profile. It still makes me sick when I think about it. The man refused to shower, and my persuasive abilities in English weren't sufficient. He undressed and lay down on the bed, the pervasive smell of cigarettes, sweat, and urine filling the room. I began to regret not staying in Prague! I locked myself in the bathroom with Jane on the phone, where I described the situation to her: "Jane, I can't handle this. That guy's penis is covered in white chunks of something that looked like cottage cheese; it smelled like urine and sweat; he's repulsive, he doesn't want to shower, and he's forcing me into unprotected oral sex. He has dragon breath rotten teeth, and wants me to kiss him. I can't do it."

Manipulative Jane quickly reminded me of my place: "Sweetheart, wipe it off with wet wipes and do what you must. Remember, you owe us five hundred euros, and you're broke. If you don't do it, we won't like that you're losing clients and we're losing money. Think carefully about it!"

With tears in my eyes, I emerged from the bathroom, set the timer on my phone for thirty minutes, and with enormous self-denial, I got to "work". Rough hands touched me everywhere, the dry skin on his lips scratched me, and it was far from anything pleasant. He put his dirty fingers on my clitoris and tried to rub me as hard as he probably saw in a porno movie, convinced that I liked it. I screamed in pain, tears dripping onto the pillow. I tried to wipe his member with wet wipes, but I can't say it helped. When I had that thing in my mouth, it took a lot of control not to vomit on him. His pubic hair had the smell of urine, it was rubbed against my face, and hot liquid flooded my mouth, squirting down my throat. At this point, I couldn't handle it anymore and fled to the bathroom, where I vomited. When I came out, the man was satisfied and dressed, and without a word, he opened the door to the room and left.

I told Alex what had happened, but she just informed me that someone else was waiting for me downstairs and that I should hurry up. Ten minutes later, a slightly younger, cleaner candidate stood in front of me, thrusting money into my hand while undressing. I was beginning to feel like these men here knew how this business worked much better than I did. The room smelled of the previous client like a weasel nest, but this man didn't seem to mind. Before I knew it, more hands were ripping off my clothes. That day, I had another penis in my mouth, more pubic hair on my face, and more fingers in my crotch, trying to tear my clitoris out. The man obviously enjoyed it, and I felt like a puppet. After his climax, back in my mouth, he asked me if I was new here. After all, it was pretty obvious! I answered "Yes", to which he responded, "Hmm, fresh meat," and told me that his friend would come after him. When he said that, I began to believe Jane that maybe, indeed, one man sends another. When the fifth person was lying on top of me that day, I stopped perceiving everything, as if my brain had shut down. You just enter a phase where you don't think; you just stare into space and try to pretend you're invisible. This isn't unfamiliar to men; they have an innate ability not to think. Usually, you realise this when they look like they've had a stroke and are staring into nothingness.

Turning off the brain is a highly complex matter for women, and it happened to me for the first time that day, but certainly not for the last time.

Somewhere, I heard that during sex, we distinguish between two types of women: those who enjoy it as if they were going to die and those who died already yesterday. I felt like I was already dead for at least a week and what was coming at me must be a necrophile because I can't imagine how anyone could enjoy it otherwise.

By some miracle, I survived the first three days in Dundalk and moved to Cork, where I stayed at a hotel that resembled Hogwarts School of Witchcraft and Wizardry. When I arrived at the bus station, it was pouring rain. As an non English speaking being, I was ashamed to take a taxi, so I bravely decided to grab my suitcase and walk to the hotel in the rain. For most places in southern Ireland, everything is uphill. Soaked, frozen, and tired, I shuffled at a snail's pace with my suitcase towards the hotel in a completely unfamiliar environment. When I, wholly drenched, saw the sign with the name of what I was looking for, I almost jumped with excitement. It was an old place; the building resembled more of a Gothic cathedral than a hotel, but it had its charm, a terrifying charm. I looked like I had jumped into a pool somewhere along the way. I entered the reception, and I was greeted by a lovely man with an accent that reminded me of an English version of "Hoch Deutsch." At that time, I didn't know yet, but the probability of meeting someone in Cork whose accent is flattering is about as high as being struck by lightning. The pleasant receptionist understood my inability to speak English and agreed to communicate through a translator, which was pleasantly humorous. This whole adventure allowed me to forget for a while why I was there and what I was doing there. However, the girls from the agency didn't like that I even momentarily forgot, and with every step I took away from the reception, I felt the vibrations of phones in my pocket:

"Are you there already, Are you checked in, Do you have your room, What time do we start? When can I make the first booking?"

In my room, I replied to them; I wanted to buy food since I hadn't eaten since morning. I got up at five in the morning, and by the time I "rolled" here, it was afternoon, and the shopping options along the way were quite limited. Ireland is not as small as you can imagine from some movies.

My request was practically denied because I had an hour to prepare for the first client, and all the shops were disgustingly far away from me. That hotel was terrifying; from the window of my room, I could see a cemetery, the ceilings were high, the room was cold, and I felt like a princess locked in a tower. One would almost say I was waiting for a prince to arrive on a white horse and rescue me, but what I encountered in my 'chamber' could hardly be compared to princes. The whole three days in that hotel room were more of a horror experience for me than a fairytale with a happy ending. I don't remember all the men I met there, and I'm grateful that I forgot because there are things you don't want to remember. Unfortunately, on the other hand, there are things you desperately want to forget, but your brain has declared war on you and it is trying to keep some memories at all costs. I have two experiences with men from my first stay in Cork that I would like to erase from my system, but I'm afraid it won't happen, just like with many others. On the first day of my arrival, I met at least five men: hungry, cranky, and tired. I opened the door with a fake smile on my lips and tears in my eyes. It's hard to admit that you belong to someone; that freedom for many can be a fleeting thing. You pretend to like everything and pretend that you are flattered when an unattractive, hungry man appears behind the door, handing you money. You grit your teeth and pray for it to be quick because that's all that is left. You close your eyes, feeling your throat tighten, and try to forget what's happening, that you're someone's sexual slave, that you have something in you that you don't want there, that you feel the breath of a stranger and touches that send shivers down your spine. You don't want to be there; you don't want to perceive it, so you try to escape, at least in your mind, to some safe place where you feel good. On the very first day in this southern part of the island, I met a man of more diminutive stature; he wore a collared shirt, a brown leather jacket, and jeans. The man boasted of being overweight, with a belly where he could hide an elephant and an unpleasant odour. His face was severe to the point of being arrogant, and overall, he gave me an unfriendly impression. He decided to spend an hour with me, and for me, without realising it, it was the first step into the real Ireland, into the Ireland that most people don't see or can't see.

Without any hesitation, he pulled out a small pouch from his pocket containing a bag of white powder, a card, and a rolled-up banknote. He approached the table, without a single hesitation, started to spread his tools, and was doing his business. After a few seconds, he had three long lines of powder ready on the table, and one by one; he leaned a banknote towards each line to inhale all the content in one breath. After completing this process, he removed a silver flat bottle with an unknown liquid from his jacket and drunk it down. I stood there, shocked. He asked me if I wanted some, too, and I quickly replied, "No, thanks!"

The man wasn't happy with my statement and began to persuade me to take something with him, saying it wouldn't hurt me. I knew why I was there, slowly approaching my goal through all the suffering, and the last thing I wanted was to end up as a drug-addicted prostitute. After all my "no's" and immense dissatisfaction, he realised he couldn't get that filth into me.

This white powder has an exciting effect on men; they become eager, uncontrollably horny, but down there, it's primarily dysfunctional in most cases. This was my first experience, and causing an erection in the man was beyond my capabilities, which was very frustrating for both of us. For me, it was a prolonged, disgusting process where I had to endure an hour of trying to revive something that was long dead, and for him, it was thwarting desire, which led to raising his voice and unpleasant behaviour. I wasn't born with male genitalia, so I can't judge how awful it feels when you want to, but your best friend refuses to cooperate. Finally, after about forty minutes, he persuaded me to let him take one line from my body, and if it didn't work, he would leave. My only condition was that he didn't snort it from anywhere where I have membranes, which he didn't like but eventually accepted. I knelt down on all fours, naked, scared, and defenceless, letting him place cocaine on the lower part of my back. I don't know how much he poured there or how much he had already taken, but surprisingly, it had absolutely no positive effect on his manhood. The man left, angry and unsatisfied, and I was still shocked by what had happened.

At that time, I was innocent and had a massive aversion to drugs; it never occurred to me that I would come into contact with something like that. I saw how it destroyed girls in Prague; I saw my brother addicted to methamphetamine as I grew up. I couldn't imagine letting myself become a walking zombie. I had to report the whole thing to the agency, where Jane came on stage with a deep scolding that I didn't expect. She believed that if a client wanted me to do drugs with him, I should do it because then he would be willing to extend the time spent in the room and pay more money. According to her, I should sacrifice my health for money, but that was something I wasn't willing to accept. In the worst depression, I thought about what was most precious to me in the world, and my treasure deserved more than a drug-addicted mom. In this, I didn't listen to Jane, and I never reported any similar situation to her again; it was safer and without consequences for me. When the end of the day finally approached, and I could relax a little, I ordered some food. After some searching, I found out that I didn't understand almost anything and had no idea what I was ordering. You probably know it when you're in a foreign country and try to figure out with the help of the internet what the dish's name means and if it won't poison you. After several long minutes, I chose a meal that I thought would be edible, but what I received resembled a heart attack wrapped in a paper box. I picked up the order at the reception and unpacked it in the room. Despite not eating all day, I only had a little; I decided I'd rather be hungry than dead. Pasta buried in oil with a bit of chicken wrapped in a mysterious crust. I missed vegetables, regular meat, and moderation. Czech food isn't the healthiest, but at least it's edible. I've eaten plenty of vegetables all my life, minimal oil; in short, you try to keep your body healthy. But it seemed they didn't know anything like that here, and with every ordered box of delicious fat, you receive one nail in your own coffin as a gift.

The following day, I got up early and went to the shopping centre near the bus station, where I bought a few things, including a salad bowl. I was looking forward to having it, but it had unfortunate consequences. I don't know if it was a combination of those few bites of the oily pasta the night before or if the vegetables decided to declare war on me, but I got my second food poisoning of my life. I assume most people have gone through something similar; you start feeling nauseous, cramps in your stomach as if you were about to give birth to that salad. You barely make it to the bathroom, and you never know if you'll vomit or if you'll have to sit on the toilet. Watery diarrhoea alternated with vomiting, and I couldn't stop it; I had no medicine and no one to buy it for me. I called Jane, and I told her how I felt, that I probably had a fever and was unable to "work," but this lady didn't care; I "had to work." She promised me it would be quieter, so I tried to rebel and told her I wouldn't "work," that I wasn't feeling well, and practically just sat on the toilet. I was told that plenty of clients would still be excited about it and she hung up on me. I had a fever, was shaking, sitting on the toilet all sweaty, and the idea that this would excite someone seemed far from the truth to me. I didn't expect to have to serve men when I was feeling like I was three minutes away from death, but I was wrong. When I had barely crawled into bed. Someone knocked on the door, "Probably someone from the hotel," I thought. I opened the door wrapped in a bathrobe, probably stinking, with messy hair, looking like a monster. There was a man behind the door who immediately pushed inside, handed me money, and decided he had to spend the next thirty minutes with me. I was shocked. I tried to protest, but he replied with a deep voice, "You agreed on the phone, and we arranged this" I stood there, unable to speak, holding banknotes and starting to realise what this agency was all about.

That day, they didn't send one man after another, but it didn't end with that first one either.

With every client, I clenched my sphincter spasmodically and tried to endure it all without consequences; I had never felt this bad. I don't just mean the food poisoning, but also myself. "What the hell have I gotten myself into? What am I doing here, and why are these people so mean and greedy?"

I asked myself question after question in my head while one slime-ball after another took turns in my room. Every time I closed the door and the guy was gone, I ran to suffer in the bathroom and tried to get a bit of sleep afterwards. It was a terrible day full of pain!

Somehow, miraculously, I went through it all without significant consequences. Fortunately, it was a one-day thing, and the next day, I felt better. Perhaps I would have handled the previous day better if I hadn't uncontrollably excreted fluids around me. During my last day in Cork, I was supposed to meet another girl to whom I was supposed to give money to for the agency. The funniest thing was that this girl was at the same hotel as me the whole time, but no one from the agency asked if she could buy me some medicine.

After eleven o'clock in the evening, I carried the money to her room; a tall blonde in a black, short dress opened the door for me. The girl moved uncontrollably from side to side, restlessly waving her hands around, and there was no doubt in her face that she was on some sort of drug. She wanted to chat. I didn't want to be impolite, so I stayed for a while. The whole conversation was in the spirit of this lifestyle; she told me about her clients, money, and agency. I didn't learn anything new, so I apologised that I had to go back and pack up my things, I had to get up early the next day. We said goodbye and I ran away from her faster than a sprinter. The next stop was the City-west area in West Dublin, it was a vast, luxurious hotel in the middle of nowhere; I had difficulty getting there, and it was even more challenging to find my room.

During the expedition called "Find the Right Door," I managed to get lost at least twice and had no idea where to go. Upstairs on the stairs, desperate and lost I met a boy who was probably experienced and asked me how much I wanted per hour. Of course, I apologised to him, said I didn't understand him and disappeared from there, but that encounter was unpleasant. I didn't look like an escort, when you're staying at such hotels; you have to be very careful not to be noticed. I was elegantly dressed, my hair always tied in a bun, and I looked feminine but not provocatively. I didn't know why he asked me that or how he knew it; I didn't have any labels on my forehead, but it was uncomfortable and disgusting. I immediately contacted Linda, my operator, for the next three days. I wanted to know if she had arranged a meeting for me, but she replied that she never organises anything until the girl is in the room.

So, this meeting me will probably remain an incomprehensible mystery forever; maybe some of the gentlemen there hope that every girl with an unfamiliar accent travelling alone spreads her legs for financial reward. Linda had a pleasant older voice; until I met her, I imagined her as a polished, elegant, old-fashioned lady. She was always nice to me, claiming that she worked as an operator for her son; he was a teenager, and she could describe her situation so that you felt sorry for her. Sometimes, I sent her money when needed; I was happy to help her, and I did it until we quarrelled. Much later, I learned I wasn't the only girl who financially helped her. Linda earned over a thousand euros a month by telling sad stories. Well, I have to admit that she was good at it and with the help of sad eyes, she achieved what she wanted.

At that time, when I started to "work" in Ireland and many months afterwards, I had the most pleasant opinion of her, and it seemed to me that she was a friendly and supportive woman who really understood me. However, this world and the whole agency were entirely pretence and lies. On the third day in Dublin, I was supposed to hand over money to another girl, I never met this one before. Her name was Michaela, a black-haired girl who didn't seem to have a problem with addictive substances, which impressed me. After the previous meeting with the blonde lady in Cork, I considered this a significant positive.

In the evening, according to the agreement with the agency, we were supposed to meet in the toilets at the reception, a convenient place for handing over money. At that time, it was not in anyone's interest for two girls to meet longer than necessary, which was explained to me immediately after my delay in the room with the girl in Cork. Nobody wanted gossip or possible inconsistencies, even less so if one girl was new, like me, and the other had been with the agency for a longer time and had information she could share. All the ladies who worked as operators for the agency lived in constant fear; they were well aware that pimping was illegal, and aware of the other cruelties they committed out of their greed, they were in continual fear.

This Michaela was eager to share information; I didn't even have to persuade her. Her mouth was like a volcano, spewing one piece of information after another at me.

Besides exchanging money in the restroom, we quickly exchanged phone numbers and agreed to meet "after work" in the evening.

After eleven o'clock, I went to her, hit by the smell emanating from the room. This girl lived in chaos, with a system of organisation that made sense only to her. Clothes were scattered all over the floor, a tray with half-eaten sandwiches on the bed, food remnants everywhere. Used towels were lying on chairs; I was afraid to sit down. Her organisation didn't bother me too much; I was supposed to see her for only one evening, not ask for her hand in marriage.

She decided to share everything she knew with me openly, and after the conversation with her, I left frightened. That evening, I gained a specific awareness; I was so naive, unable to realise the actual reality of this strange world. Until now, I hadn't realised any danger, despite the bad experiences in Prague; I hoped it would be different here. I "worked" under the agency; they should ensure safety. Safety should be the main reason why I had to be in contact with the operator twenty hours a day, why I always wrote to them when the "disgusting guest" was inside my room. Suddenly, you learn that your life is practically in constant danger, terrible things happen here that nobody talks about, and for the first time, I was afraid of worse things than sexually transmitted diseases. One story after another gushed from Michaela, and before I could cope with what I had just learned, she was already spewing out news from last month. For the first time, someone showed me the real face of this world that no one else talked about.

She told me about a girl who was beaten, unconscious, robbed, and tied up with phone charger cables in a bathtub, where she was found in the morning by hotel staff. The poor girl almost didn't survive, and even though you can almost read in Irish newspapers that your neighbour bought a new car, these things were taboo, and nobody was supposed to know about them. Another story was about a girl who was attacked by two men, brutally raped and beaten, robbed of everything, including her phone, and tied up in the room. When the men left, they took her room key and said, "Those who come after us will kill you," and left.

I can't even imagine the horror she went through; she crawled to the door in a pool of blood, slowly soaking into the carpet. With her hands tied, she pounded on the door and walls, hoping someone would hear her. Fortunately, guests from the next room helped her, calling reception and then the Garda Síochána and ambulance. I heard to this story directly from the girl to whom it happened several years later, and when those words come out of the mouth of someone who has been through it, you're incapable of any reaction. Fear paralyses you, and you pray that nothing like this will ever happen to you. There was a lot of it; that evening, I just sat there silently, and Michaela kept sharing and sharing. I kept asking myself, "Where were the girls from the agency? Where were those who were supposed to watch over us?"

Last but not least, there was the story of an older bearded man who had gone several times directly to the hotel where we were currently staying. He repeatedly made a booking with girls from different phone numbers, went to the girls 'rooms, and as soon as they closed the door, he drew a knife, put it to the neck of his helpless victim, and searched for money. This man reportedly never hurt anyone, but it's still an experience no one wants to go through. That evening, I learned about a safety app that works for girls in the sex industry. You enter the client's number, and you'll find out if he's ever done anything if he's dangerous, armed, or just weird or drunk. We, girls locked in hotel rooms, didn't have access to this; it was the operators 'job to check every number of some potential client and try to ensure that the girl will not have a knife stuck in her stomach in twenty minutes. Over time, I gained access to the app, not that it protected me in any way. Maybe out of curiosity, I signed up and would like to share with you descriptions of events from girls locked in one of those hotel rooms or apartments. They are alone there, and whatever reason they decided to do this, they are still human beings who don't deserve cruel treatment.

I took him for 30 minutes and after he finished, he tried to take all my money from a drawer and he hurt my hand. Avoid him girls, he's very very dangerous. He banged my door when he left Very bad attitude!	Young Irish guy from Cabra. He came here and I provided the service and then started to shout that he wants his money back. I asked him to calm down and he pushed me on the floor and punched me. He went to the living room and stole all my money. He seems polite on the phone but don't trust him. Dangerous Young Man stay away from Him!
He showed me a knife after the time of the appointment has finished and robbed €1380 from me.	This guy came here drunk and high on drugs. Tried to rob me and attacked me with a knife.
He called me and said „what's up bi*ch, you wanna get fu*ked tonight?" What is wrong with this man? Is that how you talk to a woman?	When he called I noticed his poor English and he was asking me so many repetitive questions and made an appointment. I was suspicious about this guy but he showed up. He asked for a services I did not provide and I said no. He forced himself on me and got very aggressive. I have been writing this from hospital, please avoid him girls!!

This guy's name is Liam *****! He owns ******* Hotel! On the phone sounds very polite! He came here and everything was ok until he asked for sex with no condom because he can't feel anything! I explained him nicely this is not possible and he got mad, it turned into a fight, he tried to rape me, I slapped him and he punched me straight to my face! He is very dangerous and makes you afraid with his power. He said his brother in law is working for guards and I shouldn't report him for rape and attack!!! Please don't take this guy, he is extremely dangerous and aggressive.

This man came to my place and after the time we spent together he wanted the money back. He became very aggressive, after he called me many times and insulted me, he said Im in his country and he will come back to break my windows and door and so he did. Be careful girls with this crazy boy!

This man came here, he was smoking crack and was so violent. He forced me give him my money. I was so afraid of him, be careful girl he is so violent and he forced me to have sex with him.

Be careful girls he is very aggressive, he tried to hit me because I didn't want to do what he wanted. I had to kick him out from my place. Be careful he is extremely aggressive. He seems kind on the phone but he is rude and aggressive.

SERIOUS ROBBERY CASE THE GUY IS CALLED MATT AND HE IS IRISH MID AGED MAN. HE TRIED TO ROB ME JUST NOW AND TRIED TO RAPE ME AS WELL. STAY AWAY PLS!!!	This one is an extremely disrespectful guy, he even doesn't listen what you say. He treated me like a piece of s*it! He forced me to do things I didn't want, he was threatening me with violence. He is far from a normal man, it is your choice girls if you wanna deal with some animals like he is. Anyway I arrived on Garda station for this and I left all the details.
This guy after he made an appointment and didn't show up, I gave him a second chance and he arrived. He came here without money, offering cocaine in exchange service. When I said "No" he didn't want to leave the apartment.	This person came into the house with a hoodie on and was very suspicious. He was walking all over the house for no reason and when he found out I wasn't alone he left. Be careful, he definitely had some bad intentions!

This is just a small extract from what the girls confide in. It would take a long time and too much space if I shared everything with you. The stories of other girls could fit into three fat books. Personally, when I read such texts, I find them terrifying warnings. I know it's easy to judge someone, but even if these young women would do this "job" for the most selfish reasons, no one deserves something like this.

In some messages, you can see that the girl was brave enough to report the situation to police , but this happens only in a fraction of cases. Among us, some men choose the most vulnerable victims; many of them you may even know in your personal life without realising it. From my own experience, I can note that often, you encounter violence from gentlemen whom you would never expect. A kind, well-groomed middle-aged man with a wedding ring on his finger, children's wallpaper on his phone, and a knife behind his back.

Not all these girls "work" for the agency; some are independent, staying alone in apartments, houses, or hotels, and others live together in pairs for safety.

Before that evening, when Michaela gave me a tiny taste of what this world contained; I had no idea what was happening behind closed doors in all those places, and I think only a few people have an idea what could happen.

Even at this moment, as you read these lines, it's happening: sexual deviants are harming vulnerable beings, and many girls are terrified and in helpless situations where there is no one to help them. Another question is whether a person providing sexual services can be raped; someone would argue "No, it's not possible" and would undoubtedly claim that the girls still enjoy it when it happens. Where is the thin line between pleasure and pain? Rape is defined as an act in which the perpetrator forces the victim through violence or threat of violence or threat of other severe harm to engage in sexual intercourse, or the perpetrator uses the victim's vulnerability to engage in such an act. Any form of sexual gratification on another person's body of the same or opposite sex is considered sexual intercourse.

So yes, rape is possible even though a companion has sex with more men in a day than most people do in their entire lives, but she can still say "no" and she can refuse the man who wants to sleep with her. It's her body, her mind, and her decision; if she doesn't feel like it for any reason, it's her sacred right to refuse, just as anyone else has that right.

Unfortunately, most men don't take this refusal lightly, and it's not uncommon for them to take what they want regardless of whether the other person shares the same opinion.

You lie helpless on the floor, unable to scream; everything hurts; someone is hitting you, crushing your bones; occasionally, you hear the crack of your ribs, you see blood and don't know where it's coming from, tears stream from your eyes, and your whole body screams "STOP," but he doesn't stop! You're overwhelmed with immense helplessness; you shake, can't breathe, and every minute feels endlessly long. When he finally leaves, and you're alone, you remain in the same position he left you in, unable to move, unable to do anything, say anything; you cry and suffer in pain. It doesn't hurt any less than when it happens to anyone else, anywhere else; it's the same cruelty and the same inhumane treatment. You'd rather die than have it happen to you. Moreover, you're alone in this; there's no one you could share these horrific experiences with. All the things happened to me and no one to sincerely hug me, no one to help me. No one to give me even a moment of security. I was alone there, living with a suitcase, moving every three days, and the only people I was in contact with were the damn agency. I didn't call home very often because there wasn't time. The only time for myself I had in the mornings when my family was at work, and I finished with my "work" at night, I was looking like a soulless body, and the last thing I wanted was for my love ones to see or hear me like that.

The only goal was to save money, get out, and forget, which was slowly succeeding, and everything looked hopeful. But if we consider Murphy's Law, we know that everything that can go wrong will go wrong at the most inappropriate time, and every time I thought I was handling it and everything would be fine, unexpected events knocked me to the ground again. I was in Ireland for several weeks now, and although I've spent most of my finances on accommodation and paid the agency, I still managed to set aside some money. That something was further divided to cover my financial obligations, support my daughter, and save. I didn't have much saved up, but it gradually moved in a direction that evoked a positive thought.

I was slowly heading in the right direction, and the prospect of my happy return home and spending time with my little girl strengthened me. I pushed myself and endured pressure from the agency, the touches of disgusting men, insults, pretence, and pain in the hope that all of this would soon be behind me. But if something can go wrong, it definitely will, regardless of how hard you try, and it happened to me, too.

The plan was go to Dublin and then I was supposed to have a few days off.

Even though other girls "worked" on their periods, I took the first few months off for these few days. I took advantage of the situation to rest, went to see my brother, and spent a few days pretending to be accessible at his place. I was excited about my free time and was waiting on the bus to Dublin. I was standing at a bus stop in Limerick; a red alert was issued, and a hurricane approached us. It was raining heavily, icy wind was blowing, and hardly any buses were running. After two hours of freezing, I had had enough. I couldn't move my fingers; everything hurt; my teeth were chattering, and my palms were purple. I probably turned purple everywhere. With tears, I begged the agency to send me elsewhere, saying several buses had passed to other places but none to Dublin. The agency decided that I would wait exclusively for the one bus they found for me, so I waited. Another hour passed, and I was already in terrible pain from the cold with every movement; every muscle felt like a thousand needles. I begged to sit in the café across the street or go to the shopping centre, but I was only answered with, "Wait, it'll come." I don't know how long it took, but eventually, it came, and I got on. I could hardly move, and I looked like I had gone swimming in the sea. I arrived in Dublin in the evening, and I was at the hotel around seven o'clock. I was looking forward to getting out of those wet clothes and taking a warm bath. Do you think those beasts let me? Not a trace of humanity!

"In an hour you have a first client, it's late, so go and earn some money, babe." They knew how I felt, that I was hungry, tired, and frozen, but empathy was something none of them possessed. They probably didn't even know the meaning of that word. At eight o'clock, I met the first man, and I was shaking as I opened the door to him. Finally, the evening came, and I got into the bathtub and ordered food to the hotel room. I wouldn't normally spend money on it, but after such a day, I deserved something good and warm. Three days flew by quickly, and I could finally see my brother. He lived with his roommates, and one evening, as we were sitting in the kitchen, Laura, the wife of his roommate came to us. She was running around confusedly, raising her hands to the ceiling, and constantly shouting the word "lockdown." As I was an English-speaking person only in my dreams, I had no idea what it meant. At first, I mistakenly thought I had perhaps forgotten to lock the door, but as it turned out later, everyone wished that the word meant poorly locked doors.

I had to leave immediately back to Dublin; two hours later, I wouldn't have been able to go anywhere. There were supposed to be guards everywhere, and free movement was supposed to be restricted in connection with the pandemic.

I contacted the agency; Susan booked a hotel for me in a questionable part of Dublin, and before I knew it, I was sitting on the bus and had no idea what was happening.

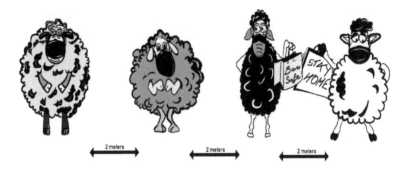

Chapter Six: COVID Madness

I found myself in front of the hotel, without any idea what awaited me, and went to the reception desk. The lobby was chaotic, with luggage strewn about and noisy guests bustling through the vestibule, mostly with phones in hand or pressed to their ears. I slowly approached the reception and demanded my reserved room. The kind receptionist, with a puppy-like expression, explained that they couldn't accept new reservations and, according to strict rules, could only provide accommodation to guests travelling for work, which needed to be proven. As a pretended tourist, I had no chance of getting a room. The cancellation with an apology was supposedly sent to my email, but Susan used fictitious email addresses for reservations, so no one knew about it. I settled into a chair, phone in hand, and in a panic, I contacted the agency, hoping they would know what to do or at least have prepared for this situation in some way. I wasn't the only girl in a similar situation, but according to my information, I was the only one left without accommodation that night. After several hours of futile attempts to find alternative accommodation and with little battery left, I was kicked out of the hotel and had to fend for myself. Someone knowledgeable decided to install charging stations at most bus stops in this country, which was useful. So there I sat, alone, exhausted, at a bus stop in the middle of the night, with a USB cable plugged into my phone, trying to figure something out. After several attempts to book a place, or even persuading taxi drivers to take me back to my brother's place, I gave up. I found a train station where I, like many others, spent the night. It was very uncomfortable, with suspicious individuals moving around me, and I was afraid that something might happen to me. After all, I had enough cash on me, and getting that money into an account was challenging for me. Sometimes, my brother sent me something and other times, I used services through Pay zone, but none of it was an ideal solution. Fortunately, no one even noticed me; I'd say that at the beginning of the pandemic, everyone was frightened and had enough of their problems. I survived that night in good health, constantly repeating that morning is wiser than the evening and I can't lose hope. Desperately, I sent several messages to property owners who offered short-term rentals, primarily for tourists, but I didn't receive any positive responses. After hours of hopeless effort, one gentleman contacted me back, agreeing to rent out his place for a few days. My heart leapt for joy; that man saved me. If he hadn't contacted me, I would probably have to stay at that train station for several more nights. I immediately headed to the address he provided, where an older and very kind man opened the door. I didn't understand everything he said, but I understood that he probably felt sorry for me. I looked awful, with makeup smeared from crying, eyes resembling a panda bear's, messy hair flying all around me, and a desperate expression on my face. I looked like something I drew with my left hand. After settling in, I took a shower and contacted Susan, explaining the situation to her. She tried to persuade me to "work" at the apartment, but I explained to her that the last thing I wanted was to risk ending up under a bridge indefinitely. Susan decided not to contribute to this accommodation and would try to find an alternative solution for me. This was the first time I hadn't heard from any of them for at least a few days, and it suited me just fine. The only thing I sometimes needed for my happiness was their absence. Several days of incredible peace were ended with my mobile phone ringing. The caller ID displayed the name "Jane," and I suspected she had some news for me.

"Hi, how are you holding up? I wanted to let you know that all the shops will be closed, and there won't be any opportunity to buy food anywhere; it's the apocalypse. Anyway, there's a girl in Dublin, Victoria; you'll go to her tomorrow morning, and you'll be living together for some time. Buy some food, so you have something to eat before the situation gets resolved."

Jane had an incredible ability to blow things out of proportion, magnify them, panic, and exert terrible pressure on people to achieve her goals. The fact that they were putting me in an apartment with another girl indicated that they were desperate and completely lost in this situation. Previously, they wouldn't even have considered something like this.

I've already introduced you to some of the members of this agency, but understanding the overall structure can be pretty challenging. Susan was the queen of the whole operation. She founded the agency with Jane, and they seemed to be good friends, but the truth was that Jane always did the dirty work, and Susan was nowhere to be seen. When someone needed to earn more money, ignore human needs, force someone to do something, or scold operators, Jane always did it, although in most cases, it wasn't her initiative. Jane was precisely the kind of person you hoped would suck the life out of someone else if you gave her a straw. She could drive you crazy, was disorganised, and made many mistakes for which you paid the price. She never admitted a mistake; she always tried to blame someone else.

Jane knew everything best and she was everywhere. Although she occasionally showed some emotions and support when you weren't feeling well, but you never knew if she meant it honestly.

Susan, on the other hand, was an organised, elegant lady.

She always spoke to you calmly and with complete understanding. You would never have guessed that the orders for the worst things came directly from her. I experienced her being angry only twice, and when it happened, even demons looked, took notes, and learned how to do it. Some women are just like this, still water runs deep. As you can see in the illustration, the other "building blocks" of the pyramid were Magda and Tina. In the final phase, before I left, they represented Jane in the organisation and also handled phone calls like other operators. I assume they still do the same, and nothing has changed. Magda, once a successful prostitute in England who dedicated her life to cocaine and sex, was one of those girls who enjoyed and was fulfilled in their "work."

When her time came and her biological clock ticked, she found a man in Prague, fell in love, and gave birth to a son. She gets blackout drunk three times a week, which was probably her way of escaping. Her personal life was not easy; her husband was a gambler, and he got them into debt and lost so much that Magda couldn't even keep track of it anymore. He spent all day at work, went to the casino after, and, to make matters worse, had sex with anything that moved. Magda had her days; sometimes, she was strict and cruel, and other times, she was understanding and supportive like no one else. She was a fantastic woman in her own way. Before I left, she had two children and found a man who, according to her words, finally stood by her, and she felt safe. Tina, on the other hand, was temperamentally similar to Susan; they were great friends in their personal lives and together decided to start an agency in Prague, which, I assume, is profitable for them. Birds of a feather flock together. I personally saw Tina only twice; she seemed a bit arrogant and selfish to me, but she was an intelligent woman, which was unusual in this industry. In addition to having a business in Prague with Susan, she provided organisational services for Jane and occasionally worked as an operator. She also occasionally decided to descend to the bottom of the pyramid and flew to Ireland, where she entertained local individuals with her alluring body. I always approached Tina with caution; she was fake and self-centred. When I had her as an operator, she could be nasty, pushing me into disgusting things and not taking "no" for an answer. She liked to manipulate people and was very goal-oriented, much like Jane. Of course, she had her bright moments, but the problem was that you never knew if she was pretending to understand you or if she meant it seriously. Maybe she was beautiful, sacrificial, and humble in her personal life, but I'll probably never know. I can't judge; I never had the opportunity to know her from that side, but what I did know was enough for me to form an opinion. She reminded me of a software update notification. Whenever I saw her name on the display, I said to myself, "Not now, for God's sake"; I really didn't feel any affection for her.

Operators are a chapter in themselves; I can't list all the names here as the girls in this position changed quite often. They left for various reasons, but most often, it was because of Jane's approach or because they couldn't handle what the job actually involved psychologically. Negotiating with horny men, sending them to rooms one after the other, checking if everything was okay, and listening to the complaints of companions to which, according to Jane's orders, they couldn't react. Mastering all this required having huge balls and sharp elbows; no wonder most of them gave up and ran away. I even remember a lady who was a Secondary school teacher and got into operator work temporarily due to health problems.

Nobody liked her, but I adored her. It was evident that she had never come into contact with anything like that, and she didn't have the aptitude for it. Her gentle nature didn't allow her to cause suffering to others, and I loved that about her. In the pyramid, I listed the ladies who stayed longer than a few weeks. I've already told you a little about Linda, a kind lady but also a manipulative individual who likes to pretend and drown in her self-pity. I liked her a lot until I saw through her. When I saw her for the first time in Prague at the airport, I thought someone is about to rob me. As I mentioned before, I imagined her as an older, elegant lady. Jane and Susan wanted us to go to the toilets on the airport's ground floor after arriving in Prague and meet an operator there to hand over the cash for the agency. After one of my arrivals, I waited for Linda there, and suddenly, a small, skinny woman with dark skin ran up to me. She had long, black, messy hair, dirty clothes, and rotten teeth and was smelling terribly with cigarette smoke and other substances. She rushed towards me with outstretched arms, ready to hug me. At first, I thought that person was going to harm me until I heard her voice. I never judge a book by its cover, but this shocked me because I imagined her entirely differently. However, that didn't change my relationship with her; only certain facts emerged over time. Even though Linda was on thin ice several times because she liked to cheat the agency, she never left them, and they never let her go due to a lack of interest from other girls in the operator job. According to my information, she still works there today, and instead of cheating the agency, she begs money from the girls who go to Ireland to sell their bodies.

Then there was Alex; she was a kind and lovely woman who did this job out of necessity. A few months after I joined this mix of mysterious beings, Alex left. She graduated and found a better job, and we never heard from her again. I really wish her to be happy; I admire anyone who can escape from this underworld towards a better tomorrow. After her departure, many other carriers chose the same false name. Even the teacher mentioned above decided on the name "Alex". I don't know why it was so popular, but the simplicity of that name worked.

Another operator who had been with the agency for some time was Margaret. She was a good friend of Tina. I had to be careful what I said; these two wouldn't let anything pass. Margaret, however, was one of the few people who built a relationship with me over time, and I'm sure none of it was fake. As much as she hated that job, she couldn't stand the clients and the agency approach to this type of work. When she had my phone and I wanted to start later or finish earlier without asking Jane or Susan, she agreed. She was really kind and understood the hardships of my "work" life.

Tammy was very similar to Margaret, at least in terms of human approach. You had to find your way to her; she didn't want to cause problems, but when she realised she could trust you, she was kind as heaven itself. Clare was one of those I never had much chance to get to know. She was dry and harsh, with an occasional dose of humanity. It probably depended on how she slept. When she answered the phone, I didn't dare to protest or say anything that could have consequences. The last lady from the operator position was Simona. Simona was a pleasant woman, but it took me a long time to realise she was addicted to methamphetamine. She was highly moody, kind and friendly one day and turned into a little devil the next day, annoyed by everything. On worse days, you were even afraid to breathe lest it upset her. I only realised she was under the influence of drugs after some time. When she wasn't high, she was absolutely amazing, had my back, and I never had to worry about her forcing me into anything. She always politely asked me, "I have a gentleman who would like to see you. Will you take him?"

This never happened to me with any other operator; all the others just wrote "client in five minutes."

Simona had a beautiful and unique daughter, but over time, her addiction became so intense that she started taking drugs even in her presence. I really felt sorry for that little girl; it's something no child deserves. Simona left the agency a few days before I left. She was constantly yelled at, just like everyone else, and did a job she didn't want to do. Unfortunately, I later found out that she started offering escort services in Finland and Sweden, and that saddened me. She didn't go for better; her drug addiction took a toll on her.

The day I was supposed to move to the lady in Dublin, I had Lena as an operator. Lena was a nice girl. She kept her distance from the girls who worked in escort services, and she kept her distance from the agency as well. She did what was necessary to survive. She had grand ambitions and didn't want to stay with this for too long; it was a temporary income during maternity leave for her until she stood on her own two feet. I sincerely hope all her plans worked out for her and she achieved everything she desired.

That day, with her help, I got to Ballsbridge, a lovely area in South Dublin, where I was supposed to meet Victoria. After a long struggle, I found the apartment and a charming raven-haired girl came downstairs to open the door for me. She was twenty-four years old, with a symmetrical face, long raven hair, and huge breasts she liked to flaunt. She was of shorter stature with feminine curves; to me, she seemed like a beautiful young woman. We introduced ourselves, and with a smile, she took me inside. There was an incredible mess in the apartment; her things were scattered everywhere, and she had hair stuffed in kitchen drawers, which scared me. I didn't have any experience with hair extensions at the time and didn't know that after a while, the bonds would start to come out. However, putting them in a drawer in the room where you eat is unbelievably gross. I pondered how someone could be such a pig, but I couldn't say a word. I was the intruder there, not her. At first, I thought it was her apartment, and it took me a while to realise it was another short-term rental. After unpacking my suitcase and settling into my room, I went to the kitchen, where Victoria was sitting at the table, painting her nails with sparkly blue polish

"I brought some food. On the way, I stopped at a small shop with a limited selection at high prices, so I ended up with a bunch of useless stuff," I said with a bag in hand as I headed towards the fridge. She stopped me with the words, "Why on earth did you spend money on useless things when all the shops are open as usual?" I fell silent and cursed Jane and her panicked, practical ideas in my mind.

This conversation couldn't lead anywhere other than the topic of "Jane," and Victoria had so much to tell me about this woman. It's interesting how women are forthcoming when it comes to discussing people they don't like. They knew each other personally; Victoria left her things at Jane's place in Prague and tried to convince me that she was completely different in her personal life than at "work." She portrayed Jane as a caring and friendly woman, and it took a lot of imagination for me to see her like that. She described her as if Jane had two personalities, and for now, I couldn't judge that because I only knew the side where she would take a horse dose of antidepressants. The beginning of the pandemic was challenging for our "work"; we didn't have many clients, and with what came, we barely paid the rent. I had to dip into the money I had saved, and suddenly, everything went wrong as if by magic, some black, dark magic. It wasn't bad to have a roommate; quite the opposite. After months of loneliness and staying in hotel rooms from morning till night, it was a welcome change. She opened my eyes in many ways; suddenly, I saw previously invisible things. I realised many manipulative techniques the agency used to get us where they wanted us. Victoria wasn't afraid of that; she didn't care about the agency, and in their own way, they didn't care as long as she made enough money. She would get up and leave in the middle of the day, go shopping, or just left to have a lunch, something I never dreamed of. The truth was that now, at least, it was somewhat possible because we had plenty of free time, but due to her carelessness, she often got into unnecessary stressful situations. We lacked money, no flights home, and we were cut off from the world, from everyone and everything. Desperate situations call for desperate measures, so we were inspired by the other girls and started offering something called a "duo," which was often confused with a "threesome." A duo meant that two girls devoted themselves to one man, but this devotion didn't include any lesbian show or anything we had to do to each other. We took amateur photos and had another profile set up on websites. Both of us felt weird and nervous, but at that moment, it was the only thing that came to mind. The first client was a fairly attractive guy around thirty years old, a kind of Spanish type, with big brown eyes, thick dark hair, and a short stubble that framed sharp cheekbones. Most of the men who visited us were older, smelly gentlemen with rotten teeth and slightly overweight, so when 'Adonis' appeared, it was a slight relief from what was to follow. You didn't suffer less because of the pretty face, but at least you didn't feel like throwing up when he kissed you, and I consider that a significant plus.

The gentleman requested a shower, and after twenty minutes, he emerged, fully clothed, stating that he only wanted a free shower and then ran away. We stood there with our mouths open, unable to utter a word. We should have asked for money when he entered, but for both of us, it was such an uncomfortable feeling that we always left it until the very last moment, just before the actual action. Most of the bookings we initially received were so-called "fake calls."

I 'adored' this type of call; it meant that a gentleman called, polite and kind over the phone, arranged a meeting with you, and you had to stay half undressed, ready in one place. You couldn't eat, drink, or pee;

you just sat there and waited. One such joker was followed by another, third, and fourth, so what was supposed to be thirty minutes turned into six hours. I truly wished I could bill people for wasting my time. You were shivering by cold, needing to pee, your stomach was grumbling, and you couldn't do anything at all. Even when I needed to go to the bathroom, I had to report it to the operator. Can you imagine how humiliating it is to have to ask if you can pee? After emptying yourself, a shower usually followed to avoid smelling of urine or having toilet paper stuck to your labia, and this whole process was truly exceptional. It was stressful when the phone in the bedroom buzzed, with the message content reassuring you that the client waiting outside was coming up, and you didn't know anything about it. Our privacy wasn't taken into consideration; honestly, privacy was something that didn't exist. The operator knew everything, had to know everything, and it didn't matter what you were doing. Every day, all you did was confide your activities: "I'm eating, I'm peeing, I'm showering, I'm drinking, I need to finish a message to my mom, I'm getting dressed, I'm making a coffee, I'm going to sleep…"

You constantly had to ask if what you were doing was okay, if there was any horny male waiting outside who didn't want you to eat. The client always was a priority, no matter what or how urgently you needed to do something. The client was the king, and you were a piece of cloth to be ejaculated on. After him, another and another and another, and if you were lucky, you'd eat something in a rush in four hours, while you were trying to get rid of the semen of disgusting men on your body. It's no wonder that when I left this "job," suddenly I was exposed to everyday life, and I couldn't come to terms with the fact that no one was watching everything I did. The much-desired freedom suddenly seemed unwanted. After so many long years, I wanted there to be someone I could ask if I could use the bathroom. I know how absurd it sounds, and I'm grateful that this state didn't last long; it felt like leaving prison. Suddenly, you're outside, and there's too much you have to deal with.

Nonetheless, the pandemic was still at its beginning, and I had to fight through to the end. It was lucky that I wasn't alone, and in a way, it was also fortunate that during the time of COVID, there weren't as many eager clients. I could say, "I'm going out with Victoria," and the operator couldn't say anything, knowing that the phones weren't ringing, and if they were, it was someone who wouldn't show up anyway. The first few months of COVID madness were challenging; I was doing something I wasn't sure why I was doing. That light at the end of the tunnel I used to have suddenly disappeared. What I earned went towards accommodation, advertising, and for the agency.

If I happened to have a little extra, I sent it home. It was clear that I will stay here; no one knew for how long. I prayed daily and begged for a miracle, but it didn't happen. Victoria had perfect English, whereas I was still struggling with the second language. I needed her, especially during this crazy time. Susan came up with the idea that we would pretend to be business representatives of some foreign company supplying the world with masks and disinfectants. I somewhat looked the part, considering how I dressed, but Victoria's visual aspect was significantly worse. A torn, dirty jacket, jeans with holes, and long fake eyelashes reached her eyebrows. Thick, white layers of glue under the eyelashes, and in her hand, she held a huge, flashy purse from expensive brands. Honestly, she looked more like someone who sleeps on the street and steals purses than a business representative.

Some landlords believed us, and others just closed the door on us contemptuously. They probably suspected what two girls like us could be doing in a foreign country, and no one wanted their apartment turned into a brothel. We travelled from city to city, and in each one, we searched for the cheapest accommodation, but it wasn't easy with apartments. Most landlords were afraid to rent out at that time; there was a curfew, a ban on approaching, a mask mandate, and many other bans that made your head spin. We eagerly searched for a temporary refuge and hoped to earn more money than just for accommodation and the agency. Victoria was a pleasant girl, but sometimes she was a bit too much, and she knew how to push my buttons like no one else. When you're confined with someone every day for 24 hours, your mental health can rapidly deteriorate. I bet many of you during COVID thought about physically attacking your partner or escaping somewhere. It was like house arrest without an ankle bracelet, and escape was just a dream you dared to have. I always believed in a better tomorrow, but every evening, I had slight doubts, mainly because of Victoria's loud arguments on the phone. This girl had such an unpleasant whimper. She had a partner at home who had no idea what his girl was up to behind his back. Every time he suspected that she might be in another country, which was almost every night, they would shout at each other loudly, and sometimes it went too far. Victoria had such a shriek that you either ran away or slapped her to wake her up; there was nothing in between. I don't understand how her partner didn't catch on; you know, eighty per cent of the brain is made up of fluid, and this is clear evidence that, for some, it's brake fluid.

However, I somehow survived these conversations, although exploding was coming. What I couldn't handle was her nonexistent sense of organisation. Her things were everywhere; wherever you entered, there were several clear signs that Victoria inhabited this space. Underwear on the floor, clothes on the couch, dirty socks on the table. Bowls from meals everywhere, yoghurt containers, and what annoyed me the most were open plastic bottles left unattended. It wasn't unusual for such a liquid from a bottle to damage something occasionally, and most of the time, it wasn't my thing that was damaged, so I hoped that after a few spilt personal items, she would finally start closing those damn lids. If you think it ever happened, you're wrong. This girl would rather destroy the entire contents of her suitcase than make a wrist movement and screw on the lid.

Her favourite activity was leaving used pads and tampons on the windowsills, usually in the living room, which were blood-stained and smelly. There's nothing like making coffee in the morning, coming to the living room, sitting on the couch, and realising that you're sitting on a tampon and there's a sanitary pad stuck to the window. You won't believe how it brightens your day! Her least favourite activity was washing her hair; she waited up to three weeks to treat her raven mane to a bath. Believe me, when it came to that, you didn't want to visit the bathroom. The bathtub was black, the edges lined, and at the bottom, you could see pieces of something unidentifiable. For this young lady, washing up after herself was no easy task neither, so cleaning up after her "flea removal process" was left to me.

The duo profile didn't last long. It's hard to get used to seeing someone else having sex with a disgusting guy. Smelling the stench of rotten fish and staring at her dirty crotch while another man "cleans" her with his tongue is only for strong personalities. I couldn't handle it, and after a few months we spent together, I requested the removal of this profile. Victoria and the agency didn't like it; after all, it was money. But the question is whether money is worth some things. Despite Victoria being such a mess and chaotic person, men loved her. Sometimes, I envied her how much she enjoyed it; when something like this excites you, it must be much more manageable. I never reached that stage, but I wished for it several times. Whenever a new admirer appeared at her door, she pressed her breasts together, pouted her chest, and pulled out her famous phrase "Hi there," which wasn't exciting at all, but when the gentlemen saw her huge assets, erections occurred, wallets grew legs, and they ran straight towards Victoria. For money, she would do almost anything, young, old, smelly, or clean; it was all the same to her. She viewed men only as business. Weeks with her flew by and dragged on simultaneously; sometimes, we were each other's support, and other times, enduring each other's presence was a superhuman task. We both just wanted to go home, but we had to wait quite a while for flights. Both of us were under immense tension and stress; the agency certainly didn't help, quite the opposite.

They didn't have the high earnings they were accustomed to, and there was a lot of pressure on the girls. The agency implemented measures to boost profitability, and it had a huge impact on everyone. Operators were given a list of bonus rewards if a girl locked in an apartment reached a certain number of clients. Doesn't it sound disgusting to you? A girl answering the phone forces someone else into sex to get a few extra euros. The operators 'approach changed. Many girls, based on bad experiences, excluded clients of certain races. It may sound terrible, but if a guy from Western Europe beats you up so badly that you end up in the hospital, you'll be very cautious about meeting people from similar cultural circles. After several negative experiences, I was also told that I could put certain nationalities on my "naughty list." This joyful news was first announced to me by Victoria, and Jane involuntarily confirmed it.

Operators mostly respected it, and I was glad I could avoid my subconscious troublemakers. My list contained names of many countries; you wouldn't believe it if someone saw it; they would think I was about to travel the world. With the crisis and financial rewards, it seemed that the lists of all the girls mysteriously vanished into space. Regardless of how much your wishes were respected before, now you often hear the operators' sentence, "Well, I didn't notice that accent. Are you sure he's not from Ireland? If someone spoke English with an Irish accent to me over the phone, how is it possible that he's from Africa and you can't communicate with him?" Suddenly, there were so many coincidences, and it was hard to believe their excuses. If, for example, a man of Chinese nationality comes to you, unable to understand you, and uses a translator to communicate, it's tough to believe that he spoke English like Shakespeare over the phone. Let me clarify that it wasn't any racial discrimination. Slovaks and Czechs were on my list too, most Eastern European and Asian countries. If I meet people of these nationalities on the street, we would have a perfect conversation and laugh, but when you're alone, enclosed between four walls, you must be careful and take all precautions to ensure nothing happens to you. Unfortunately, the agency didn't care about our safety as much as we did, and as I mentioned earlier, they often risked our lives for a small amount of money. Are you curious about the bonuses we're talking about? How much are some people willing to gamble with someone else's life? The attached illustration is an exact translation of the message shared with me by one of the operators. She would probably be fired if it was discovered that she shared such information with me. To explain the content of the message, "piece" means one phone that the operator had assigned to one profile, usually one escort girl. "Piece" is, therefore, an address for a woman who often risked everything she had to achieve what the operator drove her to. So if the operator answered three escort profiles, forced the girl to satisfy at least fifteen men a day, and made one girl work after midnight, she could earn up to five hundred euros daily. Wow!

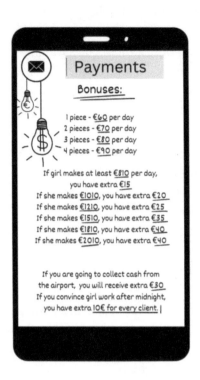

Payments

Bonuses:

1 piece - €60 per day
2 pieces - €70 per day
3 pieces - €80 per day
4 pieces - €90 per day

If girl makes at least €810 per day,
you have extra €15
If she makes €1010, you have extra €20
If she makes €1210, you have extra €25
If she makes €1510, you have extra €35
If she makes €1810, you have extra €40
If she makes €2010, you have extra €40

If you are going to collect cash from
the airport, you will receive extra €30
If you convince girl work after midnight,
you have extra 10€ for every client.

That's such an amount that you would do anything for it, right? What would be the amount you would demand to justify that you could mentally or physically mutilate someone? I don't have such an amount in mind, probably like most people, but I certainly wouldn't do something like that for five hundred euros. When the operator sits at home all day, answering phones, constantly arguing with someone, arranging something, on the brink of a mental breakdown, practically not sleeping, and trying to earn as much as possible, that amount is almost laughable. Plus, the amount she earns comes at the expense of some girl in a foreign country, locked behind walls, and with fear, opening the door to one man after another. Some of them scold her, others humiliate her and behave towards her without respect, some of them will spit in her face, yes, that happens too, and then those few friendly, kind, and quick individuals just come and go. Between individual clients, she'll be hungry, tired, and stressed. She hurriedly showered, got dressed, and redid her makeup. Then, she concealed her true feelings behind a fake smile and sought solace in the arms of another man whom she secretly wanted to crush with a baseball bat. It's stressful, especially when someone forces you to do things you don't want to do.

The pain they caused us, with their persuasion and ignorance, really wasn't worth such a paltry sum! I understand that for some people, this may be very difficult to imagine, but I assume that each of you has had sex at some point. Do you know how tired you are after one, unless your male half is trying to break the world speed record? Now imagine it ten or fifteen times with a different man each time. You can't walk, your muscles ache, you're exhausted, you can't even wash or write a message. Your brain doesn't react, and your body even less. You wait for the hour when you can message the operator that you're done, and then you see three dots, indicating that someone on the other side is writing a new message, which doesn't bode well. Your eyes are filled with tears, and you just pray that the message doesn't say, "I have another candidate in ten minutes."

Unfortunately, that's usually the message that comes, and at such a moment, tears well up in your eyes, and you write "ok," aware that refusal would have no effect. You gather your last bit of strength to get dressed and fix your face to a state of "I'm not a zombie." You can't imagine to meet someone in such a condition, and it takes an enormous effort to do that. You open the door, and another repulsive slug touches you, just to satisfy his desires. You pray it will be quick, and when he finally leaves, you almost fall asleep, standing up, knowing that tomorrow will be a new day, but it will bring the same as today.

You're controlled by fear, helplessness, and despair. Every day, you ask yourself, "How long will this last, and when will it end," you plan suicide in your mind. You think about every detail, but every time, the thought is interrupted by the realisation that you have a fantastic daughter waiting for you at home, and despite how it may sometimes seem, she would be worse off without you. My daughter has always given me the strength to continue, and I believed tomorrow will be a little better. And without her, I would have given up a long time ago. Everyone at the agency knew it was tough for me to do something like that and that I couldn't handle that "work" mentally. Despite knowing how I felt, they constantly pushed me to do things I didn't want to do and which were absolutely unacceptable to me.

Often, they used my daughter as a way of pressure, "You're doing it for her; you need money so you can be together." But this wasn't about me; it was about them. Greed is one of the worst traits a person can have. I knew why I was doing it, but when the day came when they exhausted me in such a way, I often said that the client will stay longer, and then I would deduct the money from my own pocket. Why did I do it? If they knew that there was no one with me and a horny man with a fat wallet called, within five minutes, he would be standing at the door. At the moment when I was exhausted and hungry, even thirty extra minutes provided me with rest and time to eat, which was priceless. Victoria was different in this regard; she could handle practically anything, sometimes even making me doubt if she was human. On her good days, one man followed another with her, and often I barely saw her. One left, she just picked up her clothes and put them on while grabbing an apple or something quick to eat in the kitchen. She didn't bother with a shower; as she said, if wet wipes are designed to clean a baby, they can handle cleaning a few bodily fluids and sweat. Often, she opened the door to the next one with messy hair, half-naked, and with a used condom on the bed that she forgot to throw away. It didn't matter how she looked when she opened the door; they rarely left. It seemed that to men, it didn't matter where they put their penises as long as they had somewhere to put it. Sometimes, she proudly declared herself a "workaholic," and I really envied her for that. If I could enjoy it at least half as much as she did, I would surely handle it better.

During our few months together, she benefitted me in some respects. As she used to say, something in her had died a long time ago, so it wasn't difficult for her to come to terms with the reality of the oldest profession. This probably happens to most women who work in this industry. If they do it long enough, they are no longer able to fit into normal life. At some point, something in them dies, a part of the soul that no longer screams for help. You simply silence this part of yourself after a while and accept your "work" as part of yourself. Victoria had no other education; at the age of eighteen, she flew to Holland, where she began selling her assets to stupid men thinking with their crotches. When I met her, she was so young. She had never worked a regular job; she didn't know the feeling of having a job that mattered to her. The only thing that mattered was money, and with her experience and way of thinking, she would never earn as much anywhere else.

She did whatever she did and considered it normal. We argued so many times about whether it was work or not. Technically, it's an activity you perform and receive financial compensation for, so, of course, this activity could be considered a kind of work. However, if you have your values set right, you understand that it's not entirely moral or noble, and therefore, you shouldn't consider it a legitimate job. Whenever a message came on Telegram saying, "Work in ten minutes" I almost jumped out of my skin. Tina always wrote it with great joy; the other operators preferred to use the term "client," which, for some mysterious reason, was more acceptable. Victoria was an exciting person, and on her better days, she was pleasant and kind, but on her worse days, I thought the devil possessed her. She had a tremendous sense of empathy, understood you like no one else, and supported you, which I liked about her, but her dark sides overshadowed it. Despite the increase in bonuses for operators, neither of us was very busy during COVID-19, and that had its charm. We went for long walks on empty streets and explored cities. Travelling was more challenging; every time we changed location, something went wrong. Either the driver refused to let us on the bus for failing to explain the reason for travel adequately, or we were kicked out of transportation by the Garda for inexplicable reasons. We never told the truth, but eventually, we decided to improve our invented story. Usually, we mentioned an address and said we were going to our pregnant cousin, who was due to give birth any day, and someone had to take care of her son. If there were questions about our cousin's husband, Victoria was clear: "He is in the army on a mission and can't be home".

Usually, it worked. I hate lying, but here, there was no choice. If we didn't lie, we'd sleep under a bridge, and when you need to survive, you do many things you're not proud of afterwards.

I remember when a guard walked through the bus, and everyone had to answer where they were going and the reason for their journey. One elderly lady replied solemnly that she was going to Dublin to buy a new phone because she lived in the back of Beyond, where she could never get one. The guard smiled at her, didn't even try to explain how the internet works to the grandmother, and wished her the best of luck. After a few months of uncomfortable travelling, we decided we needed a car. My brother had a friend in Dublin who owned an auto repair shop, and since he didn't have too many customers in these crazy times, he would lend us a car for four hundred euros a month. That seemed perfect; we would pay what we already paid for transportation, and everything would be more comfortable. I didn't start considering this option only just because of the excessive number of questions; we wouldn't have avoided them while travelling. My biggest problem and benefit at the same time was Victoria. She had a considerable suitcase overflowing and always bought a massive amount of food, which she then brought from place to place. When we travelled, she had a purse in her suitcase that couldn't even be closed due to the amount of nonsense she transported. On her shoulder, a heavy, huge bag full of food. She had so much food that she could feed an average family for a week. While travelling, she also carried a substantial frozen chicken under her arm. Somewhere, she read that it was the ideal place to store cash, which theoretically it could be if you didn't have to thaw that chicken six times a month. Practically, I travelled with a girl accompanied by the smell of death. So imagine a dark-haired girl dragging a giant suitcase, purse, and large shopping bag and having a frozen chicken under her arm, which had nowhere else to be placed. With my smaller suitcase and standard-sized purse, I constantly had to wait for her, sometimes even help her, and more than once, we missed our bus connection. Moreover, that chicken stank so much that the bus driver often didn't want to let us on the bus.

I remember our first big fight. By then, we had been together for several months, didn't have much money, and wanted to disappear. We were both frustrated; at that time, I started exercising and running to get rid of my depression, and Victoria, for the same reason, started overeating even more. Everyone deals with their frustration differently, and this woman lived to eat, but not as you imagine. She tortured herself! She had a medium size kitchen scale with her, weighed portions, counted calories, and meticulously recorded everything on tables, and it was a massive effort for her not to overeat. She fought with herself, and I honestly felt sorry for her. Sometimes, when she couldn't stand it anymore, she ordered pizza, hamburgers, cookies, and much more. The description of the items on the receipt practically looked like she had bought the entire restaurant. After consumption, she went to vomit, forced herself to exercise torturously all day, and then everything started over, and she carefully wrote down how much of what she had eaten.

We were in Galway in a beautiful rooftop apartment, a truly magical place. After a short stay, it was time to pack our bags and change our place of residence for a few more days. I had packed relatively early without any significant problems, and Victoria asked me if she could put some things with me because they wouldn't fit anywhere else. I really didn't have any space; although my suitcase was smaller, it was pretty extensive. After all, my life was in it, and besides a few things at my brother's, I had nothing else in Ireland.

Victoria didn't like it; her suitcase was about to explode, and she didn't enjoy hauling heavy bags around. She started to get angry, throwing things around, and all the disgust that had accumulated over the months was unleashed on me. Hysterical screaming alternated with pleading, and at first, I just stood there trying to calm the situation until a plastic honey bottle landed on me, which pissed me off. Covered in that sweet mess, I uncontrollably rushed to her stuff to get rid of her problems and throw them all out of the window. We wrestled for her crap like children in a sandbox as if we hadn't grown up at all. She threw whatever came to hand at me, and in the end, I grabbed her impressive heavy kitchen scale from the kitchen, along with that stupid bowl, and threw it out onto the street from the terrace. It landed on the ground from the top floor and was no longer usable. Moreover, it landed next to a man, almost scared him to death. I would have been the same; imagine calmly walking down the street, and suddenly, some lunatic throws a scale out of the top floor apartment window at you. At the time, I didn't think much about it, but damn that thing could have killed him. Victoria was angry, and next to the man, my shoe also landed. When he started shouting at us to calm down, we looked at each other and started laughing.

Maybe it was the release we both needed. Better than therapy, I highly recommend it. If you're at rock bottom and feel bad, get into a fight with someone close to you and throw their things out the window onto the street, but please make sure the street is empty first.

She went outside to gather the remnants of evidence in an attempted murder case while I was cleaning up the mess we had managed to create in the last fifteen minutes. This was the last straw; we desperately needed a car!

Well, that was the time when I made a mistake; I introduced Victoria to my brother. Those two were like an inseparable duo, understanding each other right from the start. Wherever we went, they were devoted to each other, leaving me feeling like a fifth wheel. During the COVID period, we had so much time that we occasionally took a day off and went somewhere, even with my brother. The agency knew they weren't losing money, so their approach was more relaxed. It was a pleasant way to escape from everyday reality. Suddenly, we had an opportunity to travel, and it was faster and more efficient. Although we couldn't avoid questions due to the frequent checkpoints, at least there was no risk of being thrown out of the car. We explored almost every corner of the beautiful island and it was a wonderful time, usually full of joy, despite the fact that I didn't have a buddy as they were acting like I wasn't there. When we were "working" and moving from one place to the other, we could stop somewhere along the way to grab some food, and no one could dictate what we could or couldn't do. If we reached our destination in time for check-in, everything was perfect, and no one from the agency had the slightest clue that we had been wandering around. And if, by chance, we arrived late at a new apartment, we blamed it on a police checkpoint, which everyone believed.

The vehicle made our travels more enjoyable. The only problem was that Victoria didn't have a driver's license, so the driving was up to me. I love driving, but sometimes it became tedious, and I must admit that at that time, it would have been helpful to have a partner who could take over. Moreover, as a passenger, she wasn't helpful at all. Once, we were leaving an Asian restaurant, where we quickly grabbed takeaway food to make it on time to our place. She had it in her lap and was distracted listening to music, which was piercing my ears. Her whole head was stuck in the window, making it nearly impossible to see anything. I shouted, "Is left side clear?" three times until she finally understood what I meant, only when another car started honking at us at the intersection, which it would likely have crossed much faster if we wouldn't be there. Absentmindedly, she glanced to the left and exclaimed, "Yes, you can go." I started moving and hit the brake so suddenly that the Asian food ended up everywhere, especially on her clothes. Someone clearly didn't understand what "is left side clear" meant. We almost got hit by some young guy in a German car. Victoria felt offended, and I explained why I couldn't check it myself. Maybe it had something to do with not having X-ray vision! Apart from a few situations when I felt like asking her to leave the car, the whole thing gave us a taste of false freedom and was a pleasant change. Weeks passed, and it was demanding: changing apartments, travelling, dealing with dozens of sleazy men - we had had enough, but it brought Victoria and me closer.

We found ourselves in the same place in Galway again but in a different apartment. It was a beautiful lakeside apartment where we could recharge our batteries if only a little. Victoria confided in me that she had a client in Cork with whom she slept without protection because he paid her a little more. I scolded her in a way you can't even imagine. Trusting a man who pays for sex that he has no diseases is like playing Russian roulette. Risking your health, the only thing you have, for money, isn't worth it. He told her he had a vasectomy and didn't see anyone else. Such words, meant with such sincerity, made me sick to my stomach. My assertion was supported by three positive pregnancy tests that Victoria had taken. So either that guy was lying to her, or he had horrible luck with a doctor who gave him a new kidney instead of a vasectomy, but the first option seems much more likely to me. The gullibility with which she trusted him shocked me! If anything was taboo in this "work," it was trusting a client and risking oneself for a few pennies. I was so incredibly angry with her; I wouldn't have expected her to do something like that. In Galway, there is a beautiful park we walked through on our way home from the store, where we bought magical future-telling sticks that were supposed to reveal the lies of that scammer to Victoria. She sat on a bench and pulled out a small plastic bottle of urine from her bag. I didn't expect that! She poured the first test in front of everyone, publicly revealing the truth. Victoria surprised me with that bottle, and probably everyone in the park, too, but she was spontaneous and impatient. Back home, she did the remaining tests and decided she would have to get an abortion. How do you do that when you're stuck in a foreign country, there's a pandemic, and you get pregnant by some random guy for a few extra euros? Victoria wasn't efficient for life, so I found the nearest clinic and booked her an appointment. She said she met a guy, they spent one night together, and now she has his DNA growing inside of her. It wasn't far from the truth, and in such a situation, being completely honest wasn't required. Victoria arrived and terminated the unwanted pregnancy with a guy named Mark, whom she didn't know much about. Of course, I went with her, partly because it was difficult for her and partly because I would do anything to avoid the agency and horny men from Galway.

Jane kept texting both of us the whole time, and they weren't exactly supportive messages; she didn't like that only one of us was going for the procedure, but we weren't both working. "Come back; Victoria will handle it; you're getting a lot of calls; you need to earn money to see your daughter."

Most of her messages were aimed at my daughter. How could she? I hadn't seen her in so long, and if it weren't for the pandemic, I wouldn't even have a chance to hear from her or call her occasionally. There was no escape from this island, and the earnings were so low that I was struggling financially. Sitting at home alone, half-naked and ready to spread my legs for a few coins for rent and for Jane and Susan? No! I just refused to do that. Besides, most of the callers wouldn't have shown up anyway; during the COVID period, it was all about time wasters who would come, grope you at the door, and run back to their car for their wallet. Those cars were probably parked far away because the men never came back. You waited for them half a day and got nothing, and what did come had to be survived. I'd rather hold Victoria's hand while she swallowed pills than spend a day at home dealing with something like that. Jane's blackmailing didn't work for this time, and when I wasn't there, she could send to the apartment anyone she wanted, and I could be a supportive friend. Victoria needed to rest for a while, so we headed from Galway to Dublin, where we rented an apartment for three days for her to recover a bit. My brother came too and was with us. Victoria didn't seem mentally affected by the abortion, so we focused on what we could. Unfortunately, we had to be cautious due to movement restrictions and couldn't afford to go on trips. It wouldn't have been a problem for us two, but my brother might have been affected by it. So we mostly stayed in the apartment, played cards, watched movies, and those two got along well, to the point where I sometimes felt like he was her brother, not mine. The idyll ended, and it was time to return to reality. Victoria didn't want to have a break longer than three days and was ready to ruin another sizeable portion of the Irish population financially. So we decided to head to a place with an unpleasant reputation, Limerick.

We arrived at an apartment that looked disgusting. It was in a terrible area full of suspicious individuals, and you were even afraid to go out shopping. I was cleaning while Victoria was "working", and she was approached by one disgusting guy after another. She took everything, making me sick, to see what she would do for a bit of cash. When the guys offered her only half, sometimes even a third, of the amount she asked for, she took it, satisfied them, and messaged the operator that they had left. That got us into a difficult situation. The operator sent more guys, thinking Victoria was available, and I would open the door for them and keep them in the kitchen. At the same time, they could listen from her room to loud moans emphasising the presence of another man inside her vagina. Paradoxically, nobody minded this, and Victoria was thrilled not to have to confess to the agency the thirty to fifty euros she collected from each man and had them all for herself. I would either kick such guys out immediately or offer them her services, of course if she happened to be available. It was already difficult enough for me, and letting another piece of my soul be stolen for thirty euros just wasn't worth it to me.

One of these evenings, when we were both done with work, I decided to exercise as every day. I put on my headphones, played loud music, and tuned off my brain. I forgot where I was, and it was my way of relaxing and escaping. These were moments when my body belonged only to me, and it helped me not to lose my mind completely.

Suddenly, I felt Victoria shaking me vigorously. I removed my headphones and looked at her, saying, "What's going on? Can't you see I'm exercising?" She stared at me wide-eyed and said, "Can't you hear it?"

I listened to the silence for a moment, then heard it: loud banging on the door. "What the hell is going on? Who is it?" In one of the most feared parts of Ireland, someone was trying to break down the door of our old apartment. We were both scared and worried. We messaged Jane about what to do, but she didn't respond. It was late, and everyone except us was probably already asleep. Suddenly, we heard a woman's voice with a strong Limerick accent yelling at us, "Let me in; I know my fella is in there!" For a moment, I suspected Victoria of hiding someone in the room, but she assured me that nothing like that was happening and reassured me that there was no one in the apartment. This was a problem; who knows who that woman was? Maybe she found our address in her partner's phone. I couldn't believe it! After about half an hour of meaningless banging and kicking at the door, her voice faded away, and the footsteps retreating from the door indicated that she had possibly given up. We both breathed a sigh of relief, and I wanted to return to exercising, but suddenly, terrible blows broke the silence. It sounded like the girl had upgraded from kicks to a metal rod.

Along with the sounds of attempting to murder our front door, her pleas to be let in and desperate cries to see her partner could be heard. This was no joke; we knew how much we were risking, but we were both terrified, so we called the Gards. They escorted the girl out and took statements from us; there wasn't much we could say. Victoria and I were both beside ourselves with fear, watching from the window as the guards escorted a small, feisty woman out of the building. She was drunk and on drugs, which matched the whole scene, but she made us scared like she was a professional security guard.

After visiting several other places, we finally received joyful news: flights had resumed, and it was possible to travel again. In a few weeks, the first flight home was scheduled, and I immediately purchased two tickets for both of us to get out of there finally. It was about time; my right eye was twitching, my hands were shaking uncontrollably, and I was getting strange stress rashes. It was time to escape! We eagerly approached, leaving the land of leprechauns and good whiskey back to the land of a lousy economy and cheap beer. But a few days before the departure, we received an email saying our flight had been cancelled. This was a disappointment! Tears, loud crying, hair-tearing, and screaming accompanied it. We didn't know what to do. Jane added several fake stories about other cancelled flights and how no one could travel. Supposedly, we weren't the only ones. Unquestioningly, we believed her and continued our activities amidst painful depressions and a path through Irish towns and cities.

Sligo, Mullingar, Maynooth, Dublin, Ballina, Kilkenny, Belfast... I don't even remember where else we went, but almost every one of these places was accompanied by stories as pleasant as hell. In Sligo, the worst was probably when a short Indian man came to see me, despite the operator knowing full well that I didn't want to meet anyone this nationality.

I didn't have good experiences with Indians; they usually started to act weirdly, pressing you hard, squeezing you tightly, biting your skin, holding you in a painful embrace like a firm octopus that attaches itself to you. Usually, after their visit, I had bruises, marks on my skin, hickeys, and scraped skin. Overall, my experiences were more reminiscent of wrestling than intimate moments. I reluctantly accepted that man, not wanting to start any conflict situations, and I was convinced that I would somehow survive that hour. He grabbed me right at the door, hugged me tightly, and dragged me to bed while I smelled a strong odour of sweat. When I say strong, I mean strong, it's the kind of sweat where you try not to faint. After throwing me on the bed, he tried to have intercourse while I was still in a tight grip. I tried to convince him to use a condom, but he didn't seem interested. He hit me in the face so hard that I started bleeding from my lip. He grabbed his penis and tried to force it into me with all his might while I kept my legs tightly closed and screamed for help. Victoria ran in and opened the door. I don't know what she was doing, but it took her a while. She immediately threw the guy off me. He was in shock, probably hoping I was alone. I grabbed my robe and ran to the door, where I stopped and uncontrollably shook. I looked a bit like someone with Parkinson's disease. I screamed at him to pack up and leave immediately, or I'd call the police. He stood there, looking like he didn't understand what was happening; maybe he was confused by my English.

Victoria quickly understood the seriousness of the situation and began to argue with the pervert for me. "Why should I leave? I paid. So give me my money back!" The man shouted back at me. This angered Victoria; the audacity to think he owned me for the paid time. She gave him thirty seconds to grab his stuff, threatening to put on her heels and kick his ass. Nobody wants a scar on their butt from a lady's heel for life. The guy ran away, and thank God, I never saw him again. In a country where such things are illegal, it's almost admirable that he was more afraid of a pissed-off black hair woman than a police officer.

Victoria was excellent; I felt the need to wash that scumbag off me, and she helped me clean up the mess after him. I was all flushed and bloody. This was probably the worst story that happened to me during our unexpectedly extended time in Ireland.

After Sligo, we went to Ballina, a place in the middle of nowhere, and that's how it looked. I don't understand why the agency sent us here; we mysteriously got there, but the place where we were supposed to have an apartment was quite far from the parking lot. Parking nearby was impossible, so we had to grab our things and walk. It was unpleasant; Victoria had a broken wheel on her suitcase, so she dragged it behind her. Since the suitcase was broken, the part that should never have touched the road dragged along the asphalt and made cruel noises. That doubled the time for the entire journey, and what should have taken ten to fifteen minutes took us over half an hour. The apartment was pleasantly located, and as a place to stay for a few more days, it seemed suitable despite being chilly. That was the problem with almost all properties in this country. The heating barely worked; in some places, only cold water ran, so in most apartments, we were like two icicles slowly forming frostbite.

Throughout our stay in this little town, we met only two clients, which didn't even cover the rent. However, we had plenty of time to walk around and explore, and Ballina has absolutely stunning nature. After a few days in a town in the middle of nowhere, we left for Mullingar. In the morning, we were packing up again, followed by a walk with suitcases to the car in a relentless downpour. We were in it together, so I obediently got wet and waited. Yes, I could go ahead to take the car and pick her up, but then I wouldn't be able to blame her and force her to buy a new suitcase. The journey was long, but it wasn't bad. In Mullingar, we arrived at the scene; it was an elephant house. Why elephant? The owner was a big fan of elephants, so everything was in the shape of elephants, practically almost every item you can imagine. We met her, and she was a charming woman; I felt sorry that we were going there to do what we would do. A lovely, friendly, and kind lady in her prime showed us the house and let us settle in. The operator, of course, pushed us to work, and without the possibility of resting, we had to start.

It was inhuman how fast we had to operate; she sent us one man after the other and after Ballina, where we even lost money, I must admit that financially, it was good but utterly inhumane. Each of us had at least eight hundred euros daily, so it was enough to pay the agency, cover the rent, advertisements, and work supplies, and save up for rent in the next city.

It wasn't worth it, absolutely not worth it. Having three days of peace and then let the whole country abuse us for three days just because we hadn't earned anything before. It wasn't a good prospect, and there was nothing to look forward to. No flight date to go home, no promise of a better future, simply nothing to give me strength. For Victoria, it was easier; money gave her strength, and the more she had, the happier she was, so those days were pleasant and satisfying for her. Among all the clients I had, there was one unforgettable individual. A boy no older than twenty. He snorted one line of cocaine after another, was paranoid, anxious, and didn't know what to do with himself. He decided to hide in the closet and playing with his little tool while I was supposed to watch him, and masturbate, which wasn't that bad. But it lasted long, and it was starting to feel endless. He was leaving the closet repeatedly, his drooping penis still in his hand, kept giving me money and extending the time. After he paid me, he stuffed himself back into the closet and continued his seemingly endless self-gratification. Victoria found it suspicious after about three hours, and since it was almost time for us to finish, she decided to knock on the door and see if everything was okay. That caught the man's attention, and since I hadn't achieved any great success with him in terms of his climax, he decided to negotiate with Victoria that he would now watch her from the closet. Of course she agreed, which made me thrilled. I left the room as quickly as I could and sent a message to the operator that the man had left. Victoria was delighted because she got money she didn't have to mention to anyone, and the man was in seventh heaven, probably just from how many drugs he had taken. It reached a point where, around eleven at night, he was in a trance, and Victoria and I got his address out of him and called him a taxi. We didn't want to be responsible for this, and we had to work with the possibility that it wouldn't end well. Heart problems accompany cocaine; if something happened, how would it look? I can see the newspaper article: "A man had a heart attack in a house with two prostitutes and two thousand elephants?" No, that wouldn't work! If anything, the taxi driver would take care of him; we told him he was a friend and got very drunk. It was evident that he wasn't feeling well, so

122

we asked the driver to take him home and gave him extra money in case he vomited in the car.

With this appalling story, we left Mullingar and fled to Kilkenny. It was a magical place; I loved it there about as much as most people. It is a favourite place for tourists and Dublin residents—a place with a reputation for long parties and short skirts. We didn't go to parties there; honestly, we didn't go anywhere. Firstly, the current situation didn't allow it as everything was closed. Secondly, we spent most of our time at home or on long walks, which allowed us to see places where we probably will never be again.

The owner of the apartment in Kilkenny, like one of the few, knew what will be happening in the apartment, and for a small extra fee, he didn't mind. During COVID-19, the agency found several such places and owners who were happy to avoid paying taxes and supported prostitution. This was one of them. He was an older gentleman, kind and without prejudice; he accommodated us as usual, took cash, and left us there to face our fate.

It was a ground-floor apartment in a building with about eight flats. The gentlemen had to pass through a gate with bars, forcing them to enter a code. Some weaker individuals couldn't open this gate, even after a detailed description from the operator. We encountered this often. Mostly good-looking and seemingly intelligent men who couldn't fulfil the most primitive tasks. They probably already had all their brain cells in their penises, and their ability to think was at the level of a goldfish in a round aquarium. Some gave up, and others decided to overcome themselves and fight their way to our apartment. It was unnecessarily lengthy and unpleasant. When they were not able to enter the gate, there was a huge chance that some neighbours could see them which was freaking me out.

One afternoon, something happened in the building, and the fire alarm siren went off loudly. We started to panic along with it! Immediately, we dropped all activities and rushed to hide our work equipment where it wouldn't be visible. We dressed at lightning speed, grabbed only the essentials, and pushed out with the crowd of scared people. The alarm was blaring like crazy, giving us pounding headaches and feeling partially deafened. When we finally reached the street, firefighters rushed in, and everyone outside was confused. We had to send a photo to the agency as proof that we didn't make it up, which was absurd and waited to see what would happen. We were outside for about two hours; the rescue teams were trying to evacuate the building, significantly hindered by a lady who lived directly above us. She had taken such strong sleeping pills that she didn't hear anything at all. Those must have been damn good pills if they couldn't wake her up from that crazy, ear-splitting alarm.

The funny thing was, a few months after this incident, Jane contacted us, claiming that the landlord was convinced we had set the blanket on fire with a candle to avoid working. This triggered the fire alarm, and now he was demanding an extra thousand euros for damages, and the agency wanted us to pay for the day of work allegedly lost

124

because of us. I still wonder, what kind of blanket could possibly cost that much money? There was no fire in the building; it was just some short circuit that triggered the alarm. We were genuinely scared, and doing something so crazy never crossed our minds. We didn't pay anything to the landlord, but we had to reluctantly pay the agency for that day, when we dared not work with firefighters behind our windows and all neighbours in front of the building. Sex would be accompanied by loud fire alarm sounds, how exciting. When it comes to money, people will do anything to get it, and that doubled in this world. Susan didn't like this part and decided that I was a liability to her. That day, we had a terrible argument; she told me to work from nine in the morning until ten at night and not go anywhere. In her mind, Victoria could do all the shopping for me or I could get up every day earlier. Maybe for some people it can be enough to sleep five hours per night, but not for me. I didn't want to be confined to the apartment for fourteen hours daily when I knew it was for nothing. There were no clients, nobody was coming, and I was also missing money. I was stressed, and the only thing that gave me a sense of normality was our walks and the brief feeling of freedom. Susan decided that if I didn't do what she said, she would split us up, and we would each have to work alone. This was absurd, audacious, and inhumane. I was just a walking asset to her, obligated to do whatever I was told. Working from nine in the morning meant returning to the apartment by half past seven or earlier to prepare and getting up before six while going to bed after midnight. Trapped in the apartment, unable to go anywhere, and completely drained of energy, waiting with a fake smile for potential clients interested in my vagina. I didn't want to put up with it, but I didn't want to be separated from Victoria either. Despite not always seeing eye to eye, it was nice to have someone to talk to, to feel safe with, and someone I could cry on the shoulder of if need be. Plus, she spoke English, which helped me a lot and was an invaluable skill, especially during the period when there were police checks on every corner. Victoria heard every word of my conversation and was genuinely saddened by how Susan treated me. I decided to remain a good girl and obey Susan, so early rising and endless all-day fatigue began for an extra two hundred euros. The people from this agency were inhuman monsters with sharp elbows. We often considered breaking free from their clutches and "working" for ourselves, but it wasn't possible. This idea was accompanied by many stories about how they treated girls who decided to do something like that. The first thing was that we would have to buy back our profiles from them. Our photos, reviews, regular clients – everything behind that one profile was hidden, and they would never give it to us for free. Another demand from them was that we would always had to inform them where we were going, how long we would be there, and give them at least twenty per cent of our earnings for three months because they showed us all the places to go. These were the facts, and we knew that was how it worked, but then there were things we only heard about and weren't sure if they were true, but we didn't want to risk it. Girls who refused to give them a percentage of their profits after they left practically opted for public execution. Susan and Jane had copies of every girl's passport, addresses of all of us, and everything they needed to destroy us. If a girl did something they didn't like, they would contact her family, find her on social media, and publicly shame her. They sent everyone unedited photos from escort websites and evidence of what she was doing in Ireland and how long she had been doing it. Many women had children or partners, and whether it was moral or not, no one deserved this. We always wanted discretion, and risking someone taking away even the last bit of our dignity would be absurd. Victoria had a plan in mind, and with her personality type, she might have been able to pull it off. She was ready to fight the agency and explain that just as they knew information about her, she also learned about them. Prostitution and tax evasion probably wouldn't sit well with anyone, but we knew that fighting dirt with dirt was not the solution. Both of us would get our hands dirty, but the difference was that Susan would like it. As I mentioned, Victoria had a boyfriend, and he meant a lot to her. She didn't want to get involved in something that could hurt him, so we let it go and were obedient girls.

Shortly after the argument with Susan I had a regular client who always came to see me when I was in Belfast. He was a nice guy, as nice as someone who sticks his fingers into your vagina can be. When we finished, we were chatting, and suddenly, terrified Victoria burst into our room. Before we could even cover our naked bodies, she blurted out, "Get rid of him; we need to get rid of the clients. The neighbour is knocking on the door and calling the police." While I was in shock and absentmindedly started putting on my pants, the guy next to me had no idea what was happening. Victoria somehow forgot to translate it into English, so the poor guy sat there in silence for another two minutes before I realised I should explain it to him. The service with a considerable dose of adrenaline was even better. Victoria also had a client she was trying to get rid of, so the two gentlemen met on the stairs. Maybe they went for a beer afterwards; it's hard to say, but first, we had to eliminate them. That lady kept banging on the door as if trying to break it down and made videos of what was happening in the house through the mailbox in the door. There was no escape through the main entrance! That is unless the gentlemen wanted to become internet stars. We had a small backyard, but we didn't have keys to the gate. We suggested they could climb over the fence and sneak out unnoticed through the dark alley toward the main street. The guy who spent his ten minutes of pleasure with a busty black hair Victoria jumped into the garden and ran as if someone with a gun was chasing him, climbed over the fence, and disappeared into the bushes. We looked at each other and didn't know what to think. The guy with me kissed me on the cheek, and amid the neighbour's threats, which could be heard through the door, he said goodbye and slowly fled. We tidied up everything, and within fifteen minutes, our house looked like nobody lived in it, and we informed the operator about the situation. She was aware of what was happening, but not from us. With her quick thinking, she scheduled more appointments, and two gentlemen sent her a video with an angry woman outside the house and a caption stating that an evil dragon guards the princess tower. We had to look for accommodation elsewhere, and when the lady finally gave up, we decided to go out and enjoy a free night. While the agency arranged accommodation for us, we were drinking at the bar and chatting with random passersby.

After a while, two significantly drunk Irishmen joined us, both from Newry. I don't know if you've ever heard this type of accent, but it's not worth it. No matter how well you speak English, if someone from Newry decides to talk to you, you're lost, especially if the person's accent is enhanced by alcohol, which significantly impairs their already poor speaking ability. After attempting to start a conversation, we were chatting for a while, eventually the gentlemen gave up, saying that apparently, we couldn't speak English, and went to find someone who could understand them. That evening, we quietly returned home, and the following day, we moved to an apartment nearby. An interesting fact about Belfast is that it is divided into safe and unsafe areas, which you won't find out until you're there. Due to the not-so-distant history when Northern Ireland was in turmoil, many residents took sides, and the city was divided accordingly. As tourists, unaware of what was happening there, we naturally stayed in suspicious neighbourhoods and encountered even more suspicious men. The new apartment was much more attractive than the previous one, cosy in a high-rise building, and there seemed to be no neighbours to disturb our plans, which were to survive a few days there and disappear. The previous house was nearer to the city center which was a huge positive. For a while, everything was easy; Victoria and I "worked" according to the agency's instructions, and after the last conversation with Susan and knowing what she was capable of, we didn't dare do anything that could deviate from the rules. Until one day, I had a client, an older man around age of sixty. He sat on the bed, we were chatting, and suddenly, he had a tightness in his chest and couldn't move. Yes, you guessed it, he was having a heart attack, and I was grateful that he didn't have it while he was on top of me. I had heard stories about how some men even died during sex with an escort, it must be extremely unpleasant when you can't tell if it's an orgasm or a heart attack. It's awful, but many men would wish for a death while they are having sex with someone.

This gentleman sat on the bed, and at that moment, I was incapable of doing anything, as if the world had stopped. My shock was awakened only by the significant ringing of the phone, where the operator asked how long he would stay and if I was okay. I called Victoria and opened the window. Victoria hesitated to go inside at first, but when she saw the disaster holding onto his chest and suffering from obvious pain, she realised that we had to act. We quickly got dressed. I think it was a new record, and while we carried him downstairs, Victoria called the emergency services, saying that we found a man in such condition on the street. We sat him on the doorstep and waited for someone to arrive and help him. Yes, we could have called an ambulance to come to us, but he still had a pulse and was conscious. Plus, we didn't want to risk it. The man had a wedding ring, which could also cause significant problems. Not that we were protecting married slimeballs, but we weren't there to judge. Anyway, the truth was that men with wedding rings were thrown at us a lot, and although we felt sorry for their wives, we couldn't reject them just because of that. Was it immoral? Yes, it was! Their marriages wouldn't be saved by us anyway, and if we rejected them, they would go somewhere else. Sometimes, it seemed that men didn't care where they stuck it as long as they stuck it somewhere. After this unpleasant incident, we were both terrified and worried. After a few days Victoria started laughing and joking about how men have heart attacks because of me. She used to say, it's the best compliment. We got over it, but I wouldn't want to experience it again; it's such a feeling of helplessness and fear that accumulates in you. It was time to move on and continue "working."

Honestly, even if the man had died, it wouldn't stop the agency from sending us more individuals craving sexual satisfaction. The very same evening I experienced that 'compliment', I also met a guy named Johnny. He was a nice, kind, and friendly biker. He lived in an unhappy marriage with two children and stayed only because he was told that if he left, he would never see his children again. He always paid me for three hours and came to chat with me; sometimes, I even cooked for him or served him hot whiskey, which I knew how to prepare very well. Sometimes, it even led to sex, which had to be endured. Although he had a good heart, he wasn't attractive, and it took him over an hour to climax. He was an obese man in his forties with long hair. During sex, he sweated in such a way that when I lay under him, everything dripped into my face, into my eyes; it was disgusting. A mysterious fluid flowed from his penis, which stained my hands whenever I touched it, and under his weight, I struggled to breathe. Intimate moments were torture, but he wanted them minimally, so most of the time, we talked, which was nice. I had someone to improve my English with, and he had enough patience to repeat everything he said to me or wait until my chicken brain with insufficient vocabulary understood it. With Johny, we had been seeing each other for a long time, he became my friend. He even bought me motorcycle boots, which I still have to this day, and once he was so kind that he drove me to the airport so that I wouldn't miss my flight. I occasionally took him out for breakfast and spent much time with him. He was indeed a nice and kind man; I gave him my personal number, and we stayed in touch, talking about his troubles, relationship, and children. That was the only positive thing this involuntary extension of our stay brought. Unfortunately, he fell in love with me over time, and it became more than evident. He didn't hide it, and with my "job" and hectic life, I couldn't tie myself to a man with a wife and kids. Actually I wouldn't do it even if I had better life. So, no matter how painful the decision was, cutting off contact with him was necessary. The essential thing was that we couldn't be friends, and forgetting about each other was the best for us. Belfast always paradoxically brought some stories; it was a city of events, and I don't think I ever left there without some experience.

Again, the day of departure and handing over the money came. Money was usually transferred through Payzone, but if there was a chance to give it to someone physically, it was better for the agency. On the way to Wexford, we stopped in Dublin at a girl's place who enthusiastically told us she is about to fly home. That shocked us completely. "How is it possible that you're flying home when no flights are available?" Rule number one: never trust Jane! That girl had been here during COVID times before; all it took was to get a PCR test and fly through Germany. Oh boy! I don't think I've ever been so angry; Victoria and I burst into tears, both of us, and we didn't talk about anything else the whole journey down to Wexford.

Finally, we could go home; there was a chance! How could she hold us against our will when she knew how hard we were coping with the whole situation? We could forgive everything that happened, but there was no way we did that. Such a manipulative hussy. We left Jane some nasty voice messages; at that moment, we didn't care about anything. We were frustrated, stuck in a foreign country, forced to spread our legs to dubious creeps every day, all because Jane needed to buy who knows what. No way! En route, we stopped at a café and bought plane tickets, ordered a test, and immediately sent everything to Susan and Jane. We were supposed to have the flight in fourteen days, and we were determined to fly home this time! Susan was angry, trying to lie that it wasn't safe, that we wouldn't be allowed cross the border because many girls weren't allowed through. A lot of nonsense! We didn't listen, filled with adrenaline and a sense of insult; we only saw ourselves getting on the plane and heading home. When a woman decides on something, nothing can stop her!

In Wexford, we stayed in a small apartment with one bedroom. It was a bit uncomfortable for "work"; we had to share the room. Victoria pushed me into a small room with a children's bed, from which the slats stuck out, and it was really uncomfortable to sleep on it. She needed a bedroom for herself to video chat with her partner in the evening, or at least that was her excuse. I was humble and didn't want to argue, so I accepted the future of broken backs and moved my suitcase into that small room. After all, it was only for a few days, and it could be survived. At least I didn't have to sleep in a bed where countless men had left their hair, cum and brown stains. A shared bedroom wasn't the only problem with this apartment. Another was the oven; if you turned on the stove to make food, the oven automatically turned on as well, without having to set anything. We both knew that and were careful, so it shouldn't be a problem. But Victoria didn't think through the consequences of situations, and informing someone about their actions was beneath her level. After Belfast, she got rid of the stinking chicken, which did us both an extraordinary service, and she decided to come up with an alternative solution. She put the money in a plastic bag in the oven without telling me, and it was well hidden, so you couldn't see it just by looking through the glass. That was, of course, the purpose. With cash comes responsibility and fear, so we both hid the money in safe places to prevent someone from stealing it. It was like a nightmare, the thought of someone robbing you and losing everything. It wasn't paranoia; it was happening daily, just fortunately not to us. There was at least one story every week. But she definitely should have consulted me about this hiding place. I got up earlier than her in the morning, just for the already mentioned conversation with Susan, and after morning hygiene, breakfast preparation usually followed.

That morning, I fried some eggs, and the oven, of course, automatically turned on as well.

After a while, a smell appeared, and I couldn't figure out what was happening.

That smell also woke up Victoria, who, half-naked and sleepy, ran into the kitchen. "What the hell are you doing? I have money in the oven!" she yelled. And damn, so the smell was the smell of ten thousand euros melting in a plastic bag. It doesn't smell nice! I immediately took action: I turned everything off and carefully took out the contents from the oven. All the melted plastic was stuck to the banknotes, and it took a long time to clean that. My roommate was, of course, angry with me, but I didn't feel guilty. She should have told me, and if she had, I would have taken everything out of the oven before I decided to make such a rich breakfast. She just yelled at me that day; it wasn't pleasant. Fortunately, she calmed down soon, when she figured out her money wasn't hurt, and we could spend the rest of our stay relatively peacefully.

Since time was pressing, and we were about to head home soon, we decided to offer the duo one last time in case anyone was interested. Unfortunately, I wasn't as lucky as Victoria in saving up as much

132

money, and although I wished her well, I felt a bit down. On the other hand, I knew what she could do for money, so I was somewhat proud of my way to be the poorer one between us. There wasn't much interest in the newly offered service. There wasn't much interest in any sexual services in Wexford in general. Women of Wexford, most of you have probably broken or faithful men at home.

One man approached us, wanting to try out two partners at once, and we didn't have many other options but to comply with his request. This man had absolutely no idea what to do with us. It was as if men had some twisted idea from porn, where they saw two actresses pretending and suffering pain, playing with his intimate parts with disgust and reluctance. Most of them yearned for something they had seen somewhere without realising that reality was far from their imagination. It was tedious, and the truth is, he made us scream, but with pain which is not the same as pleasure. He bit through Victoria's nipple, and he pressed on both of our clitorises in such a way that tears streamed down our faces. Every move he made was uncoordinated and painful. We didn't want him to stay there, but we persuaded each other that we could handle it while holding hands. We tried to satisfy him quickly, but it wasn't working. Ultimately, Victoria rode him like a Texan on an electric bull while I squeezed his testicles because he seemed to like it, according to his own words. I couldn't take it anymore, and I shouted, "Just fecking finish already," in Czech and behold, it worked. The man ejaculated like a garden hose, and Victoria collapsed next to him, completely exhausted. He looked at me, stroked my face, and with a solemn expression, he said, "It's not my fault; your language is so sexy. Otherwise, I could have lasted even longer." My language? If I had known, I would have started speaking Czech to him upon arrival, and we would have avoided this nonsensical suffering. We weren't interested in anyone lasting longer. The quicker he satisfied himself, the quicker he was gone, and those who managed it within five minutes, including a shower, were the most beloved by us!

We left Wexford behind us, and after a short journey and a few days, the last stop awaited us. Dublin! As soon as we arrived, we went for PCR tests, and we were thrilled to fly home.

The next place was a comfortable apartment near Stillorgan Village. The final place before our escape, and we were swamped here. Men in Dublin weren't as afraid of COVID-19, so from morning till night, we spread our legs until we collapsed from exhaustion. Victoria had a very interesting client at this place who brought her stockings and whipped cream. She put on the stockings, and the man sprayed about half of the can between her legs. He imagined it was the sperm of other men, and he was licking it for about an hour. Some people have strange ideas, which reminds me that I also had one of my first experiences at this place. A very polite, charming gentleman of mature years. He was a lawyer who worked in Dublin and came dressed in a suit, carrying a small paper bag. People from various social backgrounds approached us with different desires: doctors, lawyers, politicians, actors, rugby players, labourers, sales associates, drug dealers, basically a bit of everything, and it was not uncommon for us to recognise our clients from television. The most courteous ones often had the strangest requests and desires. Specifically, this guy brought lingerie in his bag and asked me if it bothered me. I mistakenly assumed it was something for me to wear, so I replied that if it was clean, I didn't mind. However, there was a misunderstanding, and the man took his bag to the bathroom. When he came out, I looked at the bald, pot-bellied sixty-year-old man with amazement as he wore pink women's underwear. The hardest part in such a situation is to maintain decorum and try not to laugh or ridicule the person in any way. It was the first time I encountered something like this, but certainly not the last. Mostly, it was older, well-off men who dressed in seductive women's lace. Some even wore their wives' lingerie because they felt like they were with their other half while they were cheating, so technically, they weren't cheating in their sick heads—strange ways to deceive one's conscience. Apart from gentlemen with unusual tastes, this apartment also brought the most significant argument between me and Victoria. One day, we finished earlier, and everyone from the agency knew about it. We planned a barbecue, and my brother was supposed to come. The raven-haired girl stuffed her money into a bag of charcoal, fully aware that we were going to have a barbecue. My brother, while preparing the fire, poured out the contents into the grill, and in the darkness, it was pure luck that he even noticed the presence of banknotes. This girl had a problem! On the one hand, I was thrilled that we didn't have to travel with that disgusting chicken anymore, but on the other hand, Victoria was too inventive when it came to hiding cash. Fortunately, there was no further harm to her banknotes, but it was close. The lousy mood soon subsided, and we joked about how expensive the dinner could have been. And in the morning, our last working day awaited us before we left for Berlin. I was excited like never before and determined to handle everything that day would bring. However, what those two had prepared for me was challenging.

In the morning, when I woke up, my brother was still in the living room; it was early, so I didn't bother asking when he planned to leave. Victoria arranged with him behind my back that he would stay until our departure, which I didn't know. I was supposed to prepare for my first client, but my brother was still present. Although he knew what I did for "work," it was pretty uncomfortable for me having him involved in any way. Ten minutes before the first client interested in buying love was supposed to arrive, I learned about their plan. Fortunately, he was sensible enough to leave for a walk and return later. I was angry. I understood that Victoria had a completely different relationship with him than I did, that she wasn't ashamed of her work, and she didn't care who listened to her during sex. It didn't bother her, but I didn't want him there.

I enjoyed spending time with him, but this was too much! Around two o'clock, the clients stopped calling, and we had a moment of freedom. Men usually liked to enjoy themselves, especially during lunch breaks at work and after work before heading home. There were as well days when we didn't meet people at all, especially when the rugby was on. Sometimes clients were coming after and before the game. The busiest time was summer and they also loved to treat themselves around Christmas. January and February used to be quite months.

My brother returned, and in total attendance, I could finally unleash my anger on Victoria. It angered me that neither could empathise with my position and realise how difficult it was for me. I wanted to maintain at least a shred of dignity, but I encountered incomprehension. Victoria sat on the couch in the living room, staring blankly at me and didn't understand why it should bother me that my brother would be in the next room while I would be selling my body and pieces of my soul to unknown, penis-thinking creatures.

Me:" This is irresponsible of you; it's extremely humiliating for me."

V: "Calm down, Elis. Nobody's doing anything to you, and I don't understand why you're getting so upset."

Me: "Why am I getting upset? He's my family, and you arranged for him to be behind me while I walk around in underwear and do what I do. Doesn't that bother you?"

V: "Jesus, he's your brother, not your partner. He's just here! Or are you jealous that we get along so well?"

Me: "Yeah, I'm jealous, but that's not the point! You wouldn't want your boyfriend to be here either!"

V: "Don't drag him into this, and he's not your boyfriend."

Me: "Victoria, shut up! Just because you're so proud that you spread your legs for money doesn't mean everyone feels the same way! You know why I'm doing this, and tomorrow I'm going home; after six months, I'll see my daughter, and I don't intend to spend the last day with a feeling of guilt."

V: "Yeah, so if he stays, you're not working?"

Me: "Exactly!"

V: "You know what? Kiss my arse, you vain cow!"

Victoria blurted out! She yelled at me in such a way that I didn't understand a word; my eardrums were slowly melting! I couldn't understand anything, and I just held back from exploding at her until I heard: "You're still a terrible mother; no mom will do this to her child".

Oh God, I couldn't handle it anymore. She pissed me off so much that I lost my self-control, and we just went at each other. We were fighting like crazy, and it wasn't a Barbie-style fight. Aside from the pulled hair, I had a broken tooth and a battered head from a broom handle. We were both in a similar state and when our brother finally separated us, Victoria needed all her attention. She sat on the floor in the kitchen, clutching her chest and screaming, "I can't breathe, you're such a bi*ch. I'm going to die now!"

Her whimpering ended with my suggestion to call emergency services, and she got angry. With screams and numerous curses, she stormed off to her room. Do you also have that one person in your life who, when they leave the room, the world seems brighter? She was like an actress! In my agony, I explained the situation to the agency and told them I will be not working anymore. Victoria decided that a bit of blood wouldn't stop her and threw herself headlong into making even more money as long as possible. I took my brother away. We went for a walk, went to the beach, and had something to eat; I just had a free afternoon. Well, did I? The agency bombarded me with messages, telling me to return immediately and that it wouldn't be so bad. Still, after my colourful explanation of the situation, to which I added several photos, Jane showed little sympathy. That day, I didn't have to see any more guys. In a way, it seemed convenient to me; I was glad to have a break from those antics for a while and didn't have to go through it. In the evening, I returned home, and Victoria and I sorted things out, made up, and in the end, we laughed about it. It was good that neither of us could stay angry for too long. This shared trait of ours was priceless. We both agreed that we didn't need this and decided not to return to Ireland anytime soon. We spent the whole night talking, and none of us slept. The following day, probably from exhaustion and stress, I started feeling sick! Oh God, I was afraid I had caught Covid. My joints hurt, I felt like I was burning all over, and it was awful!

The next day, we rushed to the airport. Finally, the moment had come; I couldn't believe it. I was going to see my family, and I couldn't wait. I prayed that no one would notice anything about me, and I hoped they would let me go without any problems. I got to Berlin without any issues, but I felt like I had the worst flu ever. I just wanted to sleep! I fell asleep on the plane and then on the train from Berlin to Dresden. The problem arose when we arrived in Dresden. We didn't expect such a massive train station, and neither of us spoke German. We didn't know how to find our platform, and no one wanted to talk to us in English. When we found it, it was too late, and the train had left. The unpleasant woman at the window told us the next one was in two days, which was unacceptable! She as well offered that we could take a boat, which we hoped was a joke or a translation mistake. Our phones were dying, and we didn't know what to do. I gathered the last bit of courage and called my dad to see if he could come for me. He was old and sick.

I didn't want to involve him in this, especially when I wasn't feeling well, but we didn't have many options, and only someone from the family could cross the border. Stupid Covid! Eventually, we managed to find a suitable alternative. Jane's dad worked for a taxi service, so he had the opportunity to come and pick us up. The problem was that we had to wait for almost five hours before he came to get us, and it cost us a few hundred euros. All the restaurants and shops were open in Germany. I might have enjoyed it, but I wanted to curl up and die.

Every movement, every muscle, and every joint hurt. If Victoria hadn't been with me, I probably would have fallen asleep on that train station bench somewhere. The raven-haired whirlwind found luggage storage and decided to pass the time with shopping. Completely unable to notice my pain, she ran from shop to shop while I slowly dragged myself behind her like a bundle of misery.

She was full of energy, enthusiasm, and freedom, while I was full of pain and convinced that I will die there. That time, I bought a dress there that still reminds me of a miserable day. At the same time, it was a joyous day because, after a long wait, where every minute seemed endlessly long, our taxi finally arrived. We stuffed our luggage and a billion paper bags into the trunk and set off. I slept the whole way to the border; I was utterly exhausted. They woke me up before the border and I had time to pretend that I was okay; otherwise, they might not let us go home. This was my life's acting performance, and I deserved an Oscar. I even flirted with the officer while suppressing my inner pain. By a miracle and with God's help, we crossed the border, and we were finally home. I was dropped off at Emma's, where I immediately collapsed on the couch after a brief welcome and slept until morning. That morning, I felt better than ever; all the travelling and sleepless nights convinced my body that I was sick. Honestly, I was afraid I might have Covid, but I didn't want to admit it. The goal was clear: to get home safely. In the morning, I was excited that it wasn't some dramatic, deadly illness! The next day, I went straight to my parent's house and spent a month with my daughter, family and friends, which seemed like a dream. But dreams end, and it was time to return to reality.

Chapter Seven
Prague - The City of Sin

As mentioned with Victoria, we decided not to return to Ireland for a while and instead chose Prague as our next destination. We agreed to try setting up our own advertising and work for ourselves. Victoria started this earlier than I did, so had the opportunity to see if it was just a waste of time and money or if there would be a chance to earn something. In a month, Victoria saved around thirteen thousand euros, she "scoped out the terrain". After barely surviving in Ireland and keeping the bare minimum, at least for me, it was nice to imagine that I might soon save enough to get out of this awful world of prostitution. When my holiday was done, Emma drove me to Prague, where Victoria picked me up. We were supposed to stay there for two months, the whole summer, and then she was supposed to fly to see her man and me back home. If I could earn as much as her, I could quit this "job" and be free. That was my biggest dream; I wanted nothing more than freedom.

The first step was to get a phone and a disposable SIM card, then set up advertising, and I could get started. I had to answer the phone myself, and that was when I first experienced how terrible it was. You can't even imagine it: lots of creepy guys calling your phone number.

They kept asking the same questions:

"What are you wearing?" "Do you like sex? Do you like it rough?" "I know you're horny. Do you want to fuck for free!" All their questions and statements made me sick.

Almost every other man felt that women were offering these kind of services because they were horny and eager. If I was such a nymphomaniac, I would find a lover, but I wouldn't degrade myself to something like that. Sometimes, men tried to lure me by sending a photo of his manhood. Who does that? Do men think I've never seen a penis in my life or that theirs is so unique that they have an irresistible urge to share it with the world? Honestly, when I receive a photo of a mushroom

140

covered in foliage, it's just like when a cat brings me a mouse. I see the man is proud, but why should I touch it or like it? Victoria was handling everything very well as usual; by the time I arrived, she had a busy schedule for the next two weeks and proudly arranged more and more meetings. I was a desperate person who did it with reluctance. The agency, in a way, was good for me; they pushed me into things I didn't want to do. I'm not saying it's okay, but at least I had "work."

Of the people who wrote to me, every other one seemed suspicious; one grammatical mistake in the text was enough for me to dismiss them. The truth was that it wasn't about the individual's way of expressing themselves but about me looking for excuses not to spread my legs. Victoria didn't like it; sometimes, she took my phone and arranged meetings so I could at least earn something. When she heard me talking to someone on the phone, she laughed at me. She said I sounded like a lawyer arranging a meeting with a client. I was always proud of my communication skills, and the truth is, probably no one expected to talk to a girl who would speak to them on the phone like a banker about derivatives, but I couldn't help it. I despised the whole world of sexual services, and it seemed disgusting to me to lose myself for money.

Sometimes, of course, I had to "work," and it took a lot of persuasion to convince myself. It was necessary to send money home, to pay rent for housing in Prague, and I had to save something as well. After a few days, I convinced myself I had to start functioning and responding to every stupid message. I didn't want to, but what could I do?

If I didn't want to see my daughter only once every six months and do something I hated for the rest of my life, I had to grit my teeth and start "working".

I felt sick, but I already had a fictional smile trained in Ireland, and I had Victoria as my support there. I started to try and earn a little, but accommodation was expensive, and we were staying in short-term rental apartments for now. Victoria had no shortage of clients and suggested that we go together to one of their clients because he wanted to see me as well. I wasn't thrilled about it, but there was no choice; I had to do something. He was a bald man with glasses in his forties; he seemed slimy to me, but he paid well. We went to hotels with him, where he tried to ply us with alcohol, which we didn't drink. He always got drunk so much that he liked to tell us about his life in detail. He was a mayor of an unnamed town, had a wife and kids at home, and whenever he came to the city of sin, he hired one or two companions to liven up his alcoholic party. I felt sorry for his wife; no one deserves to have such a jerk at home.

As a client he was demanding, but was paying well. In the following days, Victoria introduced me to Jane, who surprised me with her insight. I don't even remember how I imagined she looked, but I certainly didn't imagine her like this. We met her in a café; she was a short-haired forty-something, smiling, but wrinkles were visible on her face. She had curves, really a lot of curves, and she had a little son with her. Her son was rude and incredibly noisy. He was one of those neglected children. She would buy him anything, but she couldn't devote herself to him. She constantly forgot about him while dealing with her phones. She had a client on the phone while dealing with why some girl was kicked out of a hotel, and as compensation, she handed her son an ice cream instead of lunch and bought him everything he pointed at. I felt sorry for that boy; I'm not saying she was a bad mom, but maybe she needed to work on some things. When she dealt with work, she didn't perceive the world; she was trapped in the world of her screen, and everything that happened in Ireland was much more important than reality. Anyway, this woman helped us with a cheaper accommodation option. She knew Susan, and Susan knew the owner of a hotel that offered short-term accommodation mainly for girls who worked in prostitution in Prague.

I didn't want to do it, but economically, it made sense. They showed us our apartment; it was two rooms separated by a small corridor, and there was another set of doors in the corridor leading to the bathroom. That was all; I don't remember how much they wanted for it, but compared to other short-term rentals, it was cheap. The location was pleasant; we were close to everything, and the metro took us wherever needed. We spent a month in this apartment, and I was ready to earn at least as much as Victoria. Unfortunately, as it often happens, just when I started to be hard on myself, interest in the services we offered dropped to a minimum. Suddenly, both of us struggled to find any clients at all. There were better days and worse day as in Ireland.

Jane often visited us, and we spent much time with her. At that time, I was mentally unwell; every day, I contemplated suicide and started drinking heavily to suppress my anxiety. God, I feel ashamed of the person I was. Today, I know that when life is hard, you try even harder, but back then, it was just too much for me.

Once, Jane and I went for a drink with Victoria, and I wasn't in good condition. We had a massive argument near the Astronomical Clock. I confided in Victoria about my mental issues ages ago, so it's no wonder that she brought it up during our first argument and called me a "psychologically unstable lunatic with suicidal tendencies." That's what friendship is; people always bring up the most painful things to dig as deep under your skin as possible. We yelled at each other, and I don't remember how it happened, but when she called me suicidal psycho, I tried to defend myself. The entire centre of Prague found out that I wanted to commit suicide because I couldn't be with my daughter, I had nightmares, trouble concentrating, my psyche was slowly killing me, and mainly because I had slept with about three thousand men, which ordinary people just don't do. I remember how all the passersby were staring at me, and I'm happy I was drunk because otherwise, I would probably remember it even more vividly. Did I want too much? A normal life? I've always been so ambitious and goal-oriented! What happened to that girl? I had to go through it; it made me a stronger person, but at the time, it was hard to see it as a positive. The more I tried, the worse it got. At first, I even hoped that someone would come along and rescue me, someone who would help me, but I was alone in this, and I couldn't rely on anyone. I had no one but myself! The world was just black and white for me, and I lost the will to live. Don't judge me; I never belonged in this, and perhaps the awareness that this wasn't my world made it all complicated. Yes, my daughter, that's why I'm still alive after everything that happened, the reason I never gave up when I wanted to so many times. Days and nights dragged on, and neither I nor Victoria were financially well. I had sunk below my standards and took almost anything. Even regular clients were coming to see me, financially keeping me alive. I remember driving to see an Italian guy;

he was a kind fifty-year-old. I usually spent about three hours with him. He always complimented my elegant dresses and cooked dinner for me; we had delicious Italian coffee. I helped him with Czech language; it's a complex language, not easy to learn! He let me feel normal for two hours; I felt like a human being.

JANE

Unfortunately, there was also the aspect of my "job" that had to be endured. During the last hour, I squeezed his balls while he pushed his erect penis into me and drooled on my face. Lovely! I felt like vomiting, but I had to handle that. The sexual part was always like a nightmare! Eventually, he opened up to me and talked about his ex-wife, their relationship, and his friends in Prague, where he goes for beer. Maybe because he wasn't a stranger to me anymore, the whole hour of torturous sex became even more unbearable. Other regular clients came to see me at that hotel, I mean the place where we used to live, with Victoria. There was a truck driver who sweated terribly and smelled unbelievably bad. Ultimately, I stopped seeing him because he fell in love with me. That happened often, and if I were wicked, I might choose a wealthy man to run away with, but I did all this to be independent one day and choose a man out of love. It might sound old-fashioned, but the last thing I want is to bring my daughter into a relationship where I'll be unhappy and teach her values I don't believe in. Moreover, this hairy truck driver wasn't my type. It wasn't just about how he looked, but he couldn't handle too much intelligence either, and as absurd as it may sound intellectually, we really wouldn't match. There were a few foreigners and several Czechs between my clients, but I saw each of them only as disgusting animals paying for sex. I didn't want to judge them, but it was easier to keep my distance from them, and if I didn't see them as walking wallets but as living beings, it would be even more challenging for me. Jane, no matter what it was tried to be helpful. I was glad when she took us out somewhere for fun; that moment when I could forget everything was worth it. We met in the most exciting bars in Prague; in one, they even called me "Miss Mojito". It was one of those places where they mix a cocktail based on how you feel, which for me would probably be something called 'the black death' and contains about eighty per cent whiskey. I walked in there, not knowing how it worked and heroically ordered a Mojito. The bartender laughed and joked about it every time I went there. He was a nice guy. I could pretend to be someone completely different than I was, and I liked that. I created a lie around myself in that bar, where I was a successful, independent woman building her career and doing well. Outside, I was a prostitute selling my own body to support my family and pay off past debts and there I was confident and happy woman. Eventually, the bartender grew fond of me to the extent that he let me stay long after closing, and in return, I helped him with cleaning. I'm not particularly proud of this part because there are undoubtedly many other things to do past midnight than scrubbing toilets in a bar, but in a way, I enjoyed it. It's hard to explain that, but it felt refreshing. Jane spent much time with me, so she took over my work phone and replied to messages I didn't want to respond to. Despite all my efforts, there were individuals where my intuition screamed, "This is not right!"

She simply dismissed it, saying that money is money, and with her favourite line, "Think about your daughter," she sent me to idiots who broke all the rules I had set for why I definitely wouldn't take such clients. Occasionally, I went on outcalls to someone who sent me across Prague, only to not show up. Hilarious, right? Once, a client wanted me to tear tremendous dildos into his backside; I told Jane I definitely wouldn't do that. She persuaded me to go, saying it didn't matter if I didn't do it. On the way, that guy kept texting me to buy a cucumber or something. I told him "We'll see", but every sense in me screamed, "Don't go there, forget it!" When I arrived at the address he gave me, he wasn't even there. I paid for the taxi there and back, just for someone to make a joke out of me. I learned that money was so hard to make, and it depressed me. On the way back, I always felt like crying. The last straw was when she sent me to some junkie who offered me drugs in exchange for sex. At that time, I was completely untouched by all this, and it irritated me that someone thought every girl would like to sell herself for two grams of who knows what. Eventually, Jane arranged for cash in advance with him, and despite my protests, she called a taxi for me, again using her favourite line about my child. At least this time, he showed up and took me inside; his apartment looked like a den of teenagers. He handed me a glass of water and announced that I should wait for a while as he went to get the money. When he returned, he told me his wallet was at work and I could go there with him to collect that. I didn't like that! I wanted to get up from the couch and leave, but my head started spinning. I don't know what he put in that drink, but I was ultimately out of it. When he started touching and undressing me, all I could manage was to hand him a condom. I didn't have the strength to leave; I was incapable of any reaction, just lying there like a corpse, tears streaming down my face, waiting for him to finish. I don't remember much, but mysteriously, I got home by taxi. Besides condoms, all the money I brought with me disappeared from my handbag. It wasn't much, but it was something. When we got home, I had to call Victoria to pay the taxi driver. She ran over, and after my brief story about what happened, she helped me crawl into the apartment. I slept it off, but it didn't diminish my feeling of disgust, and the stuff he put in my drink wasn't strong enough for me not to remember anything at all. It's such a disgusting feeling when you're lying somewhere, and a stranger is lifting your skirt, someone you've never seen before. When you can't move, can't escape, you can't do anything to stop it.

SUSAN

You perceive everything, you know what is happening, but you cannot control your body. You are trying, but no part of you is listening at all! After this incident, I never let go of my work phone, and Jane was forbidden to come near it.

Once in the lobby, I ran into Susan; it was the first and last time I saw her in person. She was chatting with the hotel owner; I assume she had some commissions for referring girls who needed accommodation. Victoria liked to claim that Susan looked like a sophisticated version of herself;

I never saw that much resemblance except for the countless plastic surgeries both had undergone. Susan and Jane were also like water and fire, both completely different. While Jane was stout, fiery, and a stubborn woman on whom age and life's worries had left a mark, Susan was elegantly dressed with a plunging neckline, where her vast fake breasts could only be overlooked if you were blind. She had long black hair, a fake nose, fake eyelashes, fake nails, pouty lips. I have my own opinion on this, and artificial women who let themselves be artificially "enhanced" has never appealed to me, but it's probably a trend of this century, and if it helps the lady in question to be satisfied with herself, it's probably good that we have such options. She just greeted me briefly and went about her business, which didn't bother me at all. From that moment on, I knew who I had the pleasure of dealing with, and I knew them both. Victoria once said that Jane was a completely different person in her personal life than the one I communicated with through Telegram, but I'm afraid that wasn't entirely true. Yes, she was caring, kind and tried to help in many ways, but deep down, she was the same woman. The one who always had to be correct, the one for whom the world of prostitution seemed normal, the one who would do anything for money, the one who wasn't afraid to step over corpses. With Victoria, we had a few weeks left until the end of our Prague adventure, and I was at the end of my rope. As I had been the whole time. Occasionally, I talked to Emma and confided in her about my problems. She decided I needed a vacation, and because travelling was affordable during the COVID period, we decided that I and a few other friends would fly to Mallorca to relax. I was not proud of spending money I didn't have, but no matter which country I was in, it just didn't work. I couldn't save, and I didn't know how long I would still be stuck in this disgusting business. A short break was a good plan. We had a few weeks left in Prague, then Victoria was supposed to see her partner, and I was supposed to go home to my daughter for a few days and then on vacation with my friends. The hardest part about Prague was that I constantly had to lie to everyone. I was three hours away from what I loved most, and I couldn't pick up and go. I had the urge so many times, but what would I say? My parents thought I had a great job in Dublin, and I didn't want anyone to have any suspicions about what I was doing. I couldn't imagine to disappoint my dad again! I fought with myself every day, and when my friends came up with this idea of a vacation, the first thing that came to mind was taking my child with me. I wanted to so badly, but no one was for it, and I knew it would be tough on her. I felt as guilty as a person can feel. It didn't help my mental condition, and the more I tried, the worse I felt. I blamed myself for everything and lied about absolutely everything. How much longer could I handle this? Longer than I thought, and believe me, when you think you can't endure more pain, you get even more. But we'll get to that in the following chapters. However it will be not as depressive reading as you think.

Recently, I came across an article. It was about a man whose story shook the world of prostitution in Prague. It was a man who bought all the websites offering sexual services in the Czech Republic, and his methods of dealing with the girls the services offered were illegal. If you needed to promote your body in Prague with a price tag, you had to advertise on his websites. His behaviour was awful. At that time, he wanted to pay me about three months in advance, and I knew it was absurd because I wouldn't even be there for three months. Jane helped me; her superpower of arranging things that couldn't be arranged came in handy. She cried for about half an hour on the phone pretending to be me. Eventually, by some miracle, I could pay for the advertisement for only two months, and for me, it meant saving at least something.

This part of the newspaper article caught my attention:

"People engaged in prostitution are in a much more vulnerable position. Most often, they are women facing financial difficulties, single mothers who don't become wealthy by providing sex for money; instead, this 'work 'helps them avoid falling into complete financial ruin and pay at least the most essential bills. Furthermore, they operate in an environment where the threat of physical and sexual violence against them is much higher. Not to mention the stigma associated with prostitution. Their complex situation is so easily exploitable."

Why did this part intrigue me? I've always encountered people who believe that selling one's body will make them millionaires. In Ireland, this happened to me almost constantly; every second client slipped into our conversation phrases like, "But you must be rich," or "Easy money, huh?" Even online job offers for sex workers are supported by photos of elegantly dressed women holding wads of cash or women driving exclusive cars. I've also been in situations where I believed that women in this field must be earning obscene amounts. However, the truth is quite different. Ultimately, considering all the expenses, you'd make the same amount of money working in an office in Dublin. Of course, some women earn more, but they do anything for money or have favourite clients who give them hefty tips and expensive gifts. Take, for example, the girl from Ireland who was robbed in a hotel room; she went on vacation with a stranger she found online. Although she couldn't walk after a week, she returned home with gold jewellery and designer handbags. The question is whether the risk is worth it.

I've always been afraid of this, and maybe that's why I belonged to those girls who just try not to fall to the very bottom of existence. Anyway, this article really surprised me; I never would have believed that someone realised that whether women or men offering these services are not rich, and most of them don't even do this "work" out of love but out of necessity. You might wonder why they don't choose something else, but as I mentioned, a job in an office in Dublin would be just as profitable as offering sexual services in the same city. I can't speak for everyone; I don't know the detailed life situations of these people, but from my personal "research," most people who decide to do something like this are entirely without education and in a job position that involves more than just washing dishes, which no one would accept them for. Another issue is accommodation. Finding your place to live is currently almost impossible, and in Ireland, it's nearly a lousy joke. What you would earn in that office would be spent on housing and other services, and in the end, you wouldn't even have enough for food. So it's no wonder that many people who decide to leave this world quickly return to it. Few people think of finishing their education while working in this profession to have better opportunities in the job market or to save enough money. Some can't even do that because they have three children at home and can only make money when they don't have to care for them and spend the afternoon caring for their offspring. It's a tricky situation in many cases, and you can never use the same measure for everyone working in this industry. Victoria and I mainly enjoyed the freedom in Prague, with no agency telling us what to do or not to do. That part was probably the only pleasant thing this capital brought us. Once, we went to lunch and met two men on the street, or rather, they met us. They were gentlemen from the Netherlands, like many others, taking advantage of the cheap accommodation prices during the pandemic. They met us on the street and immediately asked if they could accompany us somewhere, but neither of us was very keen on that. We had had enough of men and were primarily interested in some time for ourselves. At least that's how I felt, but Victoria had the opposite opinion. My English was terrible, so it functioned as my ears and mouth. She immediately shared her personal phone number and arranged dinner with them later. One was handsome and looked like a typical Spanish type with dark hair and a sexy look. His friend reminded me of Hagrid; he was tall, strong, and had a long beard. Victoria persuaded me to go with her and have a pleasant evening without work. An evening without disgusting horny, hairy monsters who want to stick their penis in me? That's what I've heard about. How could I say no? Dinner was pleasant, followed by a long walk in the centre of Prague, where Victoria talked and talked and talked; actually, there was nothing else to hear except her. She loved hearing her own voice! That day, we walked a lot of steps and drank a lot of fluids. When we escorted the gentlemen back to their hotel to leave, Victoria translated for me "Elis needs to pee and she can barely hold it." Hence, the Spanish beauty took me upstairs to their room—I protested vehemently against it, mainly because I have a problem peeing when someone else hears it. I don't know why it's like that; it's been like that since my childhood.

It doesn't matter how full my bladder is; even if it's seconds away from bursting, I still can't do it. I sat on the toilet for a few seconds, hoping it would work out, but the miracle didn't happen, so I washed my hands, flushed, and opened the bathroom door into the room.

Meanwhile, the dark-haired miracle had made himself comfortable and stood there completely naked, hoping that as a return favour for using the toilet, I would sleep with him. I've never run away so quickly in my life, and I don't understand how he could even think of it; he wasn't that irresistible. I ran outside, grabbed Victoria, who was even more surprised than I was, and we ran as fast as my full bladder allowed. I fondly remember this evening with humour, and I think he won't forget me easily either. I was probably the first now who said "No" to him and maybe it could be the best sex of my life which I will never find. My bad!

The end of our adventure in Prague was slowly approaching; there were only a few days left until Victoria's departure home. The day before she was supposed to leave, her boyfriend called her, saying he wanted to surprise her and that he was in Prague with his friends. A pot-bellied sixty-year-old man had just gotten off Victoria, and she had another suitor on the way, so it was a tricky situation for her. I chuckled and sympathised with her at the same time. I never judged her; although I found it extremely immoral that her partner didn't know, she tried to save all that money for their future, and I know she loved him.

We all understand love differently, and as she said, "When I started doing this job, something inside me died." I think for most of us with this lifestyle, a piece of our soul dies, but in her case, it caused such a significant rupture that she couldn't realise how immoral it was and that it wasn't a job, not a real one. I felt sorry for her in a way, and on the other hand, I admired her because, with this conviction, it was so much easier for her, and she didn't suffer as much as I did. She persuaded me to take the man on the way instead of her, as she needed time to prepare. Men usually didn't mind; they didn't care that I was someone completely different. The essential fact was that I had breasts, buttocks, and a vagina, which they considered the "highlight" of their day. I've already forgotten the guy; I don't know who came to me then, and I'm glad I don't remember him. If I didn't remember the clients, that was good. Not remembering them meant they were relatively normal. The problem arose when someone appeared at the door, and I remembered that face. I didn't always necessarily know what they had done to me, but remembering them meant they were a disgusting brute, stinking slimeballs, or aggressive troublemaker. When I got rid of that guy after our action, Victoria was ready to leave. She told me to come to them after I freshened up, gave me the address of where they would be having lunch, and asked me to reserve some apartment where she could pretend to stay. She said she would tell him that she had things at my place, and in the evening, we would pack them together. Although it seemed unpleasant, I didn't want to lie to her partner. On the other hand, what was I supposed to do, tell him the truth? I would never do that to her; I didn't want to hurt her, and it's good to follow the rule that before you hurt someone, try to imagine yourself in their shoes and see how much it can hurt! It would probably break my heart in half if I was in her place. Although we were both different and sometimes fought like cats and dogs, I loved this raven-haired tornado. I arrived for lunch and arranged everything Victoria asked me to. I sat there, but I didn't say much. Firstly, because of my English skills, and secondly, ordinary people make me nervous. After lunch, we went for a walk; I didn't particularly like his friends, but Victoria was happy and content, which was essential to me. We went to see Prague Castle, and overall, we enjoyed a touristy afternoon. In the evening, we made a stop at a bar, where we lingered for a while, and with the help of alcohol, I finally started talking. We stayed there for a while, and then it was time to go home. Her partner, let's call him Thomas, decided to accompany his friends, and we had time to pack her things. My goodness, she had so much stuff; how was she planning to get it on the plane? I couldn't wrap my head around it. It required renting a private jet for all those things! She had everything you could imagine: ice cream-making containers, pans, clothes, shoes, mugs, tools, and plenty of gifts for Thomas. I think we were both quite surprised when, after a few hours, we successfully managed to pack it all into the prepared bags and suitcase. This was almost a miracle, or at least it could be considered one. It defied all the laws of physics, but Victoria was happy, and I helped her move all her things. I felt like I was moving out a mistress. Thomas kindly cared for her; we said goodbye, and they left the next day home together. I was left alone, and there were still two days of work ahead of me; the apartment was quiet without Victoria, no annoying voice telling me what to do, and no one to support me when I didn't feel well. I was entirely determined to make as much money as possible in these last two days. I had plans, short term plans: a few days home, then a vacation, and then a return to Ireland, where I had to buy a plane ticket and pay for the first accommodation. During the day, I met about three gentlemen whom I wanted to get rid of even before they entered the door, and in the evening, I had an appointment scheduled for four hours. He was Croatian, and even though I didn't want to do it, I needed the money. The gentleman arrived, and I tried to communicate as much as possible. However, we both spoke a Slavic language, Czech and Croatian were very different, so we chose English as our common language. We sat on the couch and talked about everything possible; the gentleman brought wine, and I decided to have a glass to make it easier for me afterwards. Wine has such an effect that besides overcoming the language barrier, it can also help you lose your mind and underwear, at least usually. After the first hour, he pulled out a bag of white powder and politely asked if it would bother me. I didn't protest, but I warned him that I wouldn't take it with him. Shortly after, he started persuading me to try some, saying it wouldn't kill me and I would feel better afterwards. Of course, I refused, so he threatened to leave and demanded a refund. Although I wouldn't say I liked it, I was ready to end this appointment. He was bluffing! He didn't want to leave. Cocaine has such an effect on men that, for some reason, they think with their penis, so he changed his strategy. He told me that if I took just one line with him, he would give me all the money he had on him, and he had plenty. I thought to myself, "Damn, I need that money, and what can it do to me?" I knew cocaine wasn't heroin, and after one dose, I wouldn't become addicted. And even though it was against all my convictions, I decided to try it in exchange for the hefty sum of money he offered me. I didn't know what to expect from it and fortified myself with another glass of wine before I took the rolled-up banknote into my hand.

I followed his instructions precisely and took a deep breath. Before I knew it, I felt the bitter taste heading up my nose and into my throat. I remember being afraid; I felt like half of my mouth was numb, and it seemed like my throat was getting swollen. I was told it was normal and encouraged to have another, saying it would stop afterwards. It was true; it stopped. I was more communicative, cheerful, and relaxed. However, he forgot to tell me one thing: after that white powder, people lose self-control, common sense and become much more open. I hated myself for that evening; I shared information no one should know about me. Frankly, I don't even know what I told him. The positive thing is that our communication barrier still existed, so maybe he didn't understand half of what I said.

That white stuff can give you courage as much as you want, but a foreign language it won't teach you. I had a lot of that white powder that night and chased it down with sips of wine like lemonade. I felt superhuman and pleasant, the only side effect being that my nose kept running, which I don't consider the sexiest thing. I'm not proud of that evening, and if I could, I would go back and kick him out, but I didn't do it, so for one night, the sweet girl turned into a creature driven by a plant from the jungle. I don't know how long he was there; I lost track of time. At that moment, sitting next to the Croatian stranger, I felt like I was sitting next to my best friend. It made me completely forget about everything else; I didn't feel any worries, fear, or any other negative emotions; I was living in that moment. That night, we had a lot of sex; technically, he paid for it, everything was with protection, and I didn't do anything terrible, but practically, I broke my most important rule, which was to "always stay sober with a client."

That night, it wasn't me, but it brought me one step closer to something important to me. I could experience another demo version of spending time with my daughter, which was important. What a terrible mother I was? At that time, you could call every little taste of everyday life a demo version. I wouldn't say I liked it; after a few days of feeling like everything was fine and not thinking about anything wrong, the day you had to face reality and leave was approaching. Departures were always accompanied by negative emotions and tears that I tried to hide from my little princess. She never wanted to let me go; I held onto her, and it hurt as much as it could hurt. You can't imagine what it's like to leave that little person who cries, screams, and begs you to stay. It breaks your heart in half, and you want nothing more than to wait and hold her for the rest of your life, but you can't. Demo versions were useless, they suck! Anyway, another one was on the horizon. That evening, when the Croat left, I couldn't sleep. It was late, but I couldn't close my eyes. It was one of the effects of that crap; you can't fall asleep after it, and even when you finally convince your body that it's late and start to doze off, a terrible thirst or the need to blow your nose interrupts your attempt. The next day, I was tired and irritable. I had to tell someone that I, the most prominent opponent of drugs in the world, had done something like that. I called my brother; maybe I should give him a name since I often talk about him. Let's call my brother living in Ireland, Oliver. Just for your imagination, he's a blond, pale man with blue eyes, and his favourite family member is the refrigerator, which corresponds to the belly that has grown over time. He was shocked when I told him what I had done, but he didn't judge me, which I liked. Oliver was a good guy and always supported me, but of course, like all siblings, we sometimes had arguments. He was afraid I would get addicted to it and warned me that it would create a psychological dependency and I might not be able to say no the next time someone offered me that white powder. I didn't take him seriously; I had my priorities and knew exactly what I was doing. Oliver was supposed to join me and my friends on the trip to Spain, so the rest of the conversation was about planning, and we were looking forward to finally seeing each other. Oliver still hadn't found a job due to his previous injury, and I occasionally supported him financially. Although it bothered me, considering I didn't have much myself and knew what I had to endure for that money, but family is family. They always come first, no matter what! On the last day, I handed over the apartment in Prague, packed my things, bought a few small gifts for my family, and waited for Emma to pick me up. She drove me home from Prague, and I could enjoy my princess for a few days. Unfortunately, I couldn't stay with my parents; it never worked out, so I rented a small apartment for a few days, where we enjoyed the mother-daughter relationship.

My parents are nice people, but their house wasn't the most beautiful place you can imagine. Many times, I suffered from depression and blamed myself for leaving my child there. She was cared for fantastically and had everything she could wish for, but the environment wasn't suitable for a child. It wasn't suitable for anyone. Mom and Dad liked to collect things; everything was handy, and nothing could be thrown away. A broken flowerpot? That's useful! An old clay bucket with a hole in it? That's useful too! Hole-ridden curtains, of course, were useful as well, and I could go on like this forever. Their house and garden resembled a landfill with no sense of detail, and neither was particularly skilled at cleaning. I remember when I was little, I was fascinated by the environment in which my friends grew up, and at one point, I kept asking one question. It gnawed at my mind, and it wouldn't let me sleep; I couldn't come up with an answer until I once asked a mom of my friend's, "How is possible your carpet is visible and has colours?" I don't know what she thought, but she was probably more than surprised. I got the answer; it was vacuumed; that was the magic that turned the carpet into a clean spot. In addition to their poor cleaning skills, my parents also had other negatives; they both smoked at home.

Throughout my childhood, teachers suspected me of this bad habit because I smelled of cigarette smoke from home. My mom still believes that if the window is open, it's enough to eliminate the smell. If any of you support the same opinion, I'll disappoint you; that's not how it works! If you smoke a cigarette at home, most likely, the smell will linger there for several days and will only disappear after cleaning everything possible and properly washing fabrics. Anyway, I attach a fairly accurate illustration of what my parents 'kitchen looked like at the time. From this, you can make your own picture of what the rest of the house looked like. There were always many unidentifiable items everywhere, and no hand had touched the entire house for a long time. When I arrived, I had nowhere to sleep, and if I had somewhere to sleep, I wouldn't feel comfortable at all; I would have to disinfect everything before using it, and all my things would smell of cigarette smoke and mustiness. The only usable place in this house would be my daughter's room, which I spent quite a fortune on to make it look pretty. However, my child didn't want to sleep alone and my mom decided to make a storage room from that place for all her 'useful things'. Fortunately, short-term rentals during the pandemic were cheap, so that I could steal my angel just for myself for a few days, and we didn't have to be in that house, which we both appreciated. However, we were close enough to visit my family daily and spend as much time with them as possible. I know what you're thinking; "No wonder you ended up like this when you have such an unfortunate background." Maybe it could have been one of the factors that led me to where I got, but it also might not have been. I grew up in a loving family; many people are not so lucky. People come from different social backgrounds; some live in luxury but are estranged from their families. I always enjoyed a great time with my family and emphasised that they were my top priority. After a few pleasantly spent days in a place closest to my heart, I went on vacation. I still felt guilty that my child didn't go with me, so I didn't tell anyone; it was a secret I kept to myself. Although I didn't want to admit it, I needed a change of scenery and a bit of freedom; those few days with friends and my brother helped me think of other things and made me feel comfortable. I met up with Emma and her boyfriend when I left my family; we went to pick up another couple, Sarah and Mark. These two had known me for a long time, but neither of them had any idea what I was doing; we weren't such good friends to confide in something like that. I didn't fully trust them, but they were good people whom I had minor reservations about. Sarah didn't believe in love and didn't hide that she was with Mark primarily for profit reasons. She cared more about the house and money, attributing a value to it that she would never give to a person. Mark worked as a soldier and liked to drown his sorrow in alcohol. He was a good guy, but at some point, alcohol became a problem for him which he wasn't willing to admit. Together with them, we went to pick up Oliver and happily headed towards Berlin. The airport in Prague had extremely limited traffic during the pandemic, and Berlin was the closest airport from where we could fly despite the time constraints. Before we knew it, we were on a plane heading to Mallorca. It was my best vacation, and I enjoyed it a lot; the most interesting thing about it was that no one, including Mark, had a drop of alcohol the whole time. We rented a house in the mountains, far from everything. We had to leave early in the morning, and when we returned in the evening, we were so tired that we fell asleep standing up. Every day was full of adventures and travelling; I didn't think about anything related to my "work" because I didn't have time for it. The last day before departure, my mom called to tell me that Dad was in the hospital. They had to amputate his toes, and I was terrified, so I changed my flight, contacted the agency, and arranged to arrive to Ireland later. I told my mom I took some time off work and would fly in. At the airport, Oliver and I said goodbye; he flew to Dublin, and I continued with my friends to Berlin. Upon returning from Mallorca, I went straight to the hospital; I felt sorry for Dad, but I knew he would recover. I had the chance to spend a few more days with them, but I'm not sure if it was a positive thing. I loved them all and was immensely grateful for any opportunity to be with my family, but knowing that cruel goodbye was coming again broke my heart. I could not do anything; the parting day arrived, and I had to leave.

Seeing those little eyes filled with tears hurt me, but I couldn't stay. I promised myself I would endure and cope, and one day, I would return and never leave again! Jane told me that at the Prague airport, I would meet a young lady named Sam. Sam was an elegant forty-something woman with so much Botox on her face that she looked ten years younger. She had a distinguished demeanour and seemed like a true lady. The gym was her life, and she liked to stay fit, which showed. We immediately hit it off; I liked that she seemed level-headed, or at least she gave that impression, and she liked that I wasn't like other girls in the field.

Sam didn't have an easy life; she fell in love with the wrong man, got pregnant, and eventually he left her. Despite all his lies, I don't think it ever occurred to her that she was truly abandoned. She was a nurse, but her salary wouldn't support her and her daughter, so she made a living from whatever offered better financial opportunities. She wasn't one to settle for less; she enjoyed a high standard of living, designer clothes, cosmetic enhancements—she just liked to indulge. Plus, she was paying off a mortgage on a beautiful apartment she bought, and the thought of giving up anything was difficult for her. I didn't judge her; it was her life, and it wasn't my place. Likewise, she could have judged me, but she didn't, which I appreciated. I was to spend some time with her; it suited me not to be alone, and likely her.

Chapter Eight: Back to Ireland

In Prague, we boarded the plane together and slowly approached our destination, Dublin. We had rented the first apartment in City West, which is a suburban part of Dublin; they were pleasant apartments by a golf course where I had once been with Victoria. The location was near to the hotel where I revealed some nasty stories about the agency ages ago. Nearly this whole part of Dublin belonged to one big beast; he was rumoured to be involved in the Irish mafia and responsible for everything from drug trafficking to murders. It was a story that made sense to me, but at the same time, I didn't want to believe it too much. Trusting rumours sometimes doesn't pay off. Anyway, according to Sam, he was a dazzling and charming man; she deduced that from when he wrote to her at night, asking her for nude photos. Sam had two significant flaws; the first was that she couldn't listen to anyone but herself, and she lacked empathy. I'm not saying she was inhumane, but she rarely understood your needs. The second was that she was emotionally immature, and despite her experience and "work," she couldn't see through men, even when their intentions were obvious. She lived with the idea of a charming prince who would bring her the moon. The harsh reality, however, is that most men didn't want a relationship or to invest in a woman, especially not in one who would spread her legs for a contribution to her upkeep. They wanted sex, nude photos, and more sex. This guy didn't want anything else from her either, just to satisfy his lustful cravings, indulge himself, and then never call again. On the other hand, can we blame him? Sam wanted to date him despite his reputation, and more than for his charming eyes, it was because of his even more charming bank account. Their flirting didn't last long, and they gradually drifted apart. Men, all they want is for us to be happy and, most importantly, undressed. Around that time, someone significant to her broke up with her when he discovered what she was doing in Ireland. It was difficult for her, and she tried to bury her troubles. We women sometimes do that when someone breaks our hearts; we throw ourselves at an innocent victim whom we use as our

163

painkiller and try to soothe our pain with them. In this case, I'm not sure who the victim was, but the lesson is that a guy who asks you for nude photos doesn't want a relationship with you; he just wants to dip his stick and disappear. Besides those two qualities mentioned above, which didn't limit me, Sam was a great woman. She had her flaws, but that wasn't my problem; after all, I wasn't dating her. She had a strange influence on me; when I was with her, I was making money, and that pleased me. Given her age, she was able to ground the agency like no one else, and that pleased me. We changed several places together, but she was with me for only three weeks; it was time for her to go home, but I stayed and wanted to continue saving. It was the only way to get out of this, just save and save, but when she left, I had to move on to another girl, coincidentally Sam's friend. This woman didn't sit well with me, and we didn't stay together for long. She liked to gossip about people and only looked for the bad in everyone; she invested her money in designer clothes and men who changed in her life more frequently than socks. In Spain, she had a son whom she left there; she didn't show much interest in seeing him or spending time with him; she put herself first.

She suffered from low self-esteem; she told everyone she spoke about six languages and has a medical graduate, but after a traumatic experience, she gave up on medicine and devoted herself to the happy life of a prostitute. She didn't know anything about medicine, and when you asked her something, she couldn't answer you without an internet browser. I never understood why she didn't invest that money in studying; it would have been much more beneficial, and she could have achieved something great. Anyway, this was on her, not on me, and everyone is responsible for their own life. We'll never be able to live in a way that pleases everyone. That's why we should live in a way that pleases ourselves. She was evidently content, and that was important. One thing I liked about her was her assertive, unpolished approach. She didn't hold back and wasn't ashamed of it. When a client came to her whom she didn't like, she told him straight up and accurately what was wrong and showed who was in charge: "Your breath stinks. Is this how you come to a girl? You look like you haven't showered in a week, are you kidding me?" Most of us would opt for something gentler, but not her; she was outspoken and unafraid. Many men came after us who needed to hear something like that. Hygienic habits in Ireland were deplorable, and many people had no idea how to wash correctly or what that tiled room with a continuous supply of water was even for. Several times, I tried to devise a way to tell someone that their breath stinks, but despite all my ideas, I only came up with the old good "there's mouthwash in the bathroom" announcement. Sometimes, I even put a note on the mouthwash saying "Use me, especially if you're a smoker!"

Every girl had her own methods; for example, Victoria took them to the bathroom and introduced the act of brushing her teeth as foreplay. There's nothing like washing cottage cheese off a penis and smiling stupidly at it while you think he's the biggest jerk in the world. Someone really should come up with a sentence to tell someone they're a jerk without offending them. If you come up with something, let me know; I don't plan on returning to that industry, but it could be practical in everyday life. Anyway, this girl didn't mess around with it; old, vulgar, smelly, anything she didn't like, she immediately sent it away. She revealed to me an unwritten rule I didn't know about. If a man came for half an hour, he often asked if he could finish twice; my answer until then had been, "We can try, if you're quick"

It felt uncomfortable to kick someone out after just three minutes just because they had already finished. Although I wanted to get rid of him from the moment I found out he was coming to see me, I also didn't want to be seen as an evil lady. This girl assured me that it doesn't work like that and I have to follow the rules. If someone came for half an hour, he could finish once, and then I had to kick him out; if he wanted to finish twice, he had to pay for forty-five minutes or an hour. It didn't matter if he finished in the first five minutes; rules were rules. I've mentioned the Cork accent before; it can be challenging even for native speakers, like most Irish accents. Once, a guy came to me and asked, "Can I cum twice?" I started arguing with him fiercely "Are you insane? Of course not, it hurts, how did you even come up with that?" He was surprised that I was doing something that hurt me. Fortunately, the misunderstanding was cleared up, and of course, I was appropriately embarrassed. He spoke so fast that I understood him as

"Can I cum into your eyes?" I blushed all over, but in the end, we laughed about it. I was told that ejaculating into someone's eyes is not a thing, but in this world, I wouldn't be surprised by anything anymore. I met a man in Cork: "Before I came to see you, I made a booking elsewhere, but I had to leave." He said.

"What happened to bring you here?" I asked.

"It was strange. I called there, and some woman scheduled an appointment with me over the phone, but when I arrived, I found myself in a strange house!"

"What was so special about the house?"

I tensely urged him to continue.

"You know, there were girls, young girls, almost children. They were standing next to each other in a row and looked scared; none of them spoke, but I don't think they spoke English. The men in the room were forcing me to choose one, but I couldn't. They didn't want to let me go without paying even though I didn't have sex."

I immediately started asking where it was and why he didn't call the police, but the gentleman grunted, became suspicious and left with the words, "You're nice honey, but I shouldn't be here."

Ireland is trying to fight prostitution by all means, but they are not doing very well. I heard a similar story at least three more times, but no one helped the girls, and I was defenceless and a man who risked losing everything by helping those in need always ended up being a coward. Young girls torn from their families, perhaps sold or kidnapped, had to continue to suffer and let nasty hairy older men roll over them, as potential saviours could lose their families or be publicly ridiculed. Although I understand the fear, I secretly hope that there is a special place in hell for such people. It's not just their fault but the rules in Ireland. Their desperate attempt to intimidate and pretend that the world of prostitution in Ireland does not exist often makes people do bizarre things. The providers of these services frequently find themselves in unpleasant situations, and sexually trafficked girls lose hope that someone will save them. Perhaps there should be some protection for brave individuals in such cases. "We know you're a horny bastard, but because you made the right decision and reported it to us, no charges will be brought against you, and you will not be publicly shamed as a deterrent." The Irish are strange; rather than consider such a thing, they prefer to 'put the culprit naked in the square and throw tomatoes and rotten eggs at him like in the Middle Ages. 'So it's no wonder that many men prefer to pretend they didn't see anything, which is sad.

Men sometimes have bizarre desires, and I've encountered many things. The Spanish diva gave me a different perspective, and thanks to her, I learned to say "no" to many things. I wasn't as tough as she was, but probably no one was. So, I started kicking out clients if something didn't seem right about them at the door or if they were arrogant. They were usually offended and asked why they should leave. When a woman doesn't want to sleep with you, it can damage your ego. Of course, it depended on the specific case, but usually, I kicked them out with the line "You don't Pay me enough to make me handle your rudeness."

Once, I was staying at a hotel in Stillorgan, and a Frenchman, about thirty years old, came to see me. I always divided Frenchmen into two groups: some were extremely nice and kind, and the others fell into the category of "arrogant arseholes."

This guy was unpleasant when I opened the door; If you can hate at first sight, this would be the case! He had AirPods in his ears, gave me a disdainful look from head to toe, and put on a contemptuous expression as if someone had persuaded him to deal with an idiot. He didn't even bother to greet me, and that's overlooking some language barrier; think everyone knows how to say "hello." I asked him to take out his earphones, and he understood but replied, "You won't tell me what to do," and threw money at me. I hated this; how could someone be so vulgar? He acted as if I was forcing him to be there, but he was the one who came to my door with a hard-on. I picked up the money and threw it back at him, telling him to pack up and leave. He looked surprised and offended, "You're kicking me out; you can't be serious," but I meant it, and I was dead serious!

Out of the €220 that flew at me, after the agency cut and expenses, I might have ended up with €40. It wasn't worth spending time with such an arrogant prick.

The man protested for a moment; he was utterly shocked that I was kicking him out, but I wanted to keep at least some dignity. On the other hand, the agency wasn't pleased with my actions. They would rather I put up with even the most demanding clients to maximise their profits. They wrote a report about that guy; that's what they did. If someone was upset, they could leave me a bad review, and avoiding that was crucial for them.

Theoretically, for me, too, because too many bad reviews would scare away clients. So, if someone wronged me or I hurt someone's ego, their number was reported immediately to prevent revenge. For this purpose, there was an app mentioned in the fifth chapter. It's not easy to get into that app, but I've often wondered how many women could find dirt on their partners, husbands, or acquaintances there. So many phone numbers were blocked that it was almost impossible to count, and it's not always about what's written there. Just having a number in such a database means the guy actively sponsors girls from escort websites. I was doing my own research, just out of curiosity, almost every male's phone number in my contacts is in there, even most of them have reports as a time wasters. In many cases, clearing browser history is the key to a successful relationship as women don't use such apps. Meeting new girls was enriching; everyone liked to complain about the agency gossip, and I just sat and listened. I didn't want to gossip; lust craved information that I remembered very well and used at the right moment.

Another benefit was observing the approach to clients. The apartments we stayed in were small, and I could usually hear everything, from the greetings to the sex itself. At first, I found it extremely weird, but over time, you get used to it, and it doesn't seem so strange anymore. Victoria trained me in this; since one guy after another came to her, she followed the golden rule: "If he can't satisfy himself, just be louder."

This usually worked, along with a few other tricks. We put a little lubricant under the condom; when he didn't feel the tightness of latex, it was quicker. We tried to insert a little foreplay because it sped up the intercourse process, and he would finish earlier. Moaning convincingly was a top priority, but it must be done carefully. Most of the time, it couldn't be too loud; if it was, there was a risk of someone hearing us, and the owner would kick us out or, worse, call the police. Another good trick was remembering the guy's name if he introduced himself.

At the right time you just said his name during sex, something like "You're so huge, John," and that's it. Men and their ego, a small compliment about their penis in one sentence with their name, and they're in heaven. I'm not saying it reliably worked on everyone, but it did on most. After sex came the part that had to be endured. Some of them just went straight to the shower, got dressed, and ran home. But then there was that other group who wanted to chat with you and believe me, with most, it was an even worse experience than the sex itself. There was a small percentage of men with whom I genuinely enjoyed conversation. Those who captured my attention were sympathetic, funny, and intelligent. The other group had nothing intellectually to offer me; they mostly asked idiotic questions, and the topics they chose bored me. Do you know what guys do after sex? They annoy us and they are needless. Some of them, a lot! The ideal client was the one who came, didn't want much, quickly satisfied himself, and if he didn't have any smart conversation prepared to dazzle me, he left, and I never saw him again. It might sound cruel, but this wasn't real life; I was locked in a room and greeted strange men in my underwear. I was tired and mentally broken, and I had to smile and be nice despite any pain. Eventually, I found a way to escape mentally; each of us had a way to "Turn off" after some time. I always turned on music that could take me away from reality; I listened to songs while robotically moving parts of my body. Sometimes, I got lost in thought, lying there like a corpse, and suddenly, my brain reminded me, "Sigh, so he thinks you like it." So I sighed here and there and returned to thoughts of rugby, food, or imagined myself walking on the beach somewhere. They didn't want to hear the truth anyway; they craved lies like "You're such a man, John, I like it, no one has ever satisfied me like this, you've lost weight since last time, haven't you? No one can kiss as well as you."

God, even the thought of it makes me sick. But what was I supposed to tell them, the truth?

Something like, "I don't mind you; I just want to hit you with a shovel."

That probably wouldn't have a high success rate. Lying made it easier for both of us; if I told him he was disgusting, slimy, fat, dirty scum, and I was looking forward to slamming the door behind him, it would probably be hard to get anything out of it. I think few could handle the truth and wouldn't leave, and I still had a goal ahead of me, and by that time, I was finally able to start saving slowly again. There wasn't much I could save; I didn't have that many clients, but even that little counted. After a few days with the Spanish queen, I could be with Sam again. I was happy she came; that girl had my sympathies. We understood each other, and travelling was more straightforward; I would even say that, in some respects, I understood her more than Victoria. Both were very different; besides the above qualities, I liked Sam's organisation and cleanliness. We usually returned apartments in even better condition than when we arrived, which can't be said about Victoria. Victoria was quite the opposite; she used to have used condoms around her bed, a nasty bathroom full of dirt and hair and used tampons on the floor. She never really cared about how the place looked like and kept saying, "I paid for the rent; I'm not cleaning." Sam had a considerable respect for landlords and was thinking about what if we will ever get back here. However, Sam always stayed for a maximum of fourteen days, and then I was alone again. For some mysterious reason, I earned as long as I was with her; she probably brought me luck. When she left, strange people started visiting me, and there weren't many clients. One evening, Sam ran up to me excitedly and, with bright eyes, started telling me about someone she met. Of course, it was a client; let's call him Brian.

That evening, he visited her, and sparks flew between them; her heart turned from an ice stone into a gushing volcano that couldn't be extinguished. Do you believe in love at first sight? For me, it's pure instinct, a mutual attraction that can't be escaped. Your brain is flooded with pheromones, and hormones attack you from all sides while you slowly become a victim of a chemical reaction. You're addicted to dopamine, and that happened to her that evening, too. Back then, I didn't understand it, not that I didn't wish her well: I didn't understand how someone could fall in love with someone who pays for sex and, on the other hand, how a man could fall in love with someone who provides sex for money. I don't know how, but it happens, even though it contradicts all good morals. At that time, I told myself that it would never happen and that I would never let a client get so close to me. That's how Victoria met her fiancé, and Sam met Brian. From a few clients, I heard stories about having a relationship with a prostitute, and I always believed that it wouldn't happen to me. But when you're convinced you don't want something, you usually get it. It's like some higher power is enjoying black humour at our expense.

He is so dreamy!!!

His smile!

He smells nice!

The way he talks...

My Prince Charming

lover

Such a stud!

Of course, it happened to me, too, but we'll get to that later. Despite not understanding their love, I wished her well. She talked about him that night for hours; it happened to her for the first time in her entire life; she was so excited, her eyes sparkled, and she couldn't wait to see him the next day. Let's be honest, ladies, it doesn't matter if you're eighteen or forty; when love strikes and our 'Prince Charming' comes, we're all screwed.

No matter how much we are trying to resist it, our hormones take over and have us fully in their grip! From that moment on, we didn't talk about anything other than work and Brian; she spoke of him so often that I knew him as good as if I was the one who is dating him. She was thrilled and in love. It didn't take long, and both Sam and I started spending a lot of time with Brian. Brian was an intelligent guy around his fifties, he lived in a beautiful old, stone house near the sea, had a great sense of humour, a good job, and in his spare time, he taught me English which was necessary. With Sam, we often took time off, and we spent some nice moments at Brian's house. After a while, I began to see them as my second family. We got used to each other, and evenings by the fireplace with a bottle of wine in their company cheered me up. After a long time in a pretend world, it's challenging to recognise what's real and what's not. The friendship between the three of us felt genuine, and to this day, I hope it was. The moments spent with them have brought me so much joy, not just because I could escape reality but because we genuinely enjoyed each other's company. Everything we did was a significant relief from what I had to endure every day, which was difficult. Their friendship meant a lot to me! When we couldn't take time off, he drove everywhere to see her and drove us around Ireland. He travelled with us wherever needed, which, considering what his girlfriend did, was almost admirable. Sam hid him from the agency for a long time; we mostly pretended to take time off together to rest a little. We had to hide him; those beasts could exploit anyone for their benefit. Probably, Sam would start asking Brian to pick up money from someone, to drive someone somewhere, to be at hand when needed. We heard many stories confirming how Jane and Susan used people around them. They had high demands and expectations; manipulative techniques to achieve their goals were not unfamiliar to them. Taking time off at that time meant one free weekend per month approximately. Most people who do standard work have about four free weekends a month and work eight hours daily. So, as you can imagine, that free weekend was very welcome for both of us, and we were extremely grateful for it.

Sam always handled the organisational matters with the agency; Jane would never dare to say "no" or contradict her in any other way. Sam earned so much money that no one understood how she did it, which meant that the agency also had its "commissions" from her. If Jane just hinted at disagreement, Sam would leave and go elsewhere, and that wouldn't be suitable for their business. For this reason, everyone treated her decently. Somewhere, I heard the phrase, "When money talks, no one checks the grammar," that's what all this was about—money, money, and money. For money, girls sacrificed their own lives; for money, they risked sexually transmitted diseases; for money, they were willing to step beyond their convictions. For money, the agency treated us like a piece of trash thrown on the street; for money, they were willing to risk our health, safety, and everything else, and for money, they had a few selected girls they treated decently. It was never about people, morals, or decency. Sexual services are a tricky business, and if you don't listen to orders, you'll hit rock bottom hard. That's reality. Anyway, thanks to the fact that Sam's vagina and body were something everyone in Ireland queued up for and had to have, that girl was respected even by her 'superiors'. It's a bit funny how upside-down this world is. In everyday life, when you have a job, the most valuable thing your management appreciates is not your body or intimate parts unless you work with some perverted freak, and I really wouldn't wish that on anyone. In the world of "easy virtue ladies," it was like in some strange horror realm where many rules were upside down. Working twelve hours a day, sometimes at night, constant fatigue, understanding does not exist. Drugs and alcohol are okay if it pays off financially, and "free time" is a profane word. Sticking with Sam was beneficial for me in many ways because I didn't have to follow all the rules; she always found a way to get me out of it, and the truth was that as long as I was making money, it was all about the money, and when money was silent, Sam spoke. Brian showed us Ireland, all the beauty that we couldn't see from the hotel windows. It was magnificent; Ireland is an amazing country with beautiful places that soften your heart. I fell in love with Ireland back then, and my love for this charming country, despite all the bad things that happened to me there, has lasted until today. Gradually, that place became my second home; the friendliness of the people I met on the street, the breathtaking landscape, and the deep history I enjoyed studying in my spare time. It is a fascinating and wonderful place, almost like paradise on earth, except for the constant rain, which is nasty, unpleasant, and depressing and ruins my idyll. When you live in Ireland, you can leave your refrigerator door constantly open to warm up your house. Outside is such a low temperature that you may feel like living in Greenland. Before long, we reached a point where we shared our personal lives so closely; it seemed like the outside world was just an illusion and didn't exist at all. I was always very cautious about what I shared with others, but with Sam, I felt like I didn't have to be afraid. She knew about my child; we visited her together several times when we were both in the Czech Republic. Sam was charming despite some of the selfish qualities mentioned earlier. She and Brian had a harmonious relationship, and it reached a point where she decided to leave escorting and follow her heart. They had a plan; she would start working as a nurse at the local hospital, and he would financially support her. She would pay off her mortgage in the Czech Republic and buy a car, and even at their advanced age, they talked about wanting to have a child together, which I found fascinating. It's so difficult to leave such "work," even after several months, let alone after several years. She fell in love so deeply that she was ready to leave behind a world that, in a way, delayed her for a happier and more stable life. When she told me, I genuinely wished her well. I never felt envy or any other negative emotions; I loved her very much and was excited that she had made that decision. However, she still had a long journey ahead of her and needed to be sure she wasn't making a mistake. The days passed, and we spent much time together before her "D" day arrived. Many disgusting, slimy men were touching our bodies, but the difference was that Sam didn't mind it; she was terrifyingly similar to Victoria in that regard. She had no reason to continue this "work," but she did it anyway. Whereas I knew I didn't belong there. Perhaps it could be a reason; when you don't have to do it but want to, it's probably much more bearable to sell your body than when you have to do it but don't want to. Her presence made all my negative feelings somewhat easier to bear; I could complain to her, and she would understand or at least try to. I didn't like being alone, and her presence was beneficial. Brian helped me several times when Sam went home and I was alone. He was amazing; sometimes, he took me out for breakfast when I was nearby, and he even drove me to a hotel in Carlow. Carlow didn't have the best reputation despite being close to my beloved Kilkenny; it was my first time there. Brian helped me with my suitcase at the hotel reception, and I had to manage it independently. It's worth mentioning that although the hotels were operating, the rules were still stringent due to the pandemic, so we were more often in apartments than hotels. At the reception, an unpleasant dark-haired woman told me I had to wait for my room because I arrived too early. I asked if I could leave my suitcase to go into town, but her answer was "No."

I think she knew from the beginning what I was there for; she acted arrogantly and unpleasantly. I sat with that suitcase at the reception for another three hours until she finally informed me that my room was ready; that was a relief. It can be not easy to go through such emotions in such a situation. You're constantly on guard, vigilant. Any provocation or poorly chosen word can mean clashes with the Garda Síochána or the loss of money that no one will return to you. Locked in hotel rooms, at the slightest sound in the hallway, I ran to the door and peeked through the peephole to monitor the situation in the hallway. Constant arguments with the agency about not taking clients if there were maids in the hallway. Sometimes, even the clients were a problem; some were idiots by nature, and more than once, I received a call from reception telling me I had a visitor downstairs. It wasn't uncommon for individuals who had already accumulated all the blood from their brains into their penises to ask the maids for directions to my room, despite receiving precise instructions. And some even let the housekeepers open the door for them. Some men are arseholes! Sometimes, I had a strong urge to scream, "Hey, do you have anything in that head, or is there just a monkey playing the triangle?" Maybe being an arsehole from an anatomical point of view isn't such a hopeless situation, but in this world, it greatly complicated my life. Ireland is a conservative country, and paying for this type of service is highly illegal. Not only did they not realise it, but many were even convinced that the hotel knew what I was doing there. Some of them didn't give a damn and even compared me to the photos in the open door to decide whether to stay, shoved money into my hands, or in their loud, deep, vibrating voice, asked something like, "So how much for half an hour? Do you do oral sex without a condom?" As I sat on that couch waiting for the room, I had a million reasons to be afraid and stressed, so when they finally gave me the key to my new home for the next three days, it felt almost like salvation. The room I got was close to the reception in a hotel that possibly had four guests, including me, during the Covid period.

On the day of arrival, I was swamped; I didn't understand what was going on, but my phone kept ringing off the hook. As soon as I closed the door on one, another one was already waiting downstairs, and a different client was on the way. I started "working" at four o'clock, and by eight o'clock, I had six clients. I didn't stop. It sounds disgusting.

Don't worry; it sounds disgusting to me, too, and unlike me, you're lucky you weren't there.

Out of nowhere, the phone in my room rang, and a person with a solid Irish accent muttered something. I asked if that person could repeat it because I didn't understand a word. The command was clear: pack up and get out within thirty minutes, or they would call the police.

I obviously lost the money for the accommodation, including a hefty deposit. The agency didn't offer me any compensation, and on top of that, I had to give them a percentage of what I earned that day. It was my first time being kicked out of a hotel, and the feeling of returning the key at the reception was so humiliating. Everyone stares at you as if they know, judging you, and you try to hold your head up despite wanting to cry. Meanwhile, the agency attempted to arrange alternative accommodation, and I had to try to find another place at night. I wasn't allowed to wait in the hotel, so I stood outside in the rain for half an hour waiting for a taxi to take me to the bus stop. I was devastated, broken, tired, and angry. That evening, I went to another city, and I was afraid to go back to Carlow. Despite my fear, I went there twice more, once to a house owned by a Chinese woman. In Ireland, it was common for Asians to rent out their properties for such purposes. The houses or apartments were always in a dismal state; you felt more like you were in a squat than a home, with mould on the walls, crumbling plaster, layers of dust, mould, and other pathogens in the bathroom, a dirty shower, and an old mattress covered with a dirty and used sheet full of bacterias. The house in Carlow had a barricaded front entrance, so clients had to enter from the back, through a thin alley by the bins that led to the garden behind the house, and in the darkness, you couldn't see a step ahead. You reached a high wall, where you had to squeeze through layers of old junk, garbage, and broken bicycles to get to a similarly cluttered garden where you could see the back of the house I temporarily inhabited. The bravest ones who made it this far usually fled after seeing the house. The windows and doors were covered with black bags and tape. It looked like someone was going to tie up, kill, or torture and extort someone there. In three days, only two clients came to me, overcoming their fear of the sight. One, who was so out of the reality that he didn't even know his name. He wouldn't have minded going to the junkyard for a girl, but I had to refuse him, which was a problem, and getting rid of him was a superhuman task. Usually, in the most extreme cases, threatening to call the Garda Síochána helped, but this guy wouldn't care even if the president arrived. Eventually, after about an hour of persuasion, he realised nothing is going to happen and left. The second client was the opposite, a handsome middle-aged man with an English accent in a suit. The place terrified him just as it did me when he saw my beautiful half-rotten mattress and a hole in the ceiling above it, from which the plaster fell onto the pretend bed. He handed me the money and, with pity in his eyes, wished me all the best in life and ran away without anything happening between us. It was humiliating and sweet at the same time, but I never went back there. The last visit to Carlow occurred at the same hotel, as mentioned earlier, two years after the first accident. The receptionist was still the same dark-haired girl, and I hoped she wouldn't remember me. The hotel was fuller than when I was last there, and even my room was quite far from the reception. Despite not meeting a single client there, I received three phone calls from the reception. The first time, they sent me a bowl of fruit on the house, which was highly suspicious. I practically lived in hotels, and such things didn't happen. I thought they just wanted to see what I was

178

doing and what I was unpacking. The second call was friendly, asking if everything was okay and if I needed anything. Under normal circumstances, it would have been nice, but I was already very paranoid from having to be constantly on guard. Everything seemed suspicious, and I looked for hidden meanings in every word. At that moment, I started persuading Susan to find me another accommodation, saying that I would check out because if I took even one client, they would kick me out. They won't even refund me. If I check out myself, there's a chance I'll get my money back for at least two nights. The hotel could have had around fifty other guests; don't tell me they'll send a bowl of fruit to every room and ask how they are all doing. The third call was scarier; the hotel manager asked if I had plans for the evening, if I was going out somewhere, or if I was expecting a visit. That was the last straw; I checked out and left, no one ever saw me in Carlow again. Most girls were kicked out all the time; it only happened to me three times throughout the whole time, and I narrowly escaped it several times. There's nothing more disgusting than being kicked out of a hotel for something like that. I'm not saying they don't have the right to do it; of course, they do, but the immediate feeling of humiliation, disdainful glances, and condescending behaviour, even though no one knew my situation, are moments when you wish you were invisible. The second time I was kicked out of a hotel was in Dundalk; of course, they kept the deposit and the money for three nights despite kicking me out on the first day. I had been in that hotel about twenty times, and nothing happened, but I wasn't lucky that day. A client came to me, an older man, really very old, he must have been about eighty, almost deaf. He put money on the bed and started talking about his wife, who had passed away. I felt sorry for him, but I had some limits, and one of them was age. I planned to gently tell him that he couldn't stay and had to leave, but then someone started knocking on the door. I pushed the older man into the bathroom and quickly put on jeans and a T-shirt so I wouldn't look like a vulgar girl. Outside the door was the hotel manager with one of his colleagues, and to my amazement, he started speaking to me in Slovak. On my escort profile, I had stated that I was Slovak to minimise the likelihood of my secret ever being revealed.

Of course, I understood Slovak; it's a language very similar to Czech. For those of you who are toying with the idea that all Slavic languages are the same, let me enlighten you: they are not! For example, when I hear Polish, it sounds like "shhh" or the rustling of the wind; I don't understand Russian or Ukrainian either. Some words are similar, and sometimes I can grasp the context, but most Slavic languages are foreign. The manager's question was about the old man in my room, and in panic, I couldn't think of anything better to say than "He is a friend of mine." The manager looked at me with a smile. "I think he's a client. You can't do this kind of business in our hotel. You have a few minutes to pack up and leave; you're not welcome here." Since the older Irish man didn't understand a word we said, he had no sympathy for me returning his money and needing him to leave quickly. He tried to persuade me to be quick, tried to grab me, kiss me, and engage in similar perverse practices to get what he came for. I didn't have time for this; his money was returned, and he was sent back where he came from. The journey from the room to the reception through the lobby felt as long as a journey to hell, and it even evoked the same feeling in me. The wheels of the suitcase I was dragging behind me made a terrible noise that echoed through the lobby. All eyes were focused solely on me, and it wasn't the kind of pleasant attention most women desire. At the reception, I pleaded for my deposit or money for two nights, but after my pitiful crying, the receptionist gave me back one hundred and eighty-five euros out of nearly nine hundred. It was a "shut up and get out" amount, which I successfully hid from the agency. At that time, I said they didn't give me anything back, and Susan surprised me for the first time when she said they would give me thirty per cent back for the lost deposit. I don't know what happened to her that day, but it was kind of her. That was the last time I found myself in Dundalk, which I didn't mind. Susan tried to convince me several times to go back there, but I would have to be completely crazy to agree. The last and by far the worst place I was ever kicked out of was the hotel in Maynooth. It was a nice hotel, and I liked going there. A huge positive was that there was a supermarket beside it, where I could buy everything I needed and sneak it into the hotel. The building had a back entrance around the pool, which was necessary so that smelly farmers and dirty workers didn't have to go through the reception, although some individuals with brains the size of a coral still went through the lobby. Personally, if I went to a hotel for any purpose, I would dress nicely, put on makeup, and wash up. Not everyone thinks the same way, so it wasn't uncommon for a guy covered in manure from tending cows or a worker covered in lime in an orange uniform to approach me. They might have just stopped by on their way home to see their wives. That day, Tina kept calling me incessantly, not letting me eat, and she kept sending client after client my way. She didn't react to my paranoid remarks and told me to shut up and work. The hotel already knew what was happening there; my hotel phone rang several times, they were asking whether everything was okay and if I needed anything. The fire alarm went off three times that afternoon, always when I had a client in my room. It was unpleasant. That day, I met a client who booked me to do more than insert his penis into me. When Tina texted that he was coming, I left the door slightly ajar, as I often did to avoid clients knocking. I was always cautious and wanted to avoid trouble. The man entered the room, and as soon as the door closed, I felt the sharp edge of a knife against my throat. He demanded money and wanted to know where it was. A rational person would have told him, giving him everything to get rid of him and never see him again. Typically, I would have done the same, but people's reactions in such moments are unpredictable. Even though it would have taken very little to have my throat slit, I started screaming for help. Tears streamed from my eyes. I was scared and shaking, but it didn't stop me. The same reaction might not have had the same effect on someone else, but it scared the man with the knife, and he ran away. I curled up on the floor, holding my throat, crying, and then the door opened.

There stood the manager, finally having a reason to kick me out. Who knows if he sent that man to my room, but that would be speculation. He was repulsive mean, he despised me, and I was so repulsive to him that I was surprised he did not spit on me. He yelled at me in such a way that his vein was pulsating on his neck. I was supposed to pack up and leave immediately. He expected me to do it while he stood in the doorway, watching me. I managed to stutter out that I needed fifteen minutes and some privacy. In the shock I was in, tearful, I texted Tina and started packing. The reception was torture. I wanted to ask about a refund. Still, before I could even bring it up, the raging manager with the throbbing vein on his neck interrupted me, loudly declaring, "Don't expect anyone to give you anything back. Get out now; you're not welcome here, and you never will be. You're disgusting, disgraceful, and repulsive."

That was a delight; such a compliment was not hurtful at all. How could I leave without my money? It was hard to go and leave them such an amount. In the pouring rain, I limped to the train station and went to Dublin, where I took two days off. I needed to absorb the shock! Later, Tina told me that the hotel manager had booked me for eight o'clock as a client. He sometimes did that to be able to kick girls out of the hotel; this eviction usually involved a considerable scene. Eventually, Tina informed me that it wasn't bad because I had earned in a day what the hotel had cost me, so we weren't at a loss. If she had been sitting next to me, I would have spat in her face! Does she mean that? So, publicly humiliated, with a knife at my throat, shocked and mentally messed up, sitting at the train station in the rain, and she tells me it was a good day. She was a bitch! These were my worst three experiences of being kicked out of hotels; otherwise, I always saved the situation or got my money back and was asked to leave practically right after check-in. It happened once in Tullamore, the hotel management decided to collect me from my room, return my money and ask me to leave without an explanation. I suppose they checked escort websites, and a blonde with a big suitcase and a foreign accent is simply conspicuous.

Once, at a hotel in Arklow, I had a client who made sounds like slaughtering a pig during sex. When he was in the shower, the receptionist called me and asked about the origin of the sounds, which resembled something between ecstasy and torture. My improvisations were never good, so I told them I was there with my boyfriend; after that, the insightful receptionist informed me that he would also like to see me and my boyfriend at the reception, and we would have to pay a fee for the second person. Lovely! When the client emerged from the shower, surprisingly, he agreed and went with me to the reception, where he paid the fee for the second person in cash. Of course, I later returned the fee to him, but it was nice of him. Later, he drove me into town, and it took me an hour to crawl back to the hotel. It was a miracle that day, and the sun was shining, so I had sunburned back and blisters on my feet from the slippers. It was beautiful! Victoria always told me stories about being kicked out, and I must admit that you don't know how terrible it is until you're there yourself. She had significantly more of them than I did and never suffered from acquired paranoia, so she didn't pay too much attention. Thanks to that, she was usually kicked out at least once a week, often accompanied by the Garda Síochána.

She was even taken from a hotel in Monaghan to a bus stop, where they pushed her onto the first bus that arrived to make sure she left. Other times, they cursed her as dirty whore, and even one landlord kicked her, and the police were called on her so many times that you couldn't count them on the fingers of both hands. Sometimes, I felt sorry for her, and on the other hand, I thought about how lucky I was. When I was with Sam, they never kicked us out; we both behaved decently and responsibly and dressed modestly, so we avoided any suspicion.

Once we chose our accommodation, which Jane approved, it was a beautiful apartment in the centre of Dublin. Upon our arrival we found out, there was a reception on the ground floor, and every visitor had to announce themselves, so we gave up on that and Sam declared three days off for us. I adored that girl; with her, Susan would argue with me and send me off to the other side of the island, or she would make me "work" until I got kicked out. Brian came to visit us, and it was an enjoyable few days. During our stay, two critical things happened: first, Brian convinced me to try hot whiskey, which is a drink made of whiskey, water, cinnamon, cloves, honey, and lemon, and it became my favourite. If you haven't tried it yet, definitely do it when you're in Ireland; don't hesitate and treat yourself to this "tasty flu remover." The second thing is not as important as the first; I remember it with a smile. I was looking forward to seeing those two lovebirds, but at the same time, the frequent presence of their love made me feel the need to go out with someone, too. I downloaded a dating app, created a profile, and started messaging all the handsome young men within a ten-kilometre radius. Creating a profile wasn't that demanding; I had simple requirements since I wasn't looking for a commitment, and I wasn't going to let another horny jerk touch me.

" Looking for someone who isn't a jerk to have a good time outdoors. I don't want any drama, so only single men. By single, I mean genuinely single. No, still sleeping with your ex-single, living with my wife-single, or dating ten other girls-single."

Does that sound terrible to you? I don't know if you've noticed, but that's today's reality. Men of the twenty-first century define themselves with the phrase, "I'm married, I have two kids, three mortgages, but don't worry, it's not serious."

I had limited time, and a free dinner would have been nice, so why not try? Unfortunately, most of them were reluctant to a quick date. I wasn't looking for a relationship or sex; I was fed up with men. I just wanted to meet someone nice, with whom I would feel suitable for a while, and then never see them again. One handsome guy decided to find out if I was a serial killer, and we met in the centre of Dublin. The first observation is that the photos lie; they lie terribly! He was a head shorter than me, limping, and not very attractive, but oh well, I was already there, and it was embarrassing to leave. The free dinner didn't happen; instead, we walked around for a long time. The whole time we talked, I didn't understand half of what he said, and the part I did understand bored me to death. We run into Sam and Brian, who were leaving the shop near us. I made such a face at them that said, "Help, this is horrifying."

They came to me and introduced themselves to the gentleman as my parents, which made a significant impression on him because shortly after meeting them, he grabbed my butt and told them he would escort me home. The problem was that we had been standing in front of my place already, so he was left with no choice and had to go. I deleted the dating app, and the only thing that the date gave me was the realisation that I was fine alone, and unfortunately, even if he was the most wonderful guy in the world, it still wouldn't work with my "job." We laughed about it at home, and the success of my dating once again proved to be zero. However, it was nice to feel like a woman for a while and not like a hooker. When Sam's last day approached, I gave her a huge gift basket; I was so excited, as if it were me who was leaving. I wished her all the best in life. Honestly, I would be grateful for anyone who decided to leave the world of hopelessness and go towards personal happiness and a normal life. We were really close; once, she even picked up my child from my parents and took her to Ireland. They stayed with Brian, and I drove to see them as often as possible. After a few days, I finally got permission to take some time off, and we spent it all together. It wasn't a superficial friendship; I trusted them, and I could rely on them, which is very rare even in the everyday world. Sam and Brian started their new life with a vacation with his sisters, which could be considered another step in their serious relationship, and I stayed in Ireland alone.

Well, I was not entirely alone; I was with my depression, which gladly accompanied me every step of the way. Sam occasionally contacted me, complaining about how Brian drinks too much, which didn't set him apart from seventy per cent of the Irish population, and she shared news from her life with me. Over time, we drifted apart until one day, we ultimately bid each other farewell. I was heartbroken when she believed rumours about me; they spread like wildfire from people she didn't even know. I felt sorry for her; I loved her, but at least it revealed her true colours. As for Brian, their love couldn't withstand the challenges they had to face. First, they gave each other the feeling of butterflies, then mental health problems, as it happens in almost every relationship. She had too high demands that they couldn't meet together, and he loved alcohol more than his livers. Despite their immense love, they couldn't work on it, and it eventually faded away. Sam still works for the agency and as well in Australia for some Russian lady. I know nothing about Brian. When she left "work" back then, I wished her well and hoped they would be happy together until death, but that probably wasn't their destiny. When we said goodbye, I travelled from city to city, getting used to not having any company. There wasn't even anyone left who could send the girls from the agency to hell, so I remained alone until Jane came up with a magical idea: "A new girl is coming to Ireland, she has never been there before, it's her first time with us, and I would like you to take her under your wings."

At that time, I didn't have explicitly bad experiences, and my only condition was that she wasn't addicted to alcohol or drugs. I was in a lovely part of South Dublin in a large apartment where the girl was supposed to follow me. She was supposed to arrive late, around one in the morning, and I had to wait. It was still difficult for me to resist the agency, and there was no reason to refuse her anyway. If I hadn't waited, she would have slept on the street, so I "worked" during the day and stayed in the evening. That day, I was pretty busy, and time flew by quickly. After a few clients, I was like a robot; it was always the same routine: fake smile at the door, hug, kiss on both cheeks. Then I would lead the man to my room, let him pay, send him to the shower, kneel, give him the illusion of happiness, and then pull him into bed, where I would touch him eagerly while thinking about fried eggs or how a fly can stand on the ceiling without falling off. If I were lucky, within five minutes, white fluid would flow out of him, as if screaming "Task accomplished," and within another five minutes, I would be closing the door. In case I wasn't lucky, the painful sex would last a long time, and the guy decided to extend the time, while I angrily imagined a bus knocking him down in the street while he pushed his penis into me, and I sighed with all my might just for him to leave. When a client decided to extend the time, it was very stressful for me. First of all, of course, the idea that the sweaty, stinking fatso would roll over me for several dozen minutes longer, and secondly, to inform the agency. Otherwise, some other client might knock on the door while I was providing paid love to someone else, which happened several times. In such situations,

I was upset, the client who was with me in the room was shaking with fear, and the one behind the door was stressed and horny. Anyway, I had to inform the agency when it was extended, which was not always easy. I considered it particularly inappropriate to pick up the phone and write that the time was being extended.

Moreover, there was no explanation for it. At the agency's request, I always had to pretend I was working independently, which was challenging because the gentlemen usually had many questions! Some questions were often repetitive and irrelevant and rarely did anyone surprise me. They were traditionally asked the same questions repeatedly: "Do you have a boyfriend? Why don't you have a boyfriend? A girl like you must have a man." Yes, with all joy, I imagined a man who would deeply love me every day and simultaneously tolerate sharing me with half of his own country. They also asked about the worst, best, funniest, or most disgusting stories I had with clients. Usually, nothing came to mind at that moment, so I either made something up or tried to explain that it was a discreet secret. The cheekiest ones asked how much money I made, as this group of men usually mistakenly thought I was a millionaire, so I had to be extremely careful! I didn't want anyone to threaten my life for a few hundred euros that I had on me.

"How many guys have you had?" I loved this one; first of all, I didn't even want to think about it because I find myself disgusting just thinking about it, and secondly, who the hell cares? When you go on a date, you casually ask during dinner, "Honey, I like you, and by the way, how many penises have you held in your hand in your life?" Try it; either way, you'll always leave an impression and intrigue the person. "Why do you do this? You must love sex!"

Another ugly question, everyone thought that a girl who sleeps for money is nothing but a horny nymphomaniac. "Have you climaxed with a client?"

That's what everyone wished, but the truth is, it doesn't happen. The body resists, everything is mechanical, and most of those weirdos think that porn is the key to a woman's orgasm, so most of the time you suffer endlessly. If I loved resistance and pain, I would indeed have at least ten orgasms a day. Several times, I faked an orgasm, yes! With the sole purpose of getting him out of my room, apartment, and my thoughts. The worst were the observant ones; usually, I had dim lighting in the room and didn't want anyone to look at my belly, so my clothes included garter belts or anything that could stay on my body while someone drilled their tool into me. However, some urgently needed me to be naked, and when they saw my belly, they froze in horror. "Stretch marks!"

The way God disfigures a mother's body after giving birth to a little human. For me, it is absolutely natural and, in a way, beautiful, reminding me of a miracle. For many men, usually old, pot-bellied, and smelly men, it is a flaw in beauty for which its bearer should be publicly flogged. Some noticed it, didn't say anything, and then, during sex, asked me about my child. This isn't normal; you don't stick your tool into a strange woman while asking her questions like "How old is your child? Is it a boy or a girl, and where is it now?"

The last thing I wanted to think about in such painful moments was my daughter. Once, I even met an Indian who was convinced that I was a man because of my normally, naturally large labia. He insisted that it was a penis, that I was now post-operative, and that I should write it on my profile while angrily demanding a refund. It wasn't even uncommon for men of Muslim descent to come to girls, insisting that the girl repeat a prayer in their language before sex, which supposedly meant that the girl would become his wife for a certain period, so nothing that the man decided to do was dishonest. I immediately threw them out with the words, "I am Catholic, you idiot!"

Anyway, many men managed to put me in an uncomfortable position with their questions or requests, where I didn't want to be. Some went so far as to ask if I masturbate and how often I masturbate; they asked me about my friends, parents, and children or invited me to meetings, where my answer was always strictly "No!"

It was well known that men visiting this kind of business ask you to a date in ninety-nine per cent of cases to have free sex. As I mentioned, I was always stubborn, and the last thing I wanted was to date a client. Nobody ever intrigued or convinced me, and sometimes I was even afraid. One Romanian gentleman met me in Tralee; he liked to boast about his time in prison for violent crimes and tried to persuade me to go on a date with him. He was persistent and didn't know the word "No!"

When he started shouting at me and acting aggressively, I realised that it wouldn't work this way, and I was afraid he might hurt me. I decided to be a little scheming to get rid of him, so I agreed to dinner with him the next day. If he had been perceptive, he would have looked at my profile and found out I was leaving the following day, but my answer was enough for him. He thought he had won, and I was glad I had left, blocked his number, and never saw him again. Fortunately, I didn't find myself in such situations often, but even one such incident can scare you. That day, when I was waiting for the girl I was supposed to take care of, I didn't receive too many questions from men, and I was glad; the day passed quickly, and nothing exceptional happened until the evening. But that day, someone entered my life and turned it upside down without knowing it.

Chapter Nine:
Mr. D

That day, one man booked an half an hour with me, whom we'll call Mr. D The letter D can mean many things; I'll leave it to your imagination. Mr. D arrived like any other client; I opened the door in heels and a short nylon robe under which I was hiding a lace, sexy bodysuit. I smiled with my usual fake smile and apologised for the delay. He had waited outside for quite some time because, for me, having coffee was significantly more important than pretending to be excited about another erect penis. He was shy and a bit scattered, but he seemed nice. I led him to my room, and after taking the money I sent him to the bathroom to shower. I was assured he was clean because he had just taken a shower and lived a few apartments away. I told him to at least wash his hands. Firstly, bacterias are disgusting, which terrified me, given how many hands touched me every day. Secondly, I needed him to leave because the moment he disappeared into the bathroom, I could take off my robe, dim the lights, message the operator that he wasn't a dangerous deviant and how long he was staying, and turn on some music, without which it was impossible for me. I needed music to escape my mind anywhere else. Mr. D came out of the bathroom, looking nervous, and I helped him undress while cursing inwardly: "Can't you undress? It will take even longer! God, I'm not your lover or your mom!"

Everything was mechanical again; I went on my knees, licked his pride, and dragged him to bed, where I sat on him. I rode him for a while, and then, as always, with a smile from ear to ear, I said, "Will you take me from behind?" where he finally satisfied himself, and I could lie down and pretend how amazing it was. To be honest, the doggy-style position didn't appeal to me in any way; in this profession, no position appealed to me. Victoria once told me this position reliably and quickly satisfies ninety per cent of men, which was true. I practised it when I wanted it to be over. Mr. D's performance wasn't particularly fascinating, but that wasn't the point.

As I mentioned, this world was the exact opposite of what you want from everyday life.

The first sex with the man of your dreams in your imagination is passionate, long, and magical. The ideal sex in my "work" was the one that didn't happen. The best would be if men gave me money at the door and left just with the imagination of sex, but that's not how it works. There was something different about this guy; the conversation we had after sex amused me and gave me the impression that I could open up and talk to him, which I thought hadn't happened with anyone yet. He was a nice, kind, good-looking forty-something years old who shouldn't have stayed in my life longer than thirty minutes.

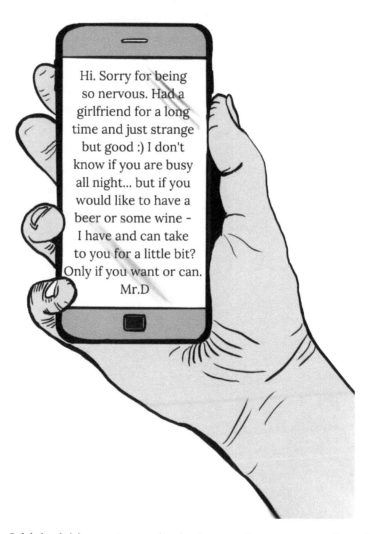

Hi. Sorry for being so nervous. Had a girlfriend for a long time and just strange but good :) I don't know if you are busy all night... but if you would like to have a beer or some wine - I have and can take to you for a little bit? Only if you want or can. Mr.D

When I kicked him out, my brain began the process of erasing memories, and I could focus on myself in peace. No one else came after me that night, so I settled on the couch and thought about cooking dinner. That's when I heard the familiar sound of an incoming message on Telegram; I expected another intruder, but instead, I received a screenshot of a message from Mr. D I had received many messages of a similar type, but for some reason, this was the first one that pleased me. I saw no ulterior motives in it, and I also considered it a miracle that the operator shared something like this with me without intending to laugh at the man or book me for overnight work. She asked me if I was interested, and after a brief consideration, I said, "Yes." That day, I was waiting for the late arrival of a new roommate, and a small company would please me.

Moreover, this man didn't give me the impression that he wanted to hurt me or that, like most others, he wouldn't consider me a nymphomaniac and decide to try again without having to pay for the service. In the picture, you can see the exact transcript of the message I received that evening, except for the signature. Damn, be careful what you say "Yes" to; one such short, innocent word can turn your life upside down, just like mine. I was preparing dinner for the girl who was supposed to arrive, and he rang the doorbell. He brought beer, and the whole evening was pleasant; despite the language barrier, we talked for hours, laughed, and joked together. I shared a lot from my personal life with him, and there was no voice in my head whispering, "Don't do it; forget about it."

Who was this mysterious Irishman? Let's introduce him: Mr. D, a charming middle-aged man who loved romantic walks on the beach, candlelit dinners, cuddling, history, and rugby. Instead of me running away, the moment when I met him and said that damned "Yes," my sanity and constructive thinking fled. On the contrary, emotions, hormones, and love arrived, and this whole gang were led by Oxytocin, which messed up all my senses. From that evening, we were in contact every day; the next morning, he took me to the sea, we had coffee, and we had a pleasant conversation. After that I had to go back to "work", but that didn't stop us from seeing each other again in the evening. The girl who arrived that evening was a nice, red-haired girl whose mouth didn't stop. She talked about everything possible constantly, so I must admit that this pleasant distraction came at a very appropriate time. After all, pretending to listen to her was enough; she wasn't demanding, but deeply annoying. I was happy, she didn't mind Mr. D in our place and everything worked perfectly. Sometimes, I took a long weekend off, and we went somewhere together. I was head over heels in love as if I were fifteen again.

Together, we could behave like children but also talk about serious matters. It's pleasant when you feel so relaxed with someone that you can reveal the craziest part of your personality without even realising you have it. It's always like that; everyone seems normal until you get to know them, and I was glad we could also discover each other's absurd qualities. We had a lot in common, and after some time, we both said those beautiful "I love you" words to each other, which brought us even closer. Of course, my "job" was a problem, and I felt guilty about it, but at that moment, there was nothing I could do about it. I hoped we would come up with something together and be able to plan a better future eventually. We enjoyed being together; I cooked Czech meals for him, gave him small gifts, and sent boxes of goodies from Northern Ireland.

He loved that stuff! They weren't bribes, but I thought of him very often, and whenever I saw something in a shop window that reminded me of him, I immediately bought it and lovingly gave it to him. On Valentine's Day, I was back in Dublin and living with Victoria then; I was delighted to share stories about this gallant guy with her, and she was genuinely pleased. Of course, she couldn't resist making occasional snarky remarks like, "Didn't you say you'd never will date an Irishman, a client, and a guy in his forties? He's like three in one!"

But that wouldn't be Victoria if she didn't occasionally tease. I knew what Valentine's Day was, but I never celebrated it much. It was a commercial holiday for me, but in Ireland, people lived for it. That day, I bought a bag full of chocolates and gluten-free food to show respect for local traditions. In the meantime, Victoria helped me cook goulash between clients, and in the evening, Mr. D arrived. The two of them met, and there was initially mutual sympathy on both sides and then we enjoyed a romantic evening together, just the two of us. When Victoria was around, it annoyed me; her English was fluent. I constantly had to pause over words using an online dictionary, or by the time I expressed myself, the conversation had long since changed topics. After several months of this mysterious relationship, during which I travelled around Ireland and spread my legs for money while he was stuck in Dublin and sent me sweet goodnight texts, a crucial turning point occurred. My period was late, again, and two magical lines appeared. I didn't know how he would react to it, but we had planned a weekend together where I wanted to tell him and discuss what would happen next. However, someone was quicker. On the Thursday before our weekend together, he didn't speak to me all day. Then, in the evening, around midnight, I received a message saying that his ex-girlfriend was seven months pregnant, and she had told him that day, despite them not being together for a long time, and he didn't know what to do. I burst into tears; it was nice that he didn't know what to do, but what the hell was I supposed to do? Why did I had such a bad luck? Moreover, I was alone again; Victoria had left me in the meantime, and I tried to describe my situation to her over the phone in early morning hours. I sent him a photo of the pregnancy test via text message, maybe so he wouldn't lack anything to think about, and we cancelled our weekend together. Mr. D reacted to it like a man in his place, and after he wrote to me, "I'm sorry, I can't do it twice at the same time," he went silent. I was ghosted, damn!

So Mr. D cancelled my weekend while he was as tender as a baseball bat! I disappeared from the Golf Apartments, but instead of continuing to "work", I took time off and went to see my brother. I was in a bad mental state and didn't want to be alone. I longed to switch off and distract myself. As you may have noticed, I'm one of those 'lucky' women who just touch men's boxer-shorts and get pregnant. What some would wish for with all their hearts was a curse for me at that moment. Although I didn't know how yet, I was sure that the "happy family" scenario wasn't happening. Oliver and I had planned a BBQ, which his roommates later banned.

The pandemic was still ongoing, and you can blame me however you want, but I didn't plan to stay sober. I stayed at a hotel nearby, and the weekend eventually turned into five days. I'm ashamed of this part, but I was foolish and traumatised, so I dealt with everything with alcohol and drugs. In the end, we had a BBQ in the forest near my hotel; my brother's friends came, we drank, and suddenly someone offered cocaine. I snorted line after line, and over those five days, I was at the hotel only twice. I was like a walking zombie with a bleeding nose, and if my brother hadn't occasionally convinced me to eat some food , I probably wouldn't have survived. You can do such stupid things when you have a broken heart. During that time, I slept about five hours, and when the day came for me to leave for Belfast, I was high, travelling across the border on the train with two grams of cocaine in my pocket. I don't understand how I could let something like that happen; I was selfish! I could tick 'the drug experience box', and although I tried it a few more times afterwards, I am grateful to God that I am not and have never been addicted to drugs. Nevertheless, this extended weekend left me with some consequences: my nose often runs, and I have to blow it. Spring has its advantages; I can blame it on allergies. My already sick heart started protesting even more, and I feel sick from myself whenever I remember the "white gold." No one should try it; you're risking your health for a feeling of euphoria.

In Northern Ireland, I arranged to take two abortion pills and end the life that was growing inside me. Deja vu! Of course, I told him about it, and in his way, he supported me over the phone, but it wasn't fair that I had to face it alone. I ended the relationship with Mr. D, devastated and frustrated, I was going through all this crap by myself, and my heart was broken. I couldn't afford to have two children; currently, I couldn't even take care of my one. It wouldn't be fair to get involved in something like this in my situation; despite my current infatuation, I still knew why

I did this job and what I wanted from life. I wasn't supposed to be alone in Belfast, the agency decided that I would take another "innocent" girl under my wing, let's call her Eva.

For me, it was even more difficult because I had to hide all my problems from her and act like nothing was happening. On top of that, I arrived completely drugged up and lost. Fortunately, she didn't notice anything. When I finally sobered up, I ordered fast food for seven people, proudly ate everything by myself in the kitchen, and went to bed. In short, I know how to make a first impression. Mr. D suddenly transformed from a charming prince into the Monday of my life. By the way, Eva is also worth mentioning. When I met her, my heart broke; she was only nineteen, and she decided to embark on this career. As for her work dedication, she was similar to Victoria; from morning till night, she could handle even fifteen clients.

On days when she was a little weaker, and I earned more money, she could be nasty. Once, she even peed in my makeup bag to get back at me because a client chose me instead of her. She constantly made my life difficult, was paranoid, and at night, she would barricade the doors with pots and pans. When something weren't her liking, she would get so angry that I locked myself in my room for my safety at night. At new apartments, she would usually steal all the towels and pretend there were none, which forced me to buy my own, which I had to leave in the apartment. When we were leaving the place I saw the pile of dirty towels lying on the floor in the room. When she wasn't sure which bus to take, she would stage a hysterical scene on the street, crying, screaming at me, rolling on the ground, or getting offended, leaving her suitcase there and walking away somewhere, so I subsequently spent hours looking for her with two suitcases. Victoria had a smelly chicken, and Eva hid money in a flowerpot and then slept with the plant. And I thought I was paranoid. I endured her for two months; I couldn't handle it any longer. Once, I asked my brother to send me money to my Czech account; Eve begged if she could also exceptionally send a thousand euros this way.

My brother agreed, so I deposited cash into his bank account and waited. A week passed, then two, I was nervous, and I realised I wouldn't receive the money. He stole it due to his poor financial situation, and after a while, he started repaying me the owed amount. I reluctantly and apologetically returned Eve's her money in cash; she was rude, mean, and unpleasant. She blamed me for her problems and accused me of trying to rob her. Unfortunately, you can't choose your family, but you can choose your friends, so the girl was sent out of my life, and my brother temporarily as well.

Eva later began spreading rumours about me, especially that I'm a thief and she was the reason why Sam stopped talking to me. People are really strange, and in the escort world, you're guaranteed to encounter a few lunatics. Anyway, after solving my problem by swallowing pills, Susan decided to send us from Northern Ireland to Dublin, right next to my dear one's residence. Vulnerable and powerless, I strongly protested, but it was useless. When Susan commands, no one can object, so after less than a week in the North, we headed back to the South. As if he knew, and I suspect he did, he messaged me shortly after we settled in, expressing that he would like to see me and we should talk. After talking with Eve about it and asking for her permission, I agreed and invited him over that evening to discuss things. I was saddened by what happened, and furthermore, I didn't fully understand everything at the time. Some things become clear over time, while unfortunately, some never do.

Being extremely trusting and convinced, I believed that all he said was true. I stayed where most women would have long escaped. Giving someone a second chance isn't uncommon for me at all. I usually provide about 1043 of them before realising what a cow I am. So after his heartfelt speech, I rationalised why all this happened, telling myself that the blame lies primarily with his ex-girlfriend, who never informed him of her pregnancy, and excusing his negative behaviour by the confusion he experienced. Poor little thing, it must have been so hard for him. With just one look, I forgot what I had been through and decided to be there for him and support him. Before long, I stared at photos of a creature I knew nothing about! Yes, that creature I mentioned in the first chapter of this book. I spent most of her pregnancy with Mr. D; he was unhappy that he couldn't be with her while she was pregnant with his child. Interestingly, it never occurred to me that I was there just to listen to his bullshits. Reassuring words of love forced me to be an even greater support to him, and suddenly, I woke up in a situation where someone I loved became a father. God must have a great sense of humour, and I was foolish to stay despite the situation so that he wouldn't be alone. Mother Teresa in action! During our time together, there were many other missteps, lies, and deceptions that hit me even harder than his offspring did. That one stupid "Yes" at the beginning brought me an immense amount of experience, scars, and pain, but also love and beautiful moments. The more I learned about him, the more crap we went through, the more I wanted to stay. Those damn hormones messed up my head, and instead of being strong and leaving, I decided to fix it because he was too good to be true, so he wasn't. Nothing was true! Do you know the book "The Little Prince"? It contains many profound and beautiful quotes. This one summarised my situation: "It is the time you have wasted for your rose that makes it so important." I didn't realise that immediately, maybe too late. I wanted to focus on our pleasant moments; he was supportive, the only support I had in this lonely world. When we were together, he was loving and considerate. He helped me with everything and would do anything for me, and the sex, the sex was fantastic. Plus, another selfish reason was my "job"; I was glad to have "something" else to focus on, someone to escape to, and someone important to me. So, despite all the bad and in anticipation of all the good, I stayed in a relationship that was wrong from the start but made us both happy most of the time. So, I decided to strengthen my legs by running away from my problems, which temporarily seemed like a fine solution. I was blind! I have reasonable suspicion that I've met some amazing man, but probably just ignored him, likely because of Mr. D So, I had no choice but to meet platonic liars, fraudsters, narcissistic lunatics, or losers. Anyway, now I had this, and when I decided to stay with him, it was necessary to work on it. I defended his bad behaviour and lies for a long time. I emphasised the positives, and let's be honest, I was head over heels in love, and as they say, love is blind. After over a year in the relationship, my friends and I planned for them to visit me; of course, I had been to the Czech Republic several times, so we had plenty of space for planning. Emma and Mark were tasked with bringing my little princes with them to Ireland. We rented a beautiful, large house by the sea in the northern part of Dublin. It was for fourteen days in July, so it rained constantly.

A few days before my arrival, Mr. D dealt me another blow over the phone, mentioning that he would like to return to the mother of his child.

Allegedly, he was offered to pretend to be in a relationship with her in front of her family so he could live with his son. I said "We will discuss it when I arrive," but you can't imagine the frustration. I was in a hotel in Belfast, alone and far away, and someone so important to me wanted to leave my life. I know what it's like to sacrifice yourself for your child, and I've heard other stories where something like this happened, but it was hard even to process the idea itself. Having him in my life was like a roller coaster, a moment up and then sharply and unexpectedly down. My friends and even my brother noticed that something was wrong in those few days. For a while, he was rude and unpleasant, and later, when my child suffered from teeth ache, he could have split himself in half open to help that little rascal.

I attributed much of the bad behaviour to frustration that he wasn't with his child and couldn't see him as often as he wanted. I knew the pain; it must have been agonising, and I knew it well. Maybe because I had been through it myself, I didn't have much trouble excusing his behaviour. He was usually golden, but when his nerves snapped, he hit where it hurt the most. For example, during those fourteen days we spent in that house, I learned that the mother of his child was better mother than I was. There's nothing better a man can do than compare one woman's abilities to another's. That's such a compliment that you deserve a punch in the face for it! Another brilliant moment was when he gave a long speech about how I shouldn't have do the "work" I did, he was yelling at me that I wanted to do that and I could choose something different and I had options. Despite knowing what led me to it and the pain I was going through. I cried to him on the phone so many times, feeling mentally drained, and then he could say something like that. Of course, he chose the appropriate sarcasm, insults, and painful reproaches, ensuring that my favourite drink, the "hot whiskey," ended up in his face. I still regret that; it's a waste of good whiskey. I listened to his nonsense for an hour without saying a word, but when he crossed a certain line and started insulting my motherly abilities and suggested that I might even enjoy my job, I exploded. In this regard, I later found karma functional, as he almost went through the same thing as me. He lost his job, couldn't find a new one, and found himself at rock bottom. His advantage was that he only cared about himself and had no children dependent on him. He often verbally attacked me in public, especially under the influence of alcohol, and passersby could hear him calling me a "dirty slut."

I understood that my "job" was awful. I didn't belong in a relationship, so for this reason, we decided that I would find a job in Dublin, temporarily move in with him, and later we would move together and bring my child to Ireland. I really believed he loved me and everything that he said was just because of his stress and my "job".

A spark of hope and happiness lit up in me; my heart rejoiced, and I looked forward to it. I was in Letterkenny then, a nasty and depressing place. There were only a few days left, and Jane mentioned on my profile that I would be leaving soon. and I was as excited as a child at Christmas. The idea of a normal life was beautiful: being with the man I love, having a normal job, and seeing my daughter. I would be cleaning the streets if necessary to disappear from there and never return.

Freedom and my daughter were what I longed for most in the world! I didn't push him into anything; he suggested I could move in with him and that he had his apartment where I had been many times. There was no reason not to trust him! Besides, why would someone lie and mess up with your life? That's a good question; why the hell would someone do that? We talked about it almost every night; we both looked forward to it, so I was astonished one evening when he called me to say it wasn't possible and to forget about it. The only explanation I received was that he didn't feel it was right. Cold sweat poured over me, my heart stopped, I couldn't breathe, and tears filled my eyes. It was as if another piece of my soul died inside me. It wasn't just that someone I loved was hurting me, but my life was much more complicated, and every decision had a huge impact not only on me but also on my child. It hurt, but I accepted that fact despite how painful it was. At the end of 2021, I was in Athlone, and terrible news came: my beloved father was in the hospital. He had been in the hospital many times, but this time was different. No one said it, but I felt he was dying. I had a flight planned in a few days, but the wait before I could fly was devastating. It also affected my physical health; suddenly, I suffered from severe tonsillitis, and an ugly eczema appeared on my body, where my skin cracked open and bled on its own. I could hardly walk because of the pain, and I was so scared. When I arrived, I couldn't even visit him; hospitals still had Covid precautions, but I often called and wrote to him. When his kidneys started to fail, both my brother and I offered to donate one of ours if possible, but the doctors didn't want to hear about it. I always bought food for my dad and left it with the nurses. It made me happy when he asked for things that would make him happy; I saw it as improving his health. After Christmas, Mr. D and Oliver flew in from Ireland and my brother slept on my couch. Mr. D was a tremendous support to me during this time. With his health improving, the news of his impending death was shocking. We were in the cinema watching a fairy tale, and after the screening, I checked my phone: one-hundred-six missed calls from my brother. I remember giggling and joking about it, but before we left the cinema, I decided to call him back. "Finally, you answered! If you want to say goodbye to Dad, come over - he's dying!" This message hit me like a lightning bolt; I felt it in every cell. My daughter refused to go to the hospital, and Mr. D took care of her while I was with my dad, holding his hand, crying and saying goodbye. How can you say "goodbye" to someone who was here for you since you were born? It was so hard! The next morning, my father passed away. The nurses in the hospital were mean and unpleasant, and it's tough to have limited time for your last "goodbye" to someone you've loved your whole life. On the day he died, I couldn't do anything; I just curled up on the floor and cried. Actually, I was in the same state for several months; I just cried. It was the greatest pain I had ever experienced; I could almost compare it to the pain of losing my little angel. The pain that appears in your heart when a loved one leaves is like an endless shadow that consumes the light of joy. It's a warm bond torn apart by an irreversible departure, and every pulse of that pain reminds you of the space left after their departure. Words become powerless, and every breath becomes a reminder of the irreversible loss that penetrates the soul like a cold gust of sorrow. Pain overwhelms you, rendering you completely immobile, unable to do anything but mourn.

I was never ready for you to leave and with you left so much of me!

On that day, on the worst possible day, Susan messaged me, deciding that on the third of January 2022, she had to plan where I would go and what I would do. It was the last thing I wanted to think about. Before returning to Ireland, I had decided that no matter what happened, I had to quit my "job", but I didn't yet know how to accomplish that. I needed a clear plan, but in those days, it felt like a fog had engulfed my soul, rendering me unable to plan, let alone think meaningfully. Upon arrival, Mr. D offered me the chance to stay with him for a few days, and I was truly grateful for such an offer. The last thing I wanted was to be alone. The pain was too great for one person to bear alone, so naturally, I was relieved that my dear one was so empathetic towards me. However, he began to behave strangely on the plane, and something didn't sit right with me. You know that feeling inside you where a loud alarm goes off in your head, and you know something's wrong before the other person tells you what's happening? That thing buzzed in my head almost the entire flight, and every time I asked, "What's wrong?" the answer was always "Nothing" until we landed. Maybe he hoped the plane would crash and he wouldn't have to explain anything. A tragedy unfolded as he stuttered, tremblingly, that he had a roommate, but the apartment was his. It didn't strike me as odd, but something else was wrong, so I kept pressing him with the question, "Are you sure it's your apartment?" Men and their egos want to lure us with expensive cars, apartments, houses, and money, but ladies, let's be honest: are you dating him or his car? I felt like I was dating him, so I wouldn't have minded if he had been honest and told me he was only renting a room. I had been in Ireland for some time, and I knew that the housing market situation was terrible, and if you live alone, it isn't easy to afford rent for an entire apartment. It was usual for even adults to resort to co-living, and it was no wonder! The price for a room in Dublin is very similar to the rent for a house in the Czech Republic. Of course, I wasn't a gold digger, so I couldn't care less about what he owned, but what bothered me was that he lied to me. Moreover, I found out by myself, just like most of his lies. When we arrived at his place, I was exhausted; all I wanted was to shower and sleep. However, on the first evening, his roommate kicked me out, saying I couldn't stay at their apartment because he didn't want Mr. D to have visitors there, so I had to leave.

I cried and was emotionally drained, experiencing immense pain over the loss of my beloved and not wanting to be alone. The idea of having to "work" also didn't appeal to me. I had calculated the money for a hotel, transportation, and food, and neither had enough for a short-term rental. I left most of my financial resources with my mom in the Czech Republic; she needed them much more in such a situation than I did. I stooped to borrowing money from my brother and reserved an apartment for us for three days.

I didn't consider this lie a huge betrayal; after all, he just wanted to impress me, and later, he didn't know how to admit it. I convinced myself that he panicked, so we went elsewhere. The second apartment, however, seemed promising. No one there to kick me out! Covid was coming to the end, and no one had any idea what was brewing in Ukraine, so we decided to give it a try. I found a job soon; I went through three interviews and was supposed to start as the head of Erasmus projects for the international college in May. I was excited, but there was one slight hitch: no housing seemed available. I had saved up several thousand euros for the move, and in the meantime, I left the apartment in the Czech Republic and moved most of my things to Ireland, where they rested in storage until we found something. I travelled around Ireland, doing what I hated and looking like a walking zombie. During that time, I met a farmer from Mullingar, a kind fifty-year-old man who took a liking to me.

He always brought me coffee and was the first person to introduce me to how difficult farming in Ireland truly is. The farm belonged to his parents; in Ireland, it was the most valuable thing, and selling it would mean shame. Farms are sold for three reasons: personal bankruptcy, divorce, and severe illness; no other options are considered. He told me stories about his friends who couldn't handle it and took their own lives; it's very lonely, and few are lucky enough to find a wife and have someone to share their world with. Most of them have second jobs. This guy worked in a factory, and he was toiling away with the cows when he wasn't working there. I enjoyed listening to his stories; he was always very kind to me and travelled long distances to see me. However, any intimate matters with him were not pleasant! He always smelled of cows with a slight hint of tar, and his kissing was so difficult that I felt like I was a contestant on a reality show called "Ten ways to do It Incorrectly."

His approach consisted of puckering his lips, sticking his tongue out, from which saliva flowed, and suspiciously waving it from side to side while strangely circling it inside my mouth. It seemed as if he wanted to win an Olympics in facial muscle exercise, and I began to wonder if he was founding a new disgusting sport. Subsequently, he started rubbing against my leg or another part of my body with his genitals while still pressing me tightly against his hairy body and drooling into my mouth. He quickly satisfied himself by rubbing his penis against my leg. He moved around my body as if he was from the Wild West. However, his speed was a huge advantage because if I had to endure something like that for more than five minutes, I probably wouldn't care that he was a nice person; I wouldn't want to meet him anymore. Many men from this country attempted unique kissing techniques that could compete with world records in clumsiness, sticking out their tongues and moving them strangely while saliva flowed. Such experiences were increasing, and I struggled with them with superhuman effort. Sadness became my best companion, and I constantly immersed myself in memories of my father, which was wonderfully depressing. I was immersed in melancholy and struggled with sadness; I was emaciated, exhausted, and broken. I felt like crying with every client; large circles under my eyes couldn't be hidden by anything, and more than one person left me when they saw how I looked. I resembled drug addicts in appearance, but my drugs were purely grief and nostalgia.

The housing search also didn't go entirely according to plan. Interest in housing was high, and with the influx of war refugees, this goal became almost impossible. Mr. D and I divided the work: I searched for apartments and wrote emails requesting viewings, and he was answering the phone and arranged viewings. The bank account where we saved money was in his name, and I sent as much as I could there every month.

208

Several property viewings took place, but it was never successful for us, even though my partner had a high income and a good job. I was losing hope and sinking into an even deeper depression. I desperately wanted to leave the world of prostitution and be with my daughter! Just for the record, I didn't perceive any man as a ticket out of this world; I was honestly, and sincerely in love with Mr. D It was too much to handle, but I was hard on myself. In a state of helplessness, I found myself in Gory, a beautiful posh hotel in a lovely little town. I "worked" as usual: I had several clients there who were relatively normal. Another client I opened the door to was a tall man with glasses, around thirty years old. He seemed nice and normal, like any classic man who wants to have fun and forget about me as soon as he leaves the hotel. Our meeting was like something from a classic novel; the gentleman paid, and I prepared for the next chapter of my day. I messaged the agency to let them know how long the hero will stay in my company. While he was using the bathroom, I prepared everything, sat down on the corner of the bed, and watched the open bathroom door as if enchanted. Finally, the doors swung wide open, and from them rose a giant cloud of steam, followed by my suitor for half an hour. He was wrapped only in a towel around his waist, and I thought, "Well, finally! He was there for ages!"I smiled, stood up, and walked towards him to start the encounter, which was supposed to be quick. Even before I reached him, I was imagining closing the door behind him when he leaves. However, the gentleman had a somewhat different idea about our time together. He grabbed me by the hair and pulled me towards him with all his strength. Pain shot through every hair root. "That hurts," I whispered. He didn't seem deterred by my pain in any way, rather the opposite.

He looked deeply into my eyes, smirking, and pushed my shoulders down, forcing me to kneel. I attempted to protest, saying it was rough and I didn't like it, but he tightly gripped my throat, making it hard for me to breathe. I gasped for air, and out of fear, I dropped to my knees. He forced his 'member' into my mouth until tears streamed down my face. He held my head with his palms and forcefully pressed it against his penis, which I felt in my throat. I couldn't breathe; I began to choke, but the predator seemed undisturbed. With each passing moment, he pushed my head closer to his body and repeatedly gratified himself with my mouth. I gasped for air and cried in pain, starting to struggle against him to let me go. Finally, he took his member out of my mouth, and I could breathe again. I knelt on the floor, clutching my throat with my hand.

The man showed no empathy; he grabbed my arm and pulled me up.

"Enough, stop, not like this!" I shouted, to which he responded, "Be a good girl and behave yourself," and slapped me across the face. He slapped me so hard that my cheeks began to resemble tomatoes. He threw me onto the bed; I lay on my stomach and tried to get up, but suddenly, he grabbed my wrists from behind and tightly squeezed both of them. In a moment, I felt another wave of pain as he penetrated me. I was as dry as the Sahara, and every movement felt like sandpaper rubbing against me. He cruelly held my hands, pulled my hair, and thrust. He kept accelerating, and every movement felt like a thousand needles piercing through me. I was unable to react; I just lay there, tears streaming down my face, completely in shock. At some point, I stopped perceiving, and everything else seemed to fade into a fog. When he finally left me, I was still in the same position for ages. I still lay on the bed, my body trembling, and the white sheets turned into a black shade from innocent white to the makeup streaks running down my face, like a sad, dramatic painting. I lay there and didn't fully understand what had happened. I felt pain all over my body; I trembled and was hurt. After a few minutes, I convinced myself I needed to get up and message the operator. That day, I had Magda. I reached for the phone, which was barely visible through my watery eyes, and messaged her that the man had hurt me. At that moment, I couldn't specify exactly what had happened, but I remember telling her that I was lying on the bed, trembling and unable to move. The response I received was very brief, almost shocking: "I'm sorry someone hurt you. Pull yourself together; you can have a little more time. Another client is waiting downstairs, but I'll send him up in fifteen minutes, so you have time to get ready."

Such unprecedented empathy, how merciful. I had been raped, shaking on the bed, in pain, bleeding from my genitals, and crying, but another man was already waiting downstairs, wanting to thrust his penis into me, so I didn't have many options. I was not too fond of the entire agency and its approach in many respects, and what's more, I hated all men. Every single one who had used me and left had been tortured or killed countless times in my imagination. This is one of the worst experiences I've ever shared, and it isn't easy to even think about it. I was still dealing with my grief; it was too soon after my father's death. Add to that the unavailability of housing, homesickness, fear, constant stress, my job, the agency and their approach, and finally, the experience with the bespectacled predator. I couldn't take it anymore; it was all too much. I spent days praying, begging for help, crying before God, pleading with him to relieve me of this suffering. Helpless, alone, and internally torn to pieces, I prayed for a miracle. Sitting in my fancy hotel room, I pondered that there seemed to be no way out of this; I needed to relieve my pain.

I grabbed a razor blade, and as I rolled it in my palm, I thought about how easy a decision would be if I chose to join my father. I wanted to be with him, not on this ugly planet without mercy. I had nothing and no one, and I was entirely determined for one deep stroke of the razor blade, I remembered my child. I remembered her vast eyes, still discovering the world, her joyful smile every time when she saw me, and her funny comments that could make the whole universe laugh. In my thoughts, I hugged her, kissed her forehead, and realised how much I wanted to be with her. It gave me new strength, and I decided to keep fighting.

At the last moment, I turned my arm and stabbed the razor blade into the back of my hand as deeply as I could, again and again. The sharp piece of steel danced slowly through my skin and muscles. I felt a sting but no pain; that came much later when I realised I had five deep, open wounds on my arm, bleeding massively from.

How on earth did I end up here..

Blood streamed from my palm to my fingers, and I felt immense relief; I could breathe deeply again. I sat in the chair and watched the red liquid drip onto the carpet.

I've always tried to be strong, and at this moment, I was at the very end of my strength. I was at my weakest point, yet I found the strength to get up and continue my fight. Such an incident never occurred again and had never happened before. The back of my left hand still bears five

212

prominent scars, reminding me of my deep pain and my strength and determination. Nothing beats sinking into depression and mutilating your body. People ask me where I got those scars, and telling the truth seems quite tricky, so I've prepared a story about a life-and-death duel with a tiger. Of course, I won, with only a minor injury to my hand, but a poor tiger. Well, he shouldn't have started it.

Later, in the city of Athlone, which isn't much to talk about, I met a nice man. He was a divorced electrician with two kids. He usually paid for two hours of my time, and we talked about life. He was kind, unlike most men who would have sex with me even if I were half dead; this guy was gentler. When I had my period, I bled in such a way that I couldn't handle anyone for longer than half an hour unless the person were into vampire play, and I believe there are such people out there. Sometimes, I bled so heavily that I couldn't "work" at all. The agency usually insisted at least try, and often, I had to send humiliating photos as proof that it wasn't possible. You know, when you're taking a shower, and in the meantime, when you leave the shower and tear into a tampon or a sponge, a puddle of blood appears beneath you, and looking at your legs, you feel like you've become a victim of some horrible crime. Someone has turned your bathroom into a slaughterhouse, so the last thing you want is for someone to shove a penis into you. When it doesn't work, it just doesn't work. I hated being forced into it or having to pay extra for days without "work" just because I'm a woman. Over time, I agreed with the agency that I would have the first two days of menstruation off because it simply wasn't possible. This electrician often paid for two hours of my time, even when I was menstruating, to have company. It was excellent; we drank tea and talked, mostly about his life. Sometimes, I gave him a massage or something similar, but otherwise, I could relax. It was worse when I didn't have my period. That guy always knocked me out; he was highly demanding, and sex was like a rodeo. He could have sex for two hours straight, and I always prayed for it to end. Everything hurt, and I counted the minutes until it was over. Of course, I smiled and said how amazing it was, but I said that to everyone. I knew why I was doing it, and no one would return to me if I told the truth. Pretending was the only way to get out of it. He rented an apartment nearby and offered to stay there if I was sick or needed to rest. I never accepted his offer; I was afraid he would want something in return, and letting someone roll on me for two hours a day and physically knock me out wasn't my idea of relaxation. It was business, not pleasure. I endured everything mentally so demanding that it couldn't even be fun. Anyway, it was nice to see that some men have good hearts and don't just see me as a piece of meat. There were more of them who treated me nicely. In Dublin, a friendly farmer used to come to me; I never met a more excellent client. Every time he visited, he brought me a bottle of wine and chocolate; he was always afraid he did something wrong, told me funny and wise stories, and his presence made me feel good. He told me his name in English and Irish, which I found pleasant. I only saw him a few times; I think visiting such services wasn't for him, but I fondly remember our conversations.

Another regular client of mine was a friendly man from Northern Ireland. He was brilliant and thought logically, sometimes too logically! We became friends over time and he helped me when needed. Even when Mr. D and I were looking for accommodation; he offered to help me with references or anything else that might be needed. There were more clients like him, but they were as rare as saffron. I met one genuinely nice person every six months, but every day brought me a new idiot ready to ruin my day.

In the meantime, while we were searching for accommodation, an unpleasant thing happened: the department where Mr. D worked was closed, and he lost his job.

He was convinced he would find a new one immediately, but Ireland had changed; the housing conditions were dismal, and the job market was overcrowded. The war in Ukraine had changed a lot of things. Remember when I was talking to a client about the unfortunate events happening in Eastern Europe and he had a very unconventional opinion: "It makes me upset so much that there's a war there. The girls from Ukraine were the best; I used to go to Kyiv for a sex vacation."

Like, seriously? I stared at him in disbelief, shaken by how someone could even utter such crap. Those girls he went to screw are probably fleeing or dead.

They're going through terrible things, and someone regrets the war there just because they can't go there to dip their stick. God, what a jerk! On the other hand, I was grateful to encounter such individuals with a brain the size of a chicken's. They could serve as a bad example and remind me of who I don't want to be and never will be. For such individuals, all the swear words are inadequate, and knowing when to shut up is a gift very few people are born with. These gentlemen and their ilk should be prohibited from speaking in public by law. Well, for some, it was annoying that they couldn't go to Ukraine for prostitutes, and for others, inflation and the almost nonexistent housing options were bothering them. Everyone has their priorities. Mr. D tried his best to find new employment, but gradually, his savings and strength ran out, and I felt sorry for him. In the end, we reached a point where I was giving him money for food, lending him money for rent, and praying that he would soon be able to stand on his own two feet. Yes, I stayed there in rainy days, guess I was a keeper or an idiot, could be the same!

Instead of love, I was just blamed for everything in his life—for his lousy relationship with his child's mother and for not seeing his son as often as he would like.

Sometimes, I felt like I could even be blamed for the rain outside, which would be unfortunate considering we were in Ireland. I was in a situation where I didn't have a job and couldn't find a new one; I sympathised with him because I knew how frustrating it was. So, without realising it, I began to be deceived and exploited. It rarely happened that he did something nice for me. There were times when he wouldn't talk to me for days, and it didn't do any good to my mental health. The worst was when he got drunk; we always had terrible arguments, and he mostly insulted me because of my "job" or vented his frustration from his own life on me. I always knew how to pick them and would pick a different kind of charming prince every time. Of course, I thought about giving up and letting him go his own way, but on the other hand, I still loved him and didn't want to leave him in the worst part of his life. I always told myself that I would like someone to stay with me if it were me. It took me a year to realise that we wouldn't live together, and when I found out after several false hopes that I was not leaving my "job", it was another blow. I was an expert, and it was as if I were attracting disappointments to myself. I cried several times and asked myself what I had done to deserve it. I sacrificed myself; I always helped others, bought breakfasts and lunches for homeless people, and went to church. So where the hell was the mistake? The mistake was obviously that I was dating errors. I was good at it! I could have my own show about "How exactly not to do it."

My earnings weren't big enough to get me home, so when Mr. D needed to pay rent, I did whatever I could and broke my rules to help him. I didn't want him to end up homeless, so I sold my body and provided at least a thousand euros a month to someone who gladly blamed me for his failures and poured his anger on me. Yes, I was an incredible cow, but it was a good lesson. Christmas was almost here, and I planned to go home. I needed every penny, but it didn't work out too well, especially with the extra support I provided to my partner. I was in Westport, a beautiful little tourist town on the west side of Ireland. Although picturesque, I never had many clients here, sometimes none. I didn't want to be without money for three days. Girls were staying here in the lovely apartment, and Susan knew the owner, who, besides renting out his apartment, also made money by owning a restaurant in Westport and renting places for sexual workers. Paying rent in this Westport apartment was quite financially burdensome, so I hoped to at least earn enough for rent, which sounds terrible. I met a regular client there who wore overalls and had a cleft lip. It didn't look aesthetically pleasing, but he was one of the more affable individuals. Another candidate who came told me he had forgotten his money.

"Classic, what else?"

Then there was a pretty nice guy around forty. After his departure, my face was so scratched that I looked like a swarm of rats had attacked me. During sex, he lay on me, hugged me, and pressed his face against mine. His beard felt like tiny, sharp needles that deeply penetrated my skin. He tore my skin as he moved his face up and down. He managed to demonstrate it for an hour, and after he left, my face was bleeding and hurt as if someone had slapped me a few times. After him came an enthusiastic male dressed like a gigolo with a passion for foot fetish. I wasn't a big fan of this fetish, but I always endured it somehow. For me,

216

it's disgusting to lick something that has walked on a dirty floor, suck toes full of bacteria, but some people love that..

Moreover, you never know when the girl last washed her feet. This young man leaned into it so eagerly that a massive wave of pain suddenly shot through my leg out of nowhere. That idiot was trying to bite off my toenail. This wasn't accidental or pleasant, so I escorted him out in a desolate state with a painful face and a bloody toe. The day was coming to an end, and as it usually happens, just before my long-awaited end of the "working" day, I received a message that a client was coming. He couldn't find the door to the apartment and mysteriously stumbled up the stairs as well. Waiting for him was like waiting for death, slow and agonising. Finally, he shuffled into the apartment, reeking of alcohol, and all he longed for was company for the evening. I don't understand this; why do drunk men and men with hangovers crave sex so much?

When I get drunk, my head spins, and I'm glad I remember my name, let alone someone else's name. And when I have a hangover, I'm honestly happy to be alive, and the idea of someone rolling on me is disgusting in itself. This man was one of those who needed to enjoy the condition of a drunkard, so he came to me. The gentleman decided to pay me six hundred euros, but on the condition that I go with him to a bar for at least an hour after sex. The sex was terrible; I suffered like a dog. It's not fun when a walking bottle of booze is rolling on top of you. After enduring that agonising ordeal, we decided to go to a nearby bar. I didn't feel like it, but I needed the money, so it was worth it. I usually didn't kiss, especially drunk men, but circumstances forced me to break this rule to earn more money. We arrived at a pub nearby, and my heavily intoxicated companion staggered to the bar, where he ordered drinks for both of us. It seemed like it would go by quickly for a while, but after a moment, he started telling me about his wonderful house nearby, how rich he was, and that I should move in with him. He mentioned it so many times that it couldn't even be taken as a joke anymore, so I discreetly checked my phone to find out when I could finally go home. He constantly tried to lick me, pushed his tongue into my mouth, and his cracked lips rubbed against mine. I wanted to leave and hoped he might fall asleep before our time ran out. I would have just left him there and run away. But he was far from falling asleep. He kept persuading me to become his girlfriend and live in his fantastic house while touching me. We all have our limits, and at that moment, he reached mine. I emphasised that "No" means no. Before I knew it, he slapped me and spat on me. I don't know what was worse. Some people from the bar tried to defend me, so he started yelling at them,

"She's a whore; I paid her to be here. She makes a living by spreading her legs!"

I felt so embarrassed; I felt humiliated. I didn't want anyone to know what I was doing, and that's precisely why I didn't go out with clients. People started staring and mocking me. I wanted to run away, but that idiot was holding my hand and explaining that we still had time and he could use it however he wanted. I know there's no contract for such cooperation, but public humiliation definitely wasn't how I imagined he would use his time. After a moment, I managed to escape, and I was afraid of being pursued. The apartment didn't have the best security doors, and I didn't want to have any problems. Fortunately, I was leaving the next day, so I could pack my things and plan my journey. It had one positive aspect. Because I allowed myself to be publicly ridiculed, humiliated, did disgusting things, and slept with a drunken bum, Mr. D could pay his rent. At that time, I didn't think about it like this, but today, knowing everything I know, I would rather go back and give him a good beating. I didn't have the money myself, at least not as much as I needed, and I knew I would have to take money from our joint savings account for my journey home. I told him what I had to do to make that money, especially in situations when I felt sick myself, and he was the only one I could tell. It was always followed by a theatrical play about how sorry he was, how it would be better if he were not in my life, how much it meant to him, how he would help me get out of that job and have a normal life, but it was all nonsense. The real blow was when I asked him to withdraw some of my money so I could go home for Christmas. Without it, I couldn't fly to the Czech republic. He told me that the money couldn't be withdrawn, that it was a special account where the bank had to be notified a week in advance, and he forgot about it. I wanted to see the balance on that account, and after days of lies, I was shocked to see there was nothing there. We had a terrible fight; I had so much money there for our common future, and he just spent it. He said he had to send child support so he could see his son, which was understandable to me, but he should have asked me. I was screwed, I felt terrible, and I needed to see my daughter. My flight was scheduled for two days, and I had to act. I sent Mr. D to get me money. So he went humbly to his parents, but of course, he didn't even make it there. That's called love; you're screwing alcoholics so he could have a roof over his head, and he's not even capable of asking for money for his girlfriend when he stole it all. I mentioned the electrician and the kind client from Northern Ireland for a reason. I turned to them humbly, asking for a loan, and without need of explaining anything, they both immediately sent me money without any guarantee that they would ever see it again and wished me a Merry Christmas with my family. Strangers could help me while my partner was robbing me. At least others had a soul when he didn't. If such an individual ever appears in your life, dear ladies, it's not worth it. Kick him in the ass before you end up with kids who look like him. I spent Christmas at home, feeling comfortable like never before. Upon arriving in Ireland, I met Mr. D again. I told him about my wonderful time with my family, and we decided to go to a bar. We met two pleasant strangers there who joined us, and the whole evening was delightful until we got home. Mr. D made a jealous scene and referred to one of the gentlemen as my new boyfriend. He stormed out, and he left the hotel; I thought that would be the end of it. But no! That jerk dared to come back, and do you know why? Because he was broke, hammered and needed to order pizza using my money urgently. I started feeling like a walking piggy bank he could use whenever he pleased. That night, while he was asleep, I checked his phone and, among other interesting things, found a conversation with a certain Monika in which he lied to impress her. He claimed to be a bank manager and was supposed to go skiing with his family, a single man who could offer her everything she desired. It would have been almost comical if it wasn't so pathetic. In the morning, I wanted to talk about it, but all I got were more lies and insults. "Monica is just a colleague; you're imagining things; she's not what you think she is; there's nothing between us." This is interesting; all men are so faithful, and it's always your fault when they seek female friends, whom you naturally see as a threat. That time, I sent him to hell, telling him it was over and Monica could lend him the money. But love is blind, and after a few days, we were in touch again. He apologised profusely, begging me to forgive him, claiming there was nothing between him and Monica. So we continued for a while in something doomed from the start. I continued to emotionally and financially support him while he pretended to love me and sucked the life out of me. It didn't take long for another blow; out of the blue, he stopped responding to me. That's what happens when the universe constantly tries to show you what a jerk he is, but you keep making excuses and ignoring all the signs from above.

A woman is always right, and even when she's wrong, the universe has no choice but to increase the dose of crap falling on you until you realise that guy isn't worth it at all. Since I always try to see the good in everyone, it took me an extremely long time to understand this, but better late than never. Mr. D received a thousand euros from me, which he was supposed to transfer to my account; the money was for my mom, and I promised her and reassured her that it was on the way. Mr. D flooded me with excuses about the bank for several days and sent several modified transfer confirmations to make me trust him. I had my doubts, but I didn't want to make a scene, considering that sometimes the bank really could be at fault. After days of lying, he gave up and stopped responding to me. I was in Ennis when I was stuck in an ugly hotel in the middle of nowhere and felt unusually abandoned. It didn't seem fair that he stopped talking to me; I was unhealthily fixated on him. Perhaps it was by the life I had, or maybe I just felt very sorry for him, and hormones clouded my senses. Anyway, he didn't respond to my messages, desperate phone calls, emotional blackmail, or ironic messages; everything was in vain.

After a few days, I reached a point where I was afraid that besides money, I would also lose my belongings that I had with him. He used my computer that I saved up for six months to purchase, and among the things in storage were remembrances of my father. Things I took from his room after he passed away. My brain created even greater panic than was necessary, and in my desperation, I decided to do something I probably should have done a long time ago. I decided to contact the mother of his son to find out what kind of person Mr. D was. I always respected his privacy and knew how fragile his relationship with his son was. I didn't want to hurt anyone, but I needed him to stop hurting me finally. That night, when I got into his phone and found the conversation with Monica, I took some phone numbers, which were neither moral nor legal. I sat in the hotel bar and had a drink to brace myself before contacting his former partner. I felt like I was doing something wrong, but I needed to free myself finally. Jane asked me to go to the gas station to deposit money and buy phone top ups, and when I paid and was leaving, I received a reply from his ex-partner. My hands trembled, and tears streamed down my face; I couldn't reason or take a step. I stood there dazed. We stayed in touch until morning, and that night, I learned many interesting facts, starting with the fact that he cheated on all his ex-girlfriends, his family knew nothing about me, most of what he said was a lie and the interesting fact that he was in prison for embezzlement. How stupid must I have been to overlook all of this? I had never emotionally sunk like this; I stopped eating, couldn't sleep, trembled, and yes, of course, I still travelled from hotel to hotel and had to expose myself to everyone the agency sent me. I could have instantly opened a counselling centre and give advices how to attract the biggest losers into your life. Tina, my dear operator, was surprisingly very kind this time; I confided in her about most of what happened, and she contacted Mr. D to explain that I wanted my things back, but that wasn't a successful move. Later, she searched for him through the escort database, and you wouldn't believe what she found out. Not only was he a lying bastard, but also a fraudster, manipulator, and user of people. From all his visits to girls, which were successful, there were also two reports where he failed to achieve what he wanted. The literal transcripts of these reports look like this (illustration), and I must say that, something like this devastated me.

These are indeed how the reports from the girls look like when you open them in the mobile app, and for me, it was something utterly painful to see there the phone number of someone I would give everything in the world to. Yes, you can blame me for not having a regular job, but I don't believe it was the biggest issue we had. I also tried to justify it this way, but it's nonsense. I did everything I could for us to be together; I gave up the apartment, found a job in Dublin, prepared my daughter for the move, and left the flat. I simply did everything for us to be together and for all the bad things to pass, but evidently, I did it for the wrong person. Of course, I never considered my "job" to be normal, and I had a huge sense of guilt, but there is a difference between doing it for survival and family or pleasure and lust. Financially, I wouldn't have been able to manage it on my own with a regular job in Dublin and with my daughter, so our plans fell apart, for which I am grateful today. Are there no decent men left out there who are capable of keeping their penis under their control? Monogamy is probably beyond the capabilities of most men roaming the world. They encountered it every day. So many men showed me pictures of their partners and children, so many proudly wore a ring on their finger while playing with my clitoris, and so many told me stories about their families. A shining example was one of my regular clients, a Slovak who married an Irish woman and had a son. They lived together in one of the wealthiest parts of Dublin, Ballsbridge; he worked as an engineer and boasted about making a lot of money for almost no work.

He spent Sundays with his wife and took his son to the stables outside the city, the model family man. Except that he tried out a new girl almost every day that appeared on the website. He had a few favourites but stuck his "dick" into anything that had a hole and breathed. I felt sorry for his wife, thinking she must be so unhappy while being cheated on by one chauvinistic jerk. I encountered such men every day and hoped Mr. D was different, so when it happened to me, my world shook, and it was a massive blow. I struggled to cope with it. Some clients noticed, others couldn't care less. After Ennis, I went to a beautiful hotel in Naas, where the housekeepers often made my stay unpleasant. It was not uncommon for them to enter the room without knocking, claiming to bring a coffee spoon or with similar excuses. Fortunately, I was extremely cautious, so I never had any problems there, but they kicked Victoria out countless times.

In my state, everything was very complicated for me, and the last thing I wanted was to spend half the day cleaning up "work stuff" and staring into spy-hole, but there was no choice. I remember one client who was very eager to learn more about my situation. He was my regular, had a job as a guard and when he kept asking about my condition I made up something about family and friends. I was ashamed of what had happened and there was no way I would talk about that with a stranger. The client listened to my speech of lies; I broke down, and tears streamed down my face. I didn't want anyone to see me like this, but despite all my efforts, I couldn't keep my composure. "When you see a girl in such a state, do you think about sex?"

I don't think about sex when I see a girl in any state, but if I saw a man crying, it wouldn't turn me on. Nevertheless, this gentleman looked at me and, with a solemn expression on his face, asked, "And now, do you wanna fuck?"

Wow, I was speechless. They didn't want me to be okay but to be naked and suck their balls. Assured that talking to me was a nice gesture, I realised my place; I couldn't see through my tears, so I knelt and did my "job". Men hurt me, abused me, spat on me. I was insulted, choked, and beaten. I contemplated suicide countless times. I was tortured in a world where there was no love or emotions. With a fake smile, I had to welcome every other man I wanted to kick out. I was raped several times, and it hurts even more today than it did back then. I was humiliated and subjected to ridicule. I still see the faces of some people who did this when I close my eyes. At night, I can't sleep, suffer, have very vivid nightmares, wake up sweaty at four in the morning and am unable to fall back asleep. You can't even imagine how I felt when I found out that the person I loved was one of those people who hurt women. He knew everything I was going through; he knew how girls must feel, or at least some, and yet he chased after them and funded his pleasures with my money. After some time, when I saw through all the lies, I stood face to face with a notorious liar with low self-esteem, and even though I knew all along that something was wrong with him, I still kept telling myself that I could fix him. None of us can fix men; they're not broken, they're idiots. If you think you can fix him, you shouldn't marry him. Not everything can be fixed, and you're not Bob the Builder.

He stole thousands of euros from me, and I lent him money, not to mention how much I spent on food for him so that poor guy wouldn't starve, without knowing that he was using it to finance his physical pleasures. On the other hand, the relationship gave me precious experience, a broken heart and self-control. What I'm grateful for, I learned English. Damn, the most expensive English lessons in my life. In marketing, you shouldn't say costly but exclusive, so if anyone ever approaches me with interest in extra exclusive English lessons, I'll probably pass on the contact. What he presented to me and what I saw in him was made up; all our relationship was like February 30th. It didn't exist!

When I was in Dublin, he finally contacted me; with a lot of aggression, he left my computer in front of his house, and we agreed that I would take things from the storage to my brother's, and he would terminate the contract. He was mad at me because I contacted his ex. I admit it wasn't right or moral, but on the other hand, many women in my situation would have done it a long time ago; I was just so stupid and I hesitated. The agency didn't forget to send me further correspondence, arranging meetings with girls or information about who he was seeing and when. His account on the Irish escort website had been active for five years and he had to keep himself happy. The girls from the agency knew we were no longer together so there was no need to send me this information, but they were so glad to hurt me under the pretext that it was for my good so I wouldn't go back to him. Seriously? Am I crazy? They were thrilled; Mr. D left, and I did my best to develop a new plan for my child and my future with her. I didn't take time off; I just functioned, survived, and, most importantly, earned money. To be able to share this story with you, I had to delve deep into the past and sift through messages with Mr. D and reread conversations with the agency. It all still hurts, and going through the past brings back things that should be dead and buried. Sometimes, you don't realise what a huge mistake you've made until you tell someone your story. We all make mistakes and I'm a champion at it. I could get a Ph.D. degree in "the world's worst relationships." How can you love someone so much that you would jump in front of a train for them while they wouldn't even step on that train for you? How can you overlook all those mistakes? It should be a basic instinct, a survival instinct, or it should be possible to find information in the handbook for young adventurers. I won't burden you with all the details of that relationship; we both made many mistakes. For example, my mistake was meeting him, and he just was a big mistake himself. I was an expert; I dated with errors, and as you can notice, I'm good at it. All I was left with was an empty wallet and a big hole in my heart that needed to be patched up. On the other hand, it gave me even greater drive and new motivation not to give up and fight until the end. I continued doing what I was doing, moving from hotel to hotel every three days and overcoming depression with exercise, swimming, and morning walks. I did everything to keep myself from going crazy. I could have turned to cocaine and alcohol, but that would have been too easy, and I preferred a more complex solution. I hadn't had cocaine for a good while by this stage, and I had no intention of touching it or anything like it. What I really liked about him was his sense of humor. I was in Enniscorthy and needed to get rid of the lint on my coat, so I was looking for one of those sticky rollers that can remove everything from your clothes. I didn't know what it was called in English, and Mr. D sent me to the store to get a "fluffer." I ran around the store asking almost every salesperson: "Excuse me, I need a fluffer, do you know where I could find one?" Most of the staff looked at me strangely and walked away. I was ready to give up, but then a young lady approached me, asking if she could help me. I told her what I was looking for, and she started laughing. "Do you mean a roller, my dear?" I felt embarrassed; "fluffer" sounded logical, derived from the word "fluff." Mr. D found it really amusing. For those of you who don't know: A fluffer is a person employed to keep a porn performer's penis erect on the set. Truly amusing!

Chapter Ten
Collection of Aliens

As I've mentioned before, I've traveled extensively, and under the influence of the agency that pushed me into many situations, it was impossible to avoid encounters with the biggest idiots who ever roamed Ireland. The parade of experts I encountered during the years of doing this "job" was quite extensive. Unfortunately, or somewhat thankfully, I don't remember most of them; only the worst, most extreme, and strangest beings linger in my memories. Since deciding to share my story, I began taking notes on the strangest perverts I encountered, so I could share them with you. In New Bridge, a house was owned by a Polish woman married to an Irishman. It was a grey house near the center at the end of the street with an unpleasant reputation.

The first time we went to that house with Victoria was during COVID, as "regular guests." Susan started sending many girls there after we left, and it didn't take long for the Polish lady to realise what was happening in the house. She negotiated favourable terms with Susan, two hundred euros per night, from which she never paid taxes, just like other apartment owners who agreed with our agency. It didn't take long before every pervert with a penis attached to his body in the area knew about the house. I encountered several exciting specimens there myself. Once, an older man came to me; he was about eighty and took ages to find the house. The man could barely move; his pants fell below his waist, and he was half-deaf. I tried to explain to him that he far exceeded my age limit, but it didn't seem to bother him much; he just smiled at me. I kept telling him he had to leave until I got nervous and yelled. Finally, I got some reaction, but not the one I expected. He sat on the couch next to the door and said he would wait. He probably thought I needed more time, but all I really wanted was for him to leave. It took me about fifteen minutes to get him out of the house, and once I finally succeeded, I called the operator to report what had happened. I don't know which operator answered the call, but I remember she didn't believe anything I said, and I had to hand over thirty per cent of the two hundred euros from my pocket to the agency. This happened so often that I was forced to pay them extra money, which annoyed me. When Mr. D and I were together, and I wanted to finish early and enjoy the evening off; it was not uncommon for the operator or Jane to calculate how many more clients I could serve by the end of the "Working hours" and I had to pay for this theoretical number.

What was I paying them for? Because I wanted to rest a bit with someone I care about because they sent me a hard-of-hearing old man who wouldn't leave? In addition, in three and a half years, I gave them thousands and thousands of euros to which they had no right, not to mention how much I paid them in total. It often happened that clients just came to look, but aware that they couldn't afford the girls' services, they left with excuses like I didn't look like the girl in the photos, they forgot their wallet in the car, or they tried to negotiate a price reduction by at least half, feeling like they were in a market somewhere in Morocco.

Anyway, another guy who visited me in New Bridge was on an entirely new level; I admired his inventiveness. An average guy around thirty who seemed nervous. He surprised me with the sentence, "You know, I've never done this before, and I don't know if I'll be able to get an erection. Do you think you could take a look at my penis first?" Did I look like an outpatient doctor? I explained to him that it doesn't work like that, and he seemed to understand what I was telling him, probably after a five-minute conversation that was quite exhausting. He asked if he could have a glass of water, which I granted him. When I returned from the kitchen with water, he was standing in the middle of the living room, with his trousers at his knees, holding his penis in his hand. He proudly demonstrated his extremely rapid masturbation skills and then fled. I stood there with the glass in my hand, completely shocked by what happened. Unbelievable! Another exciting place for encounters with strange men was a hotel in Cavan.

I liked that hotel, but Cavan was not among my favorite places. For women who want something extra in a relationship and crave uniqueness, find a man from New Bridge or Cavan, and I promise you that such a chap will surpass all your expectations. Most of the time, many farmers visited me there, which I wasn't thrilled about. Fortunately, this hotel had an easily accessible back entrance, so men with high self-esteem and low personal hygiene could slip in and out without anyone noticing. Most of the time, even though they only stayed with me for five minutes, which was about the time it took to try to refuse them and they persuade you not to, my room still smelled like I had three cows and a bull hidden under the bed or in the bathroom. I never had anything against farmers, but I had everything against the inability to shower and use shower gel. That was one regular client who liked to visit me in Cavan and wasn't afraid to travel to other places, either. I had him saved in my phone as the "I wanna cum guy" because, from the moment he stepped out of the shower wrapped in a towel and started touching me, he only said this one sentence over and over again until he succeeded, which was probably the highlight of his day. "I wanna cum, I wanna cum, I wanna cum so badly" was the only thing I heard for about thirty minutes from the moment he arrived. Despite his eagerness to climax, he was very fond of delaying his orgasm, which drove me crazy because I didn't want anything else but for him to leave! Twice, I had encounters with men suffering from dwarfism. The first time when I saw him through the spy-hole, I thought it was not appropriate to accept him, as well the housekeeper was also behind the door and saw him. Although I told the operator why I couldn't take the man, I didn't have the courage to tell him to his face. I felt sorry for him and realised that someone with such a problem probably has difficulty finding a partner. When the man appeared at my place again a few months later, I had to open the door and decided to gently reject him. He was a charming man, and rejecting him broke my heart, but if I had accepted his visit, it would have been very uncomfortable. Because of his short stature, I would have felt like a paedophile, and just the thought of it was repulsive. Anyway, I recommended Victoria to him; I knew she wouldn't have a problem with anything. Even if someone told her to have sex with a horse, she would accept it if the owner of the animal paid well. That girl had no inhibitions, and money was everything to her. In such cases, it was beneficial because when someone appeared at my place where I had boundaries that I wouldn't cross, I could recommend her. Another client in Cavan was really funny; he looked like a walking copy of Daniel Nekonecny. Google him! He had a very extravagant dressing style, spreading positive energy and unblocking chakras with scented candles; it was pretty comical.

Furthermore, in Cavan, I was blessed with mentally challenged men. I had several such visits all over Ireland. The worst part was that I usually couldn't tell immediately and it took me a while to notice. Then we reached a phase where I couldn't throw the man out anymore, so I had no choice but to endure it. The apartment in Athlone also remembers many exciting characters. There was a regular visitor, a man in overalls, who thought the shower would swallow him. I always sent him there, he always turned the water on, and he always emerged wrapped in a towel, but instead of kindly going into the shower, he went to relieve himself. When he opened the door on his way out of the bathroom, such a stench poured out that I had to open all the windows. Couldn't he relieve himself at home? Besides, I still had to send him back to the bathroom because he was so dirty and smelled like poo, that I wouldn't touch him even with tongs. Another expert who left me a huge, brown surprise in the bathroom in Athlone was about forty years old. He knew exactly what he wanted. All intimacy took place with the light on and on the floor, so the carpet beautifully rubbed me. His climax probably triggered some digestive process similar to when you have your morning coffee or smoke a cigarette, and he rushed to the bathroom, where his intestines spent about twenty minutes with very loud expressions. It was a delight to clean up after him, probably so I wouldn't get bored. I must admit that I felt really sick from such individuals, and it was a miracle that I didn't vomit.

Having it happen is human, but it's more than disgusting not to clean up after yourself. Some men probably think they're still at an age when some woman will clean up after them. Damn, gentlemen, we're not your mothers! It's like when Mr. D thought I was such a good woman and I will stay by his side no matter how much he lies, cheats, or steals. It must be realised that such a woman is your mother, not us. When I remember how many gentlemen proudly showed me photos of their wives and children, I felt sorry for those ladies so much. Why do you do this? If you love her so much, don't cheat, and if you don't love her, then leave and live your life surrounded by prostitutes. It's a decision you make, and it doesn't happen by chance or mistake. Either you want to be a good and faithful person, or you don't. She will find out anyway;

she is brilliant, and she will figure it out. With some sharper women, you can quickly recognise their dark side when they make your life hell, and you pay for your decisions. Karma represented by a woman is worse than anything else, gentlemen; keep that in mind! Now that I've explained to you that every woman has a wrong side too, we can, with a clear conscience, return to the story of how some men are unsatisfactory and how lucky you are if you haven't met any such bastard yet. Let's move on to the hotel in Dunboyne. I liked this small town behind Dublin, and most clients here were alright. There is a beautiful English-style breakfast restaurant in town with a divine outdoor terrace. Whenever I stayed in Dunboyne, I liked to go there for eggs Benedict for breakfast. There is one local alcoholic living here, and he really made my stay unpleasant. He was getting drunk in one of the local bars when he was overwhelmed by the immense desire to open an escort website. What an unprecedented stroke of luck when he found photos of a long-legged blonde in a town where usually no girls go. After a few shots, every woman was beautiful, so he decided to bless me with his presence and moved to the hotel bar, which he admitted later. He staggered from side to side and could barely speak; I wanted to kick him out right away, but arguing with someone who could barely stand on their feet somehow lacked meaning. He told me that if I kicked him out, he would go to reception and tell them what I was doing there. I couldn't afford to pay for another hotel, plus it was late at night, and the thought of travelling was killing me.

Besides the humiliation, I didn't want to face it. I took the man for thirty minutes; it was enough for him to breathe on me, and just from those fumes, I felt like I had at least two beers. As you can imagine, nothing works as it should when you're borderline intoxicated. Desperately, I did everything possible to get him out. Finally, after many unsuccessful attempts, he left, and I immediately started airing out the room. To make matters worse, the man replenished his alcohol level somewhere and decided to finish what we started that night. I was supposed to leave the next day, lying in bed in my pyjamas, when suddenly the local alcoholic started banging on the door and shouting, "Elis, I know you're in there; open up. You must be horny and I know you want me!" Of course, what else, I wanted him badly and I didn't do anything else other than fantasising about him. When he appeared, it was a completed manifestation. I immediately asked the operator how did he contact her. Magda was, fortunately, a clever girl and communicated with clients via phone calls, so the man had no evidence of what I was doing there. I called reception to inform them that some drunkard was making the evening unpleasant for me and asked if they could take care of it.

Someone from security probably helped the man out, accompanied by loud, drunken babbling. I breathed a sigh of relief and could finally go to sleep. The next day, I went to Belfast. I stayed at a hotel in a safe part of the city center. I didn't like this network of hotels, but I could be somewhat calmer there. I don't know if they suspected what I was doing there, but they never kicked any girls out. Most of the clients from Northern Ireland were civilised individuals, but of course, there were a few exceptions.

One of these exceptions was a man who called himself Tony Stark. If you visit escort websites in Ireland, you'll find a community chat option where various virtual rooms open up to you. If you click on the first option, the general chat, you'll see many different topics. Most of these chats are full of men who visit girls regularly. If you focus on some profiles, you'll see them in almost every new conversation. They live by this corrupted world. I don't judge them, and I'm not saying they're all bad, but I definitely consider the obsession of some individuals unhealthy. One such man who has an account and high activity on this immoral website is Tony Stark. In the afternoon, Margaret texted to me that a significant "escort critic" would stop by; she received instructions from Jane for me to treat the man as a regular client, not ask for any additional payments, and be as kind to him as possible. When Jane commands, even the devil listens and takes notes; l had to listen, too. "If he writes you a good review, it will greatly boost your profile. He has such huge activity on the websites that good clients will start flocking to you, and the more clients, the sooner you'll be gone."

The time for the meeting arrived, and when I opened the door, to my amazement, an ugly man of medium height with a potbelly appeared before me. He stroked his huge belly protruding between his T-shirt and pants with his hands. Appalled, I decided to survive it and embraced that ugly creature, kissed him on the cheek, and smiled at him. He showed me his yellow teeth and commented on my noisy neighbours. The smell emanating from his mouth horrified me as it resembled an open sewer. I remembered Jane's words and tried to convince myself to provide the best service to that little ugly man. I offered him a shower and mentioned twice not to be afraid to use everything he found in the bathroom, including mouthwash and deodorant, which, of course, he didn't do. He came out of the bathroom and stuck to me; I felt his hairy chest against my skin, and the combination of sweat and "oral sewage" irritated me. My nose was on fire! He started licking his lips with his tongue and buried his overbite in my upper lip while rotating his tongue in my mouth. His saliva dripped down my chin, and I just prayed not to vomit. I felt a large sore in his mouth under his bottom lip; at that moment, I decided it would be better to give him oral sex. With Jane's words in my head, I didn't put on a condom. His erection practically didn't exist, but his penis was wet and covered with a white crust.

After forty minutes of torture with his missing erection, I miraculously satisfied him with my hand, and later, we chatted about random topics. Sex didn't happen at all; it wasn't physically possible since he had no erection, and to be honest, I didn't even try. The last thing I wanted was to have sex with a walking decay. To be fair, with most of my clients, I was relieved when they left, and I slammed the door behind him.

This was one of the most disgusting experiences Belfast brought me. In Belfast, we'll stay a little longer because, besides Tony Stark, whom no one can beat, we also met, among other individuals, a very obese client. I have nothing against overweight people; I used to weigh over a hundred kilos. However, considering the service I provided, everything had its limit.

With this man, I exceeded my limit significantly. Weight: at least 160 kg, height: approximately 160 centimetres. At the slightest movement, at least half a litre of sweat poured from him; his sweat glands were working at maximum capacity. I was lucky to be lying under him when every position was a challenge. In the missionary position, I was engulfed in so much fluid from him that I felt like I had just stepped out of a shower. A very smelly and repulsive shower! Drops of sweat fell into my eyes, into my mouth, practically everywhere on my body. Plus, I couldn't move because I had a person lying on top of me whose weight was approaching that of a cow. All my bones were on the verge of breaking; I was stuck between the bed and the vast body, and with the last of my strength, I used my almost crushed lungs to pretend to sigh. I repeatedly had to answer his questions, "So, how do you like it, honey?" "I really like it, mainly just do it, or I'll suffocate down here."

The only thing I was able to focus on was my survival. Of course, I didn't like it, but what else could I say? The truth? "You're disgusting, I'm dying, get off me?"

He wasn't the wrong person, and I didn't want to be mean or nasty to him. Plus, it wouldn't speed up the process; rather, the opposite. In any case, it was always better to lie!

I wanted it to end as quickly as it started. The man thought I was enjoying it and began persuading me to have unprotected sex because, like most men, he had trouble reaching a climax with a condom. Unfortunately for him, I wasn't prepared to risk STDs for his pleasure. I felt like I could communicate better with a piece of wall than with him. What exactly don't men understand about the word "No"? The man was persistent and didn't stop persuading me, but after forty minutes of enduring torture, with sweat pools, squished and praying for it to end, I had had enough. So, I argued with the guy, and after a short exchange of opinions, he was kicked out, and thank God, we never saw each other again. I had plenty of time to meet with several girls, most of whom aren't worth mentioning, except for two. One interesting person was a girl who called herself Kate Shine. Kate was recently a family man, but at around forty years old, she decided to spend the rest of her life as a woman. I have two transgender friends who have felt their entire lives that they would like to change their gender. Being born as a man and feeling like a woman or vice versa must be pretty frustrating, and I can't even imagine how miserable life must be.

However, this wasn't Kate's case. Kate decided to change her gender so she could work as a prostitute. She first tried this even before the operation, when she started flying to Ireland as a "woman with a penis," and yes, surprisingly, there is a great demand for such a service in Ireland. Subsequently, she underwent surgery and continues to work successfully in Ireland as a prostitute. It is said that every man would like to try escort work, and I believe that might be partially true. This gentleman decided to fulfil his big dream and has successfully slept with half of this country. Congratulations buddy! Since Kate got into a woman's body at the age of forty, it seems like she's experiencing her second puberty. I only met her once at an apartment in New Bridge, but her reputation preceded her. A well-built blonde with fake eyelashes, nails so long I wondered how she could wipe her bottom, extravagantly dressed. It was nine in the morning, and she was already on her third glass of wine, claiming she did not have an alcohol use disorder. I never would have thought. I also have three shots of whiskey in the morning, and I'm not an alcoholic; it's an entirely normal process. Kate had a very masculine voice, a prominent Adam's apple, and was well-known for her stupidity. She liked to sleep with men without protection for more money, and her excuse was, "I can't catch anything; I have a rubber vagina."

In vain, I tried to explain to her that mucous membrane is mucous membrane regardless of whether you've undergone gender reassignment surgery. She didn't mind! Men ran away from her when they found out she used to be a man, and her clientele mainly consisted of gentlemen who didn't like to dress up their little friends in latex. It was her health and her choice, but I believe that if she were honest on her website and informed potential clients that she had undergone this operation, perhaps no one would run away, and maybe some would even be interested. Kate was a great friend of Victoria's; I never fully understood what those two had in common, but perhaps it was just their love for the oldest profession in the world. What fascinated me most about this lady was her decision to become a woman. Many men only dream about it, but she chooses to do everything to have sex without commitments, even ten times a day. As I mentioned, Kate had no inhibitions and was very eccentric. No girl except Victoria wanted to be with her in the apartment, and we were banned from many hotels because of her. She liked to pick up clients in erotic clothing, even at the reception, and she didn't realise how far she was from being a decent girl. Anyway, Kate is living her dream, hoping that Mr. D avoided her when we were still together. Another girl I reluctantly met was Andy. Andy and I shared an apartment in Tralee for three days. When you looked at her face, you didn't have to be very experienced to know that this girl had a drug past. What I really liked about her was her straightforwardness; this girl didn't care too much about what others thought of her. She opened the door to clients without makeup, in leggings, and often chewing something with a full mouth when she let them in. Of course, many men left her, but there were also those who liked her naturalness and stayed.

Then there were, of course, individuals who would screw anything that moves, so they didn't care who opened the door for them. Andy had no filter; she didn't understand the word privacy. She constantly told me stories about people I didn't know and didn't want to know. She didn't know when to be silent, something most girls in this industry didn't know.

When my client left, and I went to shower, she sat on the bathroom rug and kept talking. I dressed, and she was still there talking; I made myself food, and she kept talking. If only she could put together a coherent and meaningful sentence, but she couldn't. The only advantage was that she went to bed earlier than I did, so at least I had a moment of peace in the evening. Those three days with her were pure torture, and you wouldn't believe how exhausting it is when someone fills your head with nonsense. I liked Tralee, though; it was a nice town. We stayed in an apartment by the river with a beautiful view of the mountains. This place was magical, and unlike the others, I had no problem with the local accent. On the contrary, I was enthusiastic about it, and their accent seemed attractive.

Previously, girls used to stay in another apartment near the cinema. The owner was a very kind man and had an agreement with Susan. I liked that apartment; I often went there with Victoria; we were both busy, and rarely did any exotics come after us. Victoria had one client there, with whom I had the unpleasure of sharing a bed with. It happened once and for the last time! The dark-haired dragon, however, took him regularly, and it's a mystery to me how she managed it.

The gentleman looked like Gargamel from The Smurfs, to the point where it seemed he was the model for the evil wizard character.

Visually, he wasn't the most attractive, which wasn't the preference of most of our clients. What was much more disgusting was the smell of his sweat; his sweat glands were diligent, and in an hour with him, you could shower yourself and your entire room. It poured out of him like from a teapot. Susan sent one girl after another to the apartment, so it's no wonder it didn't stay hidden for long. Neighbours began to notice the queue at the door with erect penises, and we had to leave the apartment. The girls started going to a hotel in Tralee, but it didn't last long, and the 'diligent bee' Susan found another apartment, the one I mentioned already, by the river.

When I was there with Andy, I had interesting clients, from an American who boasted about his beautiful lakeside home to a man who accidentally wandered to us. This had never happened to me before; a drunk and tearful man sat on my bed, mourning. His brother had died, and I truly sympathised with him. I remember when my father died, and the last thing I wanted was to be alone. Under normal circumstances, I would have supported him and let him cry, but the operator was unpleasant and wanted me to kick him out. I decided not to pay the agency for him, and I even sent them photos of the tearful man sitting on my bed to make it clear that nothing happened between us and nothing would. When I finally managed to escort the gentleman out, he left me fifty euros for listening to him, which was very kind. I felt nauseated at the thought of kicking him out, but I couldn't play psychologist with the agency breathing down my neck. Meanwhile, while this young man visited me, Andy had an older client in the adjacent room who vomited on the floor. I think I got the better deal; I didn't want to clean up someone else's vomit. Finally, the day came when I said goodbye to Andy and went to a hotel in Tuam in Co. Galway. The journey was incredibly long, and I found the hotel myself. It was tiny, but no girls from our agency had ever been there, which suited me. I arrived on a Friday, and the first thing that hit me when I got off the bus was the omnipresent smell of cows. I was lucky and caught a taxi. In the middle of nowhere, it was a miracle, as the taxi driver told me and advised me to book some taxi in advance before leaving. Of course, no one was available, so I left the hotel in the rain and on foot while the bus was about thirty minutes late. This was classic Ireland. When the taxi driver dropped me off at the hotel, I was a little scared, but my fears dissipated as soon as I entered the reception. Everyone local came here to celebrate the weekend on Fridays, and a crowded reception was always a good sign.

I secretly recorded a video for the operator to let her know how clients would get to my room, which was standard procedure, and then I rushed to get ready.

The accent in this area was terrible; I struggled to understand, but I always managed to communicate with hand gestures. I met a friendly firefighter there who told me stories from work and several other very nice men. Unfortunately, even such a small town offers quite a collection of unusual individuals. One of them was a drunk man for whom alcohol made any attempt at an erection impossible, so he started to swallow Viagra like candies. Of course, I was aware of all the possible risks, and I directed the man to be reasonable, but he desired an erection more than his own life, so he swallowed those blue pills one after another. He asked me if I had any stay-up stockings, which was a common practice; I was about to put them on, but he snatched them from my hands and put them on his hairy legs. He looked at me with a solemn expression on his face and said, "This looks sexy on me, doesn't it?" It probably excited him, but I couldn't think of anything other than the idiot ruining my stockings, and I would have to throw them away. He wanted me to put them on after him, which I refused. I wasn't going to put on something that had been lying on someone else's hairy, smelly legs. Alcohol and Viagra are not friends, and if you want the miraculous pill to work, you should read the package leaflet.

For the slower ones: Alcohol + Viagra = erection dysfunction.

The man was, of course, frustrated because it wasn't working for him, and he started convincing me to have unprotected sex. "Darling, I haven't slept with anyone in over ten years; you have to trust me; it's safe."

If I believed every fella who told me it was safe, I'd probably be infected with everything that can be transmitted sexually. "Okay, fine, let's try anal; you must love that!"

What? That was out of the question. "No, no, no, I repeated to him. "Do you at least have any anal toys?" "No, I don't!" and at this point in the conversation, we were both angry. If anger could be seen, smoke would come from both our ears. When he tried to get up from my bed, he farted in such a way that he pooped himself. The white sheets were suddenly stained brown. The man didn't seem worried about that and hurried to grab his trousers to have another blue pill. It was probably the sixth pill, and at that moment, my nerves snapped, and I started kicking him out. "We'll spend the whole day together on Saturday. I'll give you a thousand euros, and I'll come early in the morning," he exclaimed while getting dressed. "Darling, don't take it personally, but I wouldn't spend Saturday with you even for a million euros!"

Of course, I didn't say that, but I thought it. I told him we'd see and asked him to call me, with a plan to block his phone number. I felt a little sorry for him, but I didn't want to spend another minute of my life with him. I slammed the door, blocked the man, and spent the next twenty minutes cleaning the room. Another prospective client for sexual play was a young guy under the influence of drugs. When I opened the door, he asked me if I had stockings. Tuam seemed to be full of men with a fetish for erotic accessories. Before I could explain to him that I didn't have any because it was out of the question to wear the same ones that had touched some old man's body, his actions reassured me that the man wouldn't stay. He started thrusting fifty euros into my hand and begged me for quick oral satisfaction. There's nothing quick with people on drugs, and besides, I wasn't one of those girls who would satisfy half of Co. Galway for fifty euros. Maybe it sounds absurd considering the "work" I did, but I wanted to maintain some respect for myself. The man immediately went on: "I called your friend, Amelia, a few days ago (I didn't even know that girl), she's twenty-six, right? She would surely take less money and properly screw and suck me off! She must want to suck dicks at this age. When you girls leave this business, men will have a hard time satisfying you; you're always so horny, no one can handle that!"

I listened to this for a long five minutes while I was desperately trying to kick the man out. I was glad when the evening came, and I could pack my bag and escape from Tuam.

The next place I'll take you to will be Ennis again. Not that I wanted to go there, but the hotel was relatively cheap, albeit nasty. The hotel where the girls usually stayed has an exciting story: Two sisters inherited two hotels from their parents. One hotel was in Shannon; it was beautiful, renovated, and well-maintained. The other sister inherited the hotel in Ennis, which was really disgusting. There was mould in the rooms, and once, the closet door fell on me. Too bad it didn't fall on some client! Overall, the place was so ugly that I was afraid to eat there, but it had one significant advantage: they rarely kicked anyone out, and the clients were used to coming there. Unfortunately, clients of all kinds! However, I had there a lovely guy used to visit me here; he was attentive to me. Once, he gave me sneakers to make it easier for me to travel by bus, and I still have those shoes. He was a nice guy, just lonely, and many were like him. I was also visited by a young and quite handsome man at this hotel. He was an intelligent, good looking guy studying law. "It's like hitting the jackpot," I exclaimed.

There weren't many decent men here. My excitement came too early when we got to the conversation about his fantasies; it took my breath away completely. I stood there with my mouth open, thinking I must have misheard. "I have a fantasy, and I'm looking for someone to fulfil it. I would like you to vomit on me, urinate, or defecate on me." His entire speech was inspired by some disgusting German porn film. Even if I wanted to, it wouldn't be physically possible for me, not to mention that the idea of urinating on someone is disgusting to me personally. I couldn't utter a single word, so the young man continued his monologue:

"We'll mutually fist each other and lick anal openings, then I would imagine you hitting me, cursing me, and humiliating me as much as you can." This guy was the most handsome person I had seen in weeks, maybe even months. My standards had suffered quite a bit here; it's essential to realise that ordinary and attractive men don't usually go after escorts. So, anything with the same eye size and without bad breath was considered an Irish Adonis to me. It's perverse that someone desires such practices. If any of you have similar inclinations and would like to experience someone's urine, gentlemen, we have specialised dominatrixes for such matters; don't go with such requests to girls who don't offer such services. You'll only disgust and frighten them! We'll stay in Ennis a little longer.

Ennis is very close to Limerick, and the city of Limerick doesn't have the best reputation. In the past, many violent crimes occurred here, and although it's somewhat safer now, there are still occasionally unsettling reports. I happened to be in Ennis when a Romanian girl was murdered in Limerick. It's unlikely that you have heard about this story. It was in 2023, and that poor girl was stabbed to death by a client in an apartment; yes, she worked as an escort. I dare not go into details, but her husband was also in the apartment at the time of the attack, and he survived. The woman had children and probably did this job out of desperation. It was the same apartment where Victoria and I were; maybe that's why this story touched me so much. I was there, just at a different time, but I was there. The man who rented the apartment was adept at renting apartments to girls who worked as escorts.

THE NEWS 5 Apr 2023

Agency Betrayal:
Murder of Romanian Escort in Limerick Exposes Callous Greed

In a chilling turn of events, the vibrant streets of Limerick were marred by tragedy as news spread of the untimely death of a Romanian escort, brutally stabbed to death in an apartment. The victim, whose name remains undisclosed, had been navigating life in a foreign land, diligently working to make ends meet in the bustling city.

According to initial reports, the young woman met her demise within the confines of an apartment, allegedly at the hands of a client. The harsh reality of her violent death serves as a stark reminder of the dangers lurking in the shadows of society, especially for those working in vulnerable industries.

However, what adds a chilling layer of irony to this already somber tale is the reprehensible response of the agency. The agency, which did not employ the victim directly but had other escort girls working in nearby apartments and towns, callously chose to conceal the incident. Their motive?

Fear that if other escort girls found out, they would stop working, thus impacting the agency's profits. This heartless decision exposes the true colors of the agency, revealing a blatant disregard for the well-being of those they indirectly employed and a shameful prioritization of financial gain over basic human decency. As the city of Limerick mourns the loss of yet another life to senseless violence, one can only hope that justice will prevail and that this tragic incident will serve as a wake-up call, prompting greater scrutiny and accountability for agencies that prioritize profit over people.

Who committed the actual crime?

He rented several apartments throughout Ireland, in Ennis, Dublin, and Limerick, and even the apartment mentioned above in Tralee where Andy and I stayed was rented to us by him. He had an arrangement with Susan. The rent was expensive and the girls paid outrageous amounts of money so he could buy cocaine. When we started working with him, he didn't take anything like that, but money will lead you to such things, and then it's just your choice. When the murder was being investigated, the only thing he said to the agency was that he would probably have to get rid of that apartment because the girls probably wouldn't want to go there anymore. How empathetic! All the girls who had profiles on the Irish escort websites were immediately notified of this incident and urged to exercise extreme caution. Even a video and photos of the attacker from the security camera were sent to everyone. When he entered that apartment with the intention of stabbing that girl to death, he was smiling. It's terrifying and sends shivers down your spine. Since the agency owned my profile, I didn't receive any information, no warning or photo. At that moment, no one could know if this wasn't a serial killer who, for religious reasons, was not 'cleansing' the earth and killing girls. I was the closest of all the girls then, and no one warned me. I learned about the incident from the news, and in shock, I messaged Simona to ask if they knew about it. "Yes, we know about it. We even received a video, but Susan has forbidden me to tell you until you leave Ennis because you would stop working!" Damn it!

Of course, I would stop working. How could someone risk my life for a few hundred euros? Another proof that I was just a puppet with only one task: to make as much money as possible under all circumstances. Jane used to send me to Limerick often for a client, but despite her efforts to get me to him, I only met him once. She called him "The Pharmacist" supposedly owned a chain of pharmacies in Limerick, but he wasn't Irish. He might have been of Arab nationality or similar; it's been a long time, and I'm glad I've forgotten the details.

Jane had known him from the time when she flew to Ireland to sell her enticing curves and established contact with him. Since she was working for the agency she kept sending girls to him to do whatever he desired. I didn't want to do everything expected of me, even though he paid very generously. He always appeared in designer clothing and a beautiful car and felt entitled to request special services. Jane didn't care what was happening in the room as long as she got her money. The Pharmacist persuaded girls for an extra fee to have sex without a condom, and when I later found out how many girls agreed to that, I felt sick. Since he liked to flaunt money, Jane didn't hesitate to send me to him at two in the morning, just as the gentleman pleased. As I mentioned, I only saw him once. The idea of travelling by bus at two in the morning from Dublin to Limerick for some horny jerk didn't impress me, so Jane constantly arranged new girls to charm him. Money was the only thing driving her; they were willing to risk our lives, and they would go to great lengths. It even happened that they exchanged my SIM card without my knowledge, so all the contacts I had blocked or saved as "do not answer!" could reach me again, allowing them to hurt me once more. As if going through it once wasn't enough. Several men belonged to this group who took advantage of the situation. The first one I'll introduce you to is the strange artist. You know when you meet someone and, for no apparent reason, you don't feel comfortable in their presence?

Well, that was exactly this person. When I opened the door to the room, the man, "vanilla" and self-centred appeared. His nose was so high that he could breathe the air reserved for astronauts. Immediately after payment, he began to boast, "I have two galleries, one of them in Cork, and I employ many staff. My paintings sell for enormous amounts even in America. Well, I have money, but not everyone does, so I also have to make cheap prints for people like you."

He looked at me with a contemptuous expression and smiled condescendingly. People like me? I wouldn't even buy that cheap print from him if I knew what kind of person I would support. What are such people proving when they demean others? Does it make him feel good to earn more money than a prostitute? Honestly, most people earn higher amounts. This arrogant person was utterly disrespectful, and most of his knowledge and skills in the sexual sphere probably came from porn movies.

Everything he did to me caused agony, and every touch of his was a torturous experiment. He began by pushing my nipples inward. I've experienced men pulling on them, biting them, but having someone make them inward was a new one for me. You can try it deliberately. The pain pierced through my body like an icy stream, wrapping around every nerve fibre. Every inhale was like a stab in the heart, and every exhale was like a desperate attempt to escape from endless suffering. My body became a slave to pain with each desperate attempt to hurt me further. When he inserted his fingers into me, I felt them all the way up to my cervix, where he dug his long nails, trying in vain to pull his hand out. I warned him several times that it was uncomfortable, but the man didn't care about the pain he was causing me. After my pleading for him to stop, he decided to show me what it was like to feel his nails on my clitoris, which I couldn't endure. It seemed like he was deliberately causing me all this suffering, and I kicked him out. Unfortunately, he tried to come back to me twice, and kicking him out or explaining why I chose to reject him was a very challenging process. Another man I encountered again in Athlone, thanks to Jane's decision to swap my SIM card, was an arrogant, curly-haired guy.

Upon his arrival, I knew something was wrong; a lousy feeling engulfed my entire body. I remembered his face, and it didn't bode well. He was wearing a grey T-shirt, and he didn't even greet me, let alone look at me when I opened the door. Not a single word was uttered as he headed towards the bathroom, indicating that he was very familiar with the apartment. That day, Jane was my operator, so I immediately told her I had a bad feeling about the man and would probably kick him out. It wouldn't be Jane if she didn't start convincing me to let him stay, claiming I was overreacting. Jane persuaded me, and I trembled with horror, expecting the worst. The man emerged from the bathroom and threw money at me without saying a word. At that moment, I knew what kind of jerk he was. It had been a long time since I last saw him. During our last encounter, he bit through my nipple 'tore my underwear, and when he tried to please me with his hand, it felt like a blind detective was groping me, hoping to find a lost treasure eventually. Despite his efforts to give me pleasure and arouse even the slightest excitement in me, with each step, he was closer to failing than reaching the goal.

Ladies, let's support each other, and every time it hurts, tell him. We're not guinea pigs, and how are men supposed to learn if each of us tells them how wonderful it is in the hope of surviving? The ability to stimulate with hands is desperate for most men, and if you're not sure about it or not brimming with confidence and convinced of your skills, you better avoid this activity. If you're doing it to please the woman and see that it hurts her, stop. How do you know you're doing it right? A woman who enjoys it will be relaxed, with a blissful expression on her face, "Finally, someone who's not trying to destroy my vagina."

A woman who doesn't like it will either bite your penis as punishment when her turn comes, of course, accidentally. Alternatively, she'll physically hurt you or explain that this is really not it. However, the less assertive ones will recoil from you, their faces contorted, hands pulling the covers, and you, like every selfish man, will think these are signs of an approaching orgasm and will push harder. There's a small percentage of men who can tell the difference between excitement and pain in a woman. Women are more sensitive to this, and most of us can't even watch porn when we notice that the actress is suffering, while a man thinking with his penis mistakenly believes the woman is aroused and horny. The curly-haired guy in the grey T-shirt was one of those men who believed that pain is pleasure and that my nerves are endless. After several attempts to explain this difference, our conversation reached a point where I stood at the door and kicked him out, mainly so I would never have to see him again. This final point was preceded by a long conversation about my reasons for wanting to kick him out. Seriously? Why does a woman have to explain when she doesn't want anything to do with someone?

Where should I start, with his arrogant behaviour or the fact that his touches cause me such pain that I feel like little razor blades are growing from his fingers? My reasons weren't enough, and the man thought I must be joking; with the smile of a psychopath, he spanked me. I objected to this, upon which he pressed me against the wall and held my hands so tightly that bruises formed. The man almost broke my little finger on my left hand, and I had had enough of how every man treats me like his toy. I took advantage of his wide-legged stance, and my knee touched his groin. He collapsed in pain, and I was grateful that my hands were free. Finally, I slammed the door behind him, and the aftermath of this situation: I had to ice my hand for three days. As I've said before, listening to Jane doesn't pay off, especially not in a town like Athlone. About half an hour after this man, another client selected by Jane, came. After his departure, I felt like a coke addicted guy tried to rape me, bruises adorned my body, and my little finger was almost broken from the fella who saw me before the coke guy. All the injuries seemed to me as evidence that the moment I get paid, I become a toy that people can do whatever they want. If I had known the guy was on drugs, I would never have taken him, but cocaine is one of those drugs that are difficult to recognise, and if not for that, I would probably be kicking out every other client in Ireland. The only indication that he had enjoyed the previous night was his constant fidgeting and sweating again, and he was unusually nervous and aggressive. Working with Jane was very demanding; if someone told her over the phone that he is an aggressive person on drugs, she would demand fifty euros and an extra gram of cocaine for any inconvenience. Another exciting man I encountered was Glen from Northern Ireland. He looked exactly as his name suggested, and despite being a friendly and funny guy, surviving intimate play with him was a challenge. His nipples resembled those of a nursing woman; he wanted me to play with them for at least half an hour. He pulled them, scratched them, bit them, something that not everyone would find appealing. Glen had planned precisely when and how to start and how long the activity would last. I hated it when a guy was in control and delayed climax; it was exhausting and even more annoying than regular sex. There were more guys like that, but I remember this one specifically because I saw him quite often. Another contender for the award for the biggest living disappointment is a dentist from Dublin. I met him at the beginning, in times when I couldn't argue with either men or the agency.

The dentist was of a foreign nationality, think Arab, but it's been too long. He had a big, radiant smile, a shaved head, a black beard, and glasses. He visited me before COVID-19 in hotel rooms, where he regularly paid for an hour. He wasn't interested in sex, and certainly not in satisfaction, but in the process. In his interpretation, the process consisted of providing an hour of oral sex, where he thrust his penis deep into your throat, held your head so tight that you couldn't breathe, and forced you to change head positions to find out which one gave him the greatest pleasure. After his visit, I usually caught tonsillitis, and when I stopped seeing him, which was one of my wise decisions, he started visiting Victoria. I would rather deep- throat a cactus than him! Well, started visiting is a strong word; he was with her once, and she subsequently had him blocked. When the Raven-Haired Dragon had someone blocked, it had to be serious, but she described his practices and disrespect for women as unbearable. The man eventually made it onto the blacklist of most girls because no one can endure having a penis thrust into their throat for an hour straight. Gentlemen, if you do something like that, try using a cucumber and do it to yourselves. Women, from an anatomical perspective, do not have throats adapted for someone to do that to them. It hurts us desperately in the same way it would hurt you, and if someone is also pushing your head and trying to suffocate you, it's a disgusting and cruel achievement of one-sided physical pleasure. One of the last stories I will share with you is the story of the hotel manager in Waterford City. I arrived at this smaller hotel, located by the river and relatively close to the center. I checked in, and after a day of travelling, I went to take a bath. I remember being extremely tired, and I only wanted to rest a bit before starting to work. It was the first time I stayed at this hotel, and all I knew was that the hotel manager browsed escort websites then ordered a girl as a client and kicked the girls from the hotel.

I heard from Tina stories of girls being left at the hotel if they didn't show him their breasts or didn't do some "kindness" for him. That day, I had Simona, and as soon as I settled into the bathtub, I messaged her: "Simona, please, here at this hotel, the manager orders himself as a client and subsequently kicks out the girls. Please be careful, and if you have any suspicions, let me know." Simona replied ten minutes later: "The manager called me; he's saved in all phones as 'manager ok; he asked if we could meet, so I told him to come in ten minutes, and you'll talk." Perfect, instead of handling it herself, she decided to send him to me. Simona judged that he was horny and persistent, which was hard to believe. I already saw myself packing my things and going elsewhere. I quickly got out of the bathtub and got dressed. Barely had I put on my T-shirt when the guy in a suit and glasses was already knocking on the door. I hated such situations; I was trembling with fear. I didn't want to be humiliated again. A tall, thin man with grey hair and glasses, who immediately noticed my nervousness, asked me to calm down. He asked me to confirm for his peace of mind if the girl from the website was me and reassured me that he wouldn't kick me out. I was afraid he would ask me for some favours in exchange for being able to "work" at the hotel, which I would refuse, but nothing like that happened. He very strictly gave me instructions: "You can work here from twelve noon to nine in the evening, with your last client leaving the hotel at nine. I don't want any problems, so please, only normal men and no alcohol and drugs are allowed." I stood there and looked at him with a frightened expression. "Why don't you kick me out?" I asked. "You know, I haven't been doing this job for long, and I'd like to keep this position. I tried kicking the girls out, but it solved nothing significantly. They kept coming back. So now the girls at the reception always letting me know when a prostitute comes to check in, and then I go to see what's going on and decide whether to kick her out based on that! Primarily, I care about adhering to the rules and discretion, and if you need anything, don't hesitate to contact me anytime," he said while handing me his business card with his phone number. My first impression of him was charming; when he was leaving, he kissed me on the cheek, which surprised me a bit, but as long as he didn't want anything else, I was willing to survive a kiss on the cheek. As soon as he left, Simona was already sending client after client to me. The first gentleman was a policeman from the area, who wasn't my favourite clientele. Still, he didn't do anything terrible, so I managed his presence somehow, and the next client was a lawyer, when he left me a politician arrived.

Between the first and second clients, the manager started texting Simona, asking if he could see me before going home. Subsequently, Simona asked me if I could contact him and arrange something with him.

I was very open and asked if he wanted to stop by as a client or as a manager, as I wasn't sure about his intentions, and he replied that he would like to ask me something. We agreed to meet for a coffee in the morning. Coffee went well, we walked together by the river, where there is a beautiful hotel seating area in the summer, and I answered questions about my profession. I was already at the stage where it didn't bother me; the manager behaved nicely towards me, and curiosity was natural. Every day of my stay, he bothered me more and more. I stayed in room 203, which was right across from an office. With excuses about a lady working there, he lured me out for lunch or more coffee, called me on the room phone, and later shared information with me about what he was doing. He even sent me his photos. On the last day of my stay, he even met me as a client when he decided to pay me for my services. He claimed that he had never done anything like this before, and this was his first time paying for sex.

Despite his words, girls shared their experiences with him on the app, where they subsequently described him as follows: "This man is the manager of a hotel in Waterford. On booking, the experience with him is normal. However, afterwards, he attempts to make himself directly known to you and requests sex. If you refuse, he threatens to remove you from the hotel."

I had heard such stories about him, and in the final stage, Sam contacted me, asking for information about this man. She had a similar and very annoying experience with him, based on which she decided to stop visiting the hotel. Perhaps this is one way to get rid of escort girls. Instead of kicking them out, he will make their stay unpleasant, harass them, and make sexual proposals or demand sex so that they never return. Although he seemed friendly and charming to me, he was just a disgusting creep who exploited his position.

In the early days of my career, I was with one of the girls at the house in New Bridge. Among all my visitors, there was also a bald man around forty with a strong Polish accent. He was well-dressed and even had that cute, branded men's bag. He immediately started persuading me to do an outcall, to go to his place, but I was scared. I agreed with Magda that I would stay with the client for an hour at the apartment, and if everything seemed okay, I would give her the address of where I was going and the client's name before my departure. "Even though I work independently, I'm interested in knowing your name and where you live; where exactly are we going? Ideally, if you have an ID, I could take a picture of it and share it with a friend on the phone who is not part of any agency I work for?" Yes, it sounds stupid! As I mentioned, I had to tell clients, without exception, that I was independent and never mention the agency!

After an hour at the apartment, we went to his house in Ballsbridge. We arrived in a Tesla taxi driven by his Polish friend at a family house. He led me into the living room, where there were three men drinking alcohol. They started arguing when they saw me. I don't speak Polish, but I realised that no one except the bald man was happy about my presence. It was mutual; I wasn't pleased with theirs either. I sat down in a chair, put my bag on the floor, and in a moment, I was picked up and taken to another room. My client put on a porn movie on the TV, told me to wait, watch and suggested I use my free time for masturbation, then locked the door behind me. That's exactly what I wanted: to masturbate—in a stranger's house with so many men around, locked in a strange room. I was scared; my bag stayed in the living room. I had documents, a phone, everything in there. After an extremely long time, the bald man came to rescue me and led me back to the living room. There was a massive pile of cocaine on the table; it looked like someone had spilt two kilos of flour there, and there was alcohol everywhere. His friends disappeared into their rooms, and we were left alone. He asked me if I wanted something to drink. I refused, but he was unpleasant, so 1 agreed to one glass of whiskey. The evening unexpectedly turned sour after he snorted half of the white pile and washed it down with litres of alcohol. Can the human body handle so many toxins? He started persuading me to satisfy one of his friends orally; he was so intense. Thank God his friends were asleep, so I had an excellent reason to refuse after my other reasons were ignored. I was only supposed to be there for a few hours, but he didn't want to let me go. He locked me in the bathroom and talked about his wife, who was supposed to be in Poland and he was highly paranoid. It was endless, and I was thinking about how to get back to New Bridge from there. His paranoia and aggressiveness increased; I had to whisper, I couldn't even breathe out loud, and at one point, he brought a gun. I didn't know if it was real, but it looked realistic. He walked around the apartment with it, aiming at shadows, while I trembled on the couch and begged him to let me go. In the morning, after a night full of horror, I finally managed

254

to persuade him. His friend, the taxi driver, arrived in a few minutes, and I ran out of that house as fast as I could. For several days after this experience, I had nightmares and shook with fear. I feared they saw my documents in my handbag and could find out who I was. It was a terrible horror!

Another man deserving mention is the interview guy, as I called him, alias "Mr. Ben," which was his name on the escort websites. It was one of the worst experiences I had in Ireland, and to this day, cold sweat runs down my spine just thinking about him. He first visited me in New Bridge; that day, Simona kept calling me, and due to the amount of drugs she had taken, she was in a positive mood and was luring men into our networks like flies. As mentioned above, one of the men she decided to attract was Mr. Ben. She told me he had already been with several girls from our agency and liked "role-play," which put me off. If she hadn't persuaded me, I would never have taken him. He arrived, a small, pot-bellied man in glasses with a smirk and a disgustingly foul breath, around forty years old. He seemed nice and introduced his plan for the next hour, which was very precise:

"We'll start with a little conversation, where I will ask you questions. We'll pretend it's a job interview, but the questions will be personal and sexually oriented." After the interview, he announced, " You've been successfully hired, and as confirmation of this acceptance, I'll have to spank you on the butt. You'll bend over my knee, and I'll give you twelve strokes on each cheek, increasing the intensity. Please tell me if you can't handle it, and if it is too painful. Then we'll have regular sex, and afterwards, I'll leave. Do you agree?"

I was surprised by the very detailed description of what awaited me, and although I wasn't thrilled about it, I agreed and decided I could handle it. At that time, my last weeks in this "job" were approaching, and I tried to save as much money as I could. Ben showered and dressed again, perhaps to make it authentic. Then I led him upstairs to my room, where he sat on a chair, I on the bed, and he began asking me questions he had previously written down in notes on his phone. His organisation would be fascinating if the whole situation weren't so disgusting. He asked me questions about orgasms, masturbation, and similar matters, nothing that could surprise me. I received such questions daily, just not in the form of mysterious sexual games. Among seemingly ordinary inquiries, some made me nervous, like "Have your parents ever beaten you, and if so, how?" We even had a conversation where I told him that my dad was no longer alive, and I didn't want to talk about anyone from my family. It was clear that he didn't like it, but he respected my answer, at least seemingly. He also asked me about my relationship with being beaten with a belt. I was very direct and strict about this. I told him that I have a horrid relationship with belts and similar gentle things because I was beaten with them as a child. I hoped that we had clarified this and closed the belt question. The first meeting wasn't as terrible and could be survived with a bit of self-denial. He didn't hurt me, but I had an uncomfortable feeling about him, and as I closed the door behind him, I hoped I wouldn't meet him again. Unfortunately, my wish wasn't granted, and I met him again at the hotel in Newlands Cross. Ben again devised a meticulously crafted program, which included a similar scenario to our first meeting. The only change was what we would be playing. It was a continuation, like the second part of some twisted soap opera. Again, he was my employer, sitting smugly in a chair, and I played an employee who stole cash, and he found out. I had to apologise humbly and beg him not to fire me, that I desperately needed the job. Then came the punishment in the form of spanking my buttocks; this time, I received seventeen strokes on each cheek, again with increasing intensity. Although it was only by hand, at some point, it crossed the limit and it hurt. I had to count out loud every stroke I received, which was very humiliating. After his satisfaction, he left again, and I desperately hoped I wouldn't see him again. Unfortunately, the miracle didn't happen, and we met again when I arrived at the apartment in New Bridge. This meeting was again a bit worse than the previous one. I was forced to "work off" my offence for the pretended theft and was punished again. The strokes were more vigorous again, and after this meeting with him, the first bruises appeared on my skin. I no longer had enough self-denial to pretend that Ben didn't bother me, and I blocked his number.

However, Jane foresaw this and changed my SIM card, so I met Ben again at the apartment in Tallagh. This apartment was rented by a good friend of the man who owned half of City West and had excellent relationships with Susan, and above all, he had a positive attitude towards money. I don't assume that the girls still go to that apartment; it was a small house with three or four entrances, so the neighbours likely noticed what was happening there.

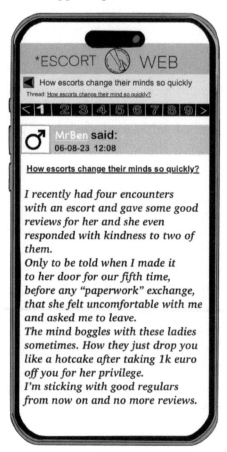

The apartment was rather nice despite being in an unattractive part of Dublin. When Ben appeared at the door, cold sweat ran down my spine, but I didn't want to cause trouble, and I told myself I would survive it again. After each visit, he wrote me a positive review, and now, with a few weeks until the start of my new life, I couldn't afford a negative reputation. That day, his breath was like an open sewer, but it turned out to be the least of my worries after a while. I was at the apartment with a friend, whom I will proudly introduce later. I tried to be polite to him. I tried, but it was difficult, given how unpleasant this man was to me. When he was in the bathroom, I went to warn my roommate not to freak out when she heard the sounds of spanking, explaining that it was a client who was doing this. Although she didn't like it much, she worriedly agreed to ignore all the sounds. I didn't want her to burst in if he started spanking me. Mentally, I tried to prepare myself for what awaited me again, but I couldn't prepare for this. He probably realised that I had blocked him on my previous SIM card and decided to retaliate: he used everything I revealed about myself during our first meeting. He prepared a performance in which he pretended to be my father, who had learned about my theft at work and decided to punish me. Seriously? I had met men who wanted me to pretend to be their daughter or the neighbour's daughter, and I had rejected them all. I still suffered from the loss of my dad and couldn't imagine playing such a filthy game. "No, sorry, but I won't play this!"

I told him and warned him that such things exceeded all boundaries. Despite my explicit disagreement, he decided to play his role as my father, and when I refused to cooperate, he took off his belt and started beating me. It probably made him feel perfect, and the whole situation excited him while I screamed "Stop, please stop!"

I begged him to let me go and pleaded with him, but it was in vain until Ben completed his precisely organised task. The moment the belt touched my skin, my heart raced, and a feeling of uncertainty washed over me, spreading throughout my body. A sense of helplessness surrounded me like a dark curtain, while every sound of the belt hitting my skin felt like a blow to the soul, evoking a mixture of pain and humiliation. My body convulsively tensed as if resisting the violence it was subjected to. These physical wounds left deep scars not only on the surface of my skin. When he left, I remained lying on the floor in tears, covered in red belt marks that later turned into bruises. I trembled in pain and shock, unable to get up. My roommate wisely decided to check on me, and when she found me in such a state on the floor, she couldn't speak. Tears streamed down her face; she heard every blow, but she wanted to respect my wish and didn't enter the room. I couldn't blame her; the only person I could blame was Ben. We reported everything to the operator, so Mr. Ben received a comprehensive report in the escort app to warn other girls to avoid him, and he was immediately blocked.

Unfortunately, it didn't stop him, and two days later, he appeared again at the same apartment. He called the operator from a different number, pretending to be someone else, to arrange a meeting. When I saw him at the door, my breath caught, and my body trembled. I immediately explained to him that he couldn't stay. "Why can't I stay? I came here by bike, work nearby, and I planned it. Let me in." I couldn't explain why he couldn't stay; it seemed obvious. He could ride that bike all the way to Scotland, and I would still say "No" after what he did to me. I was still covered in bruises, suffering from pain, and he shamelessly asked me why I couldn't take him in; he couldn't have been sincere. All I could manage was, "I don't feel comfortable with you,"

and I slammed the door. Of course, I received a negative review on my profile, which didn't bother me too much. What surprised me, however, was when Jane contacted me a few days after the incident and asked about my experience with Ben. I didn't hesitate to briefly explain to her why I would never accept or see him again. I still vividly remember every encounter and that didn't usually happen with clients. Those who remained in my memories are like my worst nightmares, and he is one of them. Ben decided to pour his heart out on escorting websites and share in an open discussion with other users how misunderstood he feels and doesn't understand why he was fired. Many men realised that the one he met was me, but his description of events was significantly different from mine. He devoted a lot of effort to getting others to pity him. When Jane told me about this discussion, I read the sympathetic responses of other men with a disdainful expression. What if he didn't lie? What if he wrote the truth there? What would the reactions be like?

I had never seen Jane so angry at a client; she took it very personally. I guessed something similar might have happened to her in the past. She was furious and decided to contribute to the discussion using my name. Her response was very straightforward:

"Hello Ben, since this has become a recurring topic and I'm posting here anyway, let's address your complaint from a girl's perspective.

I'm not certain your review/complaint is directly referring to me, however as someone who has met you a number times and has also justifiably banned you from ever visiting again, perhaps I understand her feelings. Clearly you are a Dom, surprise, I am not a Sub and likely she isn't either. Therefore, just like me, perhaps she doesn't enjoy being beaten up with a belt and restrained from moving by a much stronger individual against her consent?

Maybe she also thinks NO is a NO and paying for someone's time doesn't give automatic consent to all you want or do?

Maybe she gets questions about the bruises that still hurt? Maybe her roommate had to collect her in tears from the ground because she wasn't able to get up on her own? Maybe there was no communication issue ? As I said clearly "NO" when you asked and I screamed "NO" and "STOP" and yet you didn't care.

So please Ben find a nice submissive lady that will enjoy pain and beating and have a nice consensual session with her.

Thank you, Elis."

The gentlemen joined the conversation and, naturally, changed their opinions, emitting disdain towards Ben. There were many men here who would never behave like this towards a woman. Under the pressure of the conversation, Ben deleted his comments, but I kept the screenshots for this purpose. I wanted to show you how cruel people can be authentically. Jane pleasantly surprised me by staunchly defending me, even though she didn't have to. I would have never come across that conversation if she hadn't sent it to me herself. Still, she considered it essential for me to see how someone who had committed violence against me was seeking sympathy and understanding. The bruises have healed, but I still try to forget about Ben and many others. When you feel the need, for whatever reason, to pay for the company of others, please treat them with respect. You might strongly believe that these individuals are not human, but they are. They are sensitive and try to live their lives, and you will never know how they ended up in such a position. They feel pain, both physically and mentally, and perhaps despite the big smile on their face, these people can suffer much more than you can imagine. Please be kind! I have experienced disrespectful behaviour often, just like most of us. Once, at a hotel in Clonmel, I met with a man who didn't even bother to pretend to be respectful. With a fake smile of the highest quality, I opened the door and in walked yet another man that day. He seemed unsure but had a repulsive soul. He was a slimy one with glasses. As soon as I closed the door, he grabbed my crotch with one hand, and I felt the other on my buttocks. As soon as I managed to push him away, he made a series of demands, starting with the phrase "You sexy bitch."

I wouldn't say I liked this address; it was impolite and disrespectful. Among his demands was primarily licking the anal opening and testicles, where according to him, I could expect a half-meter jungle that I couldn't even cut with the best quality brush cutter. I kicked the man out; it wasn't just about his demands, but he had no respect, and there was nothing to negotiate about. I didn't like clients like him, and many came to me. They had an idea I couldn't fulfil; they made me feel contemptuous, and without a single blink, they considered me a thing, not a human being. However, it happened in Clonmel more often than I imagined. Despite not liking Clonmel, it brought me my personal miracle. Clonmel wasn't ugly, but the people here were depressed and pessimistic. I don't know why, but when I arrived here, I felt like I had come to a city of apocalypse survivors. Anxious people walked the streets, resembling lifeless bodies. I had been here several times, and most of the time, I got a really ugly room where I didn't feel comfortable. The view from the window was of a garden with caravans and a noisy group of local residents. I met many clients here, and I would love not to have met the vast majority of them. This place was like a mysterious, forgotten part of the world, the only city that appears in every horror movie. It felt a bit like I was back in Letterkenny. Despite the atmosphere in Clonmel, bad things happened not only here; for example, Athlone was much worse in terms of experiences. However, one experience couldn't be surpassed by anything in the world.

Chapter Eleven: Friend from Heaven

Have you ever experienced a state known as sleep paralysis? Those who have know it's one of the worst experiences that can happen to you during sleep, while those who haven't can't even imagine how terrifying it is. In the silent darkness of the night, as consciousness dives into the realm of dreams, some people find themselves trapped by strange forces. Their bodies are paralysed, but their minds are awake, trapped between two worlds. Sleep paralysis envelops them like a shadow creeping over a drowsy landscape. Time seems to slow down at that moment, and space contracts into an infinite claustrophobic refuge. Power pulses through the air, leaving behind a trail of elusive fear and despair. It's like a dance with a ghost, where one alternately fights for freedom while drowning in the chaos of infinite consciousness. This state usually lasts only a few seconds but feels like hours. It happened to me twice in the same room in the same city, and I wouldn't wish it on anyone. I lay in bed, feeling as though I had woken up with the sense that something was watching me. A dark, indiscernible figure swiftly approached my bed from around the corner with a desire to torture and instil fear. It came with the sole intent of harming me. You feel the pervasive evil surrounding you, unable to move. Lying powerless in bed, imprisoned in your physical restraints and seemingly awakened into a nightmare. Paralysed, I tried to scream, but I couldn't utter a word. I knew I was in some mysterious sleep process, but everything happening around me seemed too real. You try to convince your brain to let you move, to escape the clutches of the beast before it suffocates you. Your body is your greatest adversary, while your soul struggles for survival. It's as if your body is against you, and you're fighting a battle within yourself until you finally succeed, and all the dark shadows disappear. I sat on the bed, sweaty, exhausted, and in shock, and subsequently spent days researching information about demonic sleep and the so-called sleep paralysis. Sleep paralysis can be a consequence of long-term stress, so the ghosts I encountered during the day haunted me at night as well. One day, a man appeared in my room whom I had no idea would be significant to me. Don't worry, I didn't fall in love with a client again, although maybe differently I did, but not as the man I imagined marrying and having children with. I fell in love with a friend whom I wanted by my side for the rest of my life.

This unusual beginning of our friendship means a lot to me. It's like the sun that illuminates my path and warms my heart. A vital element of all our lives, it strengthens us and gives us the strength to move forward. Like water for life, friendship fills our souls and provides us with comfort and support in difficult times. It's a source of joy and trust that gives us energy and inspiration for everyday challenges. Sometimes, you can't explain what you see in a person. It's just how they take you to a place where no one else can. Bernard, whom I met that day, was all this and maybe even more to me. How did such a friendship begin? Probably from our first meeting. I met him after my sleepless nights full of disturbing demons at the beginning of 2023. He came into the room, guy in his fourties', nervous but smiling. It was clear he didn't have much experience with this type of company. He nervously tried to converse and complimented my scary and ugly room. I smiled and said, "I don't like this room; I don't feel good here." That caught his attention, and with a simple question, "Why not?" we started our friendship. I was honest, and he might have even thought I was crazy, but I started telling him about my experiences from previous nights. His questions showed genuine interest, and we could discuss them for hours. He also shared stories with me about strange spirit powers in his house and how he feels in their presence. Someone who doesn't believe in such things would consider us paranoid lunatics and would laugh at our conversation, but that day, I met someone who was just as "broken" as I was. Bernard was going through a divorce at the time of our meeting, and although he liked to say it was the best thing that ever happened to him, it was clear that it was one of the most difficult chapters of his life. You know how sometimes in life things unexpectedly turn upside down, and I'm not talking about a positive pregnancy test after a night spent with an attractive stranger, but wonderful things that eventually look like a puzzle taking shape, and you feel like it was meant to be from the beginning? That's exactly how I feel when I reflect on our meeting. Two lost souls traversing through painful experiences. Bernard confided in me about everything that troubled him; I became a therapist and patiently listened to him. As he later admitted, he didn't plan for another meeting with me.

Not because he didn't feel comfortable in my presence but because his life was changing, and he came to me for the same reason as most other men: he felt lonely. He never wanted to meet me again, yet we met again. The likelihood of him knowing when I would be in the zombie city again was minimal, yet a few weeks later, I returned, and he appeared at my door. "You wouldn't believe what happened to me. I wasn't looking for a company, but when I opened my internet browser to search for something, your profile showed up, and I saw you were back in town. It's like a sign I wanted to see you again." "Sure, I'll believe that it's a sign; any guy could take meeting a prostitute as a sign."

I thought to myself. I didn't say it out loud; it wouldn't have been appropriate, but we returned to that conversation several times, and with distance, his words made sense. I still think it was more of a search history than a sign, but I'm glad it happened. He spent two hours with me, and every single day of my stay, he kept coming back to visit me over and over again. I usually felt uncomfortable seeing someone so often, but I could talk for three days straight with him, and it seemed like we would never run out of conversation topics. Of course, we were doing other things too, but the conversations in the hotel rooms are all I remember with him. On the last day of my stay, he wrote his email address on paper for me to contact him when I was nearby, saying he would love to see me again. I still have that piece of paper hidden away, just like many others he gave me. We started seeing each other much more often, but I still didn't trust him. He was grouped with the people with penises whom I had stopped trusting long time ago. He was a nice client with whom I connected and enjoyed pleasant conversations. It took me several months to give him my phone number; I didn't want to share it with any jerk, and here, I could never be sure what kind of person someone was. I remember when I was visited in Clonmel, by another client. He was a tall farmer with a few extra pounds, and he scared me. He told me how he finds out when I'm flying home, that he gets into the system, finds out my name, phone number, where I live, and similar information. He said it nicely, but it still sounded slimy and scary. Then he wanted to ask me to marry him, which many others had done before him, but he was extra weird. I definitely wouldn't give my phone number to such a weirdo.

Bernard was indeed nicely unique in the best way you can imagine. So, after a while, I started to trust him and let him get closer to me. We talked about the future, about what we want from life, about spirituality, about family, about my "job," basically about everything that came to mind. I never felt that there was a topic that would be foreign to both of us. There's nothing quite like finding a friend with the same mental disorder. Bernard somewhat pursued me, driving to cities distant from him to see me. I could call him in the middle of the night because of a bad dream; he listened to me and always tried to dissect my problem into details and find the cause and relief. He wasn't like most men who would give you unsolicited advice. It was and is pleasant to have such a friend, and at this stage, I can't imagine life without him. However, when it came to the physical things, it was like with every other client, I just wanted to have it done. The more closer we were getting, the more difficult it was for me to keep separated our friendship and my "job". While we were talking, he was a friend and when we got naked, he was a client. Almost like a friendship with benefits! He never hurt me physically or done anything that would be painful, but it was still something I didn't like. The worst part was when he asked me a several time to tell him my surname while we were in the "foreplay part". He knew my real name already, he just loved the way how it sounds, which normally would be a compliment, but not there. I was supposed to pronounced the name I got from my dad out loud, while someone was about to have a sex with me. It was hard to keep it separated in my head as I was bringing something from my personal life into the ugly world I hated. He never meant it in a bad way, Bernard didn't even know I disliked that. Except for this, he was always there for me, doing lovely things. When I was in Ireland if it was even remotely possible for him, he would take me from hotel to hotel, and I fondly remember those trips. I liked his car; it was an old car, but I found something fascinating about it: the sunroof. Playing with the opening button amused me and awakened my inner child. Yeah, sunroofs, they work like a charm on women! On our trips, we mostly stopped somewhere to eat while I texted the operator that the bus was delayed so I could have more time. He was like a wifi signal in a cottage in the middle of the wood, rare and invaluable. Many times, we touched on the topic of how I ended up doing this "job" and why I didn't leave. I'm a very straightforward person, and there was no reason to lie to him; I told him almost everything about myself without ever expecting more from him than our friendship. I was again in Clonmel, and this time, I got a much better room, which I enjoyed. I didn't even know they had such rooms here; they must reserve the nicer rooms for better guests, not ruffians! Anyway, somewhere, there must have been a glitch in the system, and I ended up in this almost luxurious place that smelled of renovation. Bernard stopped by again for three hours, and we talked a lot. He waited downstairs at the bar because I'm a proper woman and everything takes me ages, especially to get ready. He had time to jot down something interesting on a hotel napkin. What he told me took my breath away; he wanted to know the amount I needed to have to be able to return to my daughter and pay for everything I needed. However, like a proper devil, he had his conditions too. The first was that if he gave me such an amount, I never return to this "job" again, and the second condition was that I help at least two women get out of the world of prostitution or, even better, convince them never to go down that path. Bernard had one fantastic quality; he never promised anything he couldn't fulfil and rarely promised things. I had to fill out the napkin with the needed amount, agree to the conditions, and sign it with a drop of my blood. No, just kidding, no blood was needed. He also emphasised that it wasn't a promise and I shouldn't count on anything. The napkin is, of course, still among my collection of souvenirs. I didn't want to count on anything; I didn't want to rely on anyone, and even though we spent a lot of time together, at that time, I wasn't completely sure about his presence.

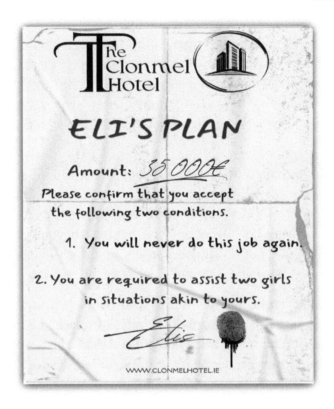

The path to my heart is thorny; it took Victoria two years before I started to trust her. Don't get me wrong; people just gave me a lot of false promises, and life has dealt me a great deal of blows. Even my clients, there was a guy from Dublin I was honest with while I was with Mr. D, he was supposed to help me find an apartment as he offered. He gave me lots of lies and was showing me fake places, but despite his promises I never had any place to live there. I've learned that sometimes, the person you open up to hurts you the most by taking advantage of your vulnerability. I didn't want to keep my distance, but I kept it. It seemed like I couldn't handle another disappointment. If I were to rely on his suggestions of money, I wouldn't just rely on that amount, but it would be a new game with my life. A new torn piece of my soul, a new desire to see my daughter and materialise the idea of us being together forever. I couldn't allow something like that to happen! I enjoy looking at that piece of paper; it looks like a funny contract on a hotel napkin.

I didn't take his words seriously; I told myself it was just curiosity, so I wrote down the amount I needed to leave. I added up my debts, something for renovation at my mom's so I could stay there temporarily, and some extra funds to reach my goals. For some people, this kind of amount is something they could immediately send away, and they wouldn't miss it, but for me, it was an amount that would turn my life upside down.

At the same time, it was too high a sum for me and my friend. I took the napkin as a provocative game, and we both laughed about it and changed the subject. However, Bernard talked about it very often, and I began to get distanced. "Why are you talking about it? I don't want anything from you, nor do I expect anything. I don't intend to cling to any false hopes; this is my life, not something you can play with."

I begged several times for him not to mention it anymore, and I occasionally glanced at the napkin. Finally, we reached a phase where he mentioned it minimally, and I appreciated that. There was no reason to play with my life, my feelings, or my maternal instinct. One day, I travelled to Athlone, where I was supposed to meet another girl. Although I strongly protested, it was of no use. "Alla only does massages, she's very nice, and she's no competition for you. You'll just be together, and that's it!"

Jane snapped at me. I was afraid that a girl who only did massages would judge me, but I was wrong. It was the year 2023, which was a year of new encounters for me. At the apartment in Athlone, on Jane's orders, I met yet another kindred spirit.

ALLA

Dear God. I beg of you. please spare me from any further suffering.

DESPITE THE BIG, BEAUTIFUL SMILE, THERE WAS AN IMMENSE AMOUNT OF PAIN HIDDEN BEHIND IT!

Remember the girl who picked me up from the floor at the Tallagh apartment? That was her. Alla was one of the most beautiful beings I had ever met. She was a beautiful woman inside and out. Her heart overflowed with love, gently mingling with the pain she carried within herself. With a massive smile on her face, joy in small things, and so much tenderness and understanding in her heart that I couldn't understand where her warmth came from. She provided erotic massages and never agreed to sexual services; I must say I admired her business skills. Most of us tried to be as lovely as possible, even to the biggest and clumsiest jerks you can imagine, but not Alla. She knew why she was doing it and for what reason she was there, which she made very clear to her clients. I laughed countless times when I heard her enticing them. I would liken it to the singing of beautiful jellyfish that mesmerises you with delightful tones until you find yourself in their

270

death embrace. In this case, Alla was fascinating by words and deceived by her body until all the money from the local playboys ended up in her pocket. She told me how it works for her and that she didn't care if clients didn't come back to her. The agency didn't like her because it was clear from what she officially earned that she didn't have many clients, but they had no idea how much that girl was earning on the side. I must admit I was a little jealous; my personality didn't allow me to do something like that, and many girls who provided similar services could learn from her. She was sharing with me how it works when she is alone with the client in her room: "Sweetie, if you pay fifty euros more, you can touch my beautiful body," she said to me with a smile on her face while she was pointing to the unsightly bulge on her stomach. Few of us are lucky enough not to be proud owners of our own tyres when we sit down. But it didn't detract from Alla's beauty!

"Touching my body obviously means that they can only touch certain parts, which they find out only after paying. I would never let them touch my vagina; who knows where those fingers have been!"

She had many other offers that horny men gladly paid for; she even invented beautifully sounding words for nonexistent services. Some might say it's a scam, but I would disagree with that claim. They paid for touching her body, but they didn't ask about the parts they could touch. They paid extra for her to undress for a massage, but no one specified that she had to undress more than her top. With extra charges, she could earn more in a day than I could in two hectic days. It was nothing more manageable for her than fooling men who think with their penises; it was just too easy, and she was simply good at it. She didn't work hard, but smartly. She couldn't do it any other way; she found this "work" difficult. Until I met her, I thought it was just me who couldn't cope with the mental struggles of this "career," but Alla showed me that her ability of handling these troubles was even worse than mine. She was very emotional, and when we met, she suffered from depression. Other girls didn't want to be with her because they felt she was too fearful and weak. I must admit that being her support was sometimes a challenge, but I gladly supported her despite the emotional toll it took on me. She was just over thirty, a single mother who thought of her son with every step she took. She was at the end of her rope, yet she fought,

fought for him. She wanted everything in the world for him and hoped that one day she would achieve the impossible and be constantly with her little prince, who made her so happy. So many sleepless nights she had, the pain she carried within herself, and the life she so hated. Despite all the burdens every day, she got up with a smile even I saw on her face that she had cried all night. Alla reminded me of what is essential in life and how we should appreciate the little things every day; we supported each other, and from the short three days we were supposed to have together, it turned into fourteen days. We said goodbye for a while; she went home, where she was happy with her little one, and then we met again. Once, when she left, devastating news came: her ex-husband died in the war in Ukraine. It deeply affected her, even though they were no longer together; they had a beautiful relationship. Alla was devastated, and with a heavy heart, she returned to Ireland after the funeral. I tried to support her a lot, but the truth is that at such moments, you don't know what to say, and every word seems insufficient. From my own experience, I know that nothing and no one can stop the pain you feel; it drains you alive, and you don't know how to face it. She felt so lost; the last place she wanted to be was Ireland, and yet she decided to face her fears and pain and came to secure herself and her son. She was never a girl who would invest her money in material things; she wouldn't spend a penny on herself, didn't care about nice clothes, brands or luxury handbags. She would sacrifice her life for her family. We are very similar in values we both have, so we were naturally drawn to each other. I had a very pronounced opinion about Ukrainians. Even before the war, I met them in the Czech Republic; no one liked them. Many of them travelled to Czechia for work, but most of them were societal waste alcoholics with minimal adaptability. Alla showed me that not everyone is the same, and she surprised me every day. She told me about their country's history, culture, and customs. It was admirable how her heart belonged to her homeland. I personally love the Czech Republic, but I couldn't write poetry about it. Nature and customs have always been remarkable to me, but I couldn't stand most of our inhabitants. I didn't want to be associated with that group of locals who just complained, hated their lives, their government, and solved all their problems with beer in the pub instead of facing them—adverse, depressive energy suckers who wore socks with sandals and carried sandwiches and pâté everywhere.

Limited racists despised other cultural customs, and every person with darker skin was automatically considered gypsy. Damn, I met some weird people. Honestly, we're not all like that, but this is the worst part of the Czech population: those perpetually complaining, dissatisfied, but proud individuals. Every country has such a bunch of weirdos, even Ukraine, of which Alla was aware. Anyway, this girl had a huge influence on me. Despite the disasters surrounding my life, I never lost faith in God, but going to church left me. She reminded me of how to open my soul to God again and go to such a peaceful place as a church. We went there together every morning, which helped me a lot mentally; I cried through most of my prayers, but it calmed me down. It is like a good therapy session! Everything suddenly became more bearable and it was an excellent way to start the day. It sounds pathetic: going to church in the morning, praying, and then spreading your legs for money, but with this approach, spreading my legs was a bit easier. You can call me crazy, but I'm grateful to her for helping me find a place for faith again, and my life began to change. The kind girl remained in my life, and we travelled together from apartment to apartment and hotel to hotel. I took her to Nenagh, not that it was a particularly captivating place, but I liked that hotel. The beautiful illuminated terrace in front of the hotel, where we drank tea together in the evening and talked about life. It had its charm, which Alla also appreciated. Bernard visited me in this place several times; we even had lunch together here, and I must admit that these two people made my life struggles much more enjoyable, and I, in turn, was there for them. Days passed, and travelling seemed much less challenging when I had my new girl-friend by my side. Everything seemed much less demanding and manageable. Bernard visited me at the apartment in Athlone and announced that he had a surprise for me. I had no idea what "surprise" meant; it could be anything. His sense of humour always fascinated me, and I could never be sure if he meant something seriously or was joking. During our usual conversation, he said, "I have a surprise in my trousers." Eww, a surprise should be positive; a hitchhiking penis is not a surprise; it's disgusting! I smiled suspiciously while he reached down there. Of course, I mean, he reached into his pocket. What did you think? He pulled out his phone and started searching for something on it, and I had no idea what was happening. "Elis, look, or I'll show you," he said, turning his phone display towards me with a proud expression. "I sold something I didn't need, and I hope it will pleasantly surprise you."

Twenty thousand euros were shining at me from the screen, it was the balance in a certain bank account. "Nice," I thought to myself, and I was genuinely grateful that Bernard managed to sell what he didn't need, and judging by the amount, I concluded that it was a successful sale. I was so proud of him, and it made me happy. "That's money for you, silly one. I know it's not as much as you needed, but hopefully, it can help you pay for what you need and go to your daughter," he said. I was in shock, unable to think; tears welled in my eyes, streaming down my face. The thought of being with my little one meant more than anyone could imagine. I couldn't believe it, and I honestly hesitated to believe him. Why would someone do this? Why would someone help me? I've met so many people, and no one lifted a finger for me. Is it even real? When the money appeared in my account, I didn't know what to do; it made my head spin. I could be at home, hugging my daughter, being free and having a life. Bernard was like an angel sent from heaven, giving me much more than a financial gift; he gave back my freedom and faith in people. Well, maybe not faith in all the people, but in some of them. Thanks to him, I am where I am, and thanks to him, I am who I am. I wanted to leave; I worked so hard on it, saved every euro, worked hard, and let myself be hurt and abused, and yet achieving such an amount seemed almost impossible. Maybe I would have left long ago if I hadn't met Mr. D, but I believe everything happens for a reason. Alla, Bernard, God, it was all like a miracle, and now this. This guy must have been crazy ever to decide to help me, but I never considered myself worthy of such a miracle. Someone cared about me; someone decided to give me a chance and support me regardless of who I was, what I did, where I came from, or how I lived. I used the money to pay off most of my debts and saved some for renovation in my mom's house as I was about to move there. The only beautiful room in that house was my daughter's room, and I needed to feel good there, too. Despite living with my mom being only a temporary thing, I needed at least a little comfort. I stayed in Ireland a little longer to save money for my new life. Meanwhile, Bernard and Alla were and still are a great support and good friends to me. I introduced Alla and Bernard, and it was only natural to share with her what had happened to me. She didn't envy or have any negative feelings. Tears of happiness flowed for me; she hugged me with a huge smile and was ecstatic. She wanted me to be with my daughter and had great understanding. My decision to leave and never return was also an inspiration for her. She left Ireland a few days before me and has not returned. I pray it stays that way forever. Every woman should have the right to be with her children her family, free, and happy. I also stayed in touch with Victoria, and although I didn't share the whole story with her, she was glad I was leaving. She left this "business" months ago. She opened a small restaurant with her partner, but when he found out how she earned money, he left her and fired her. Unfortunately, lying doesn't pay off, and she was at rock bottom, disappointed, and she returned to the oldest profession several times.

Eventually, he forgave her, and they are back together; the raven-haired dragon no longer sell her body, and I hope she never will again. I'm glad for every girl who gets out of this industry. I don't want to sound selfish, but I'm most grateful that someone helped me escape. A few days before my escape, I met a client at a hotel in Stillorgan who worked at the local hospital. He was a very kind, although nervous, gentleman. It was his first time paying for sex, and I was kind and sweet, which probably caught his attention. The next day, he brought me a gift; he gave me a new iPad and cash. I didn't understand why he did something like that, but with everything happening around me, it seemed like another little miracle. I left the iPad wrapped and gave it to my daughter for Christmas. She often sees me painting and drawing on mine, and now we can draw together. It was a very nice gesture, and besides the suspicious proposals of marriage without rings, I didn't receive many gifts. Once, I received leggings from a Chinese man to wear when we had sex together. Victoria and I once received perfume from a kind man, and once a client forgot smelly socks in my bathroom, which is not a gift you long for. My last days in Ireland were filled with excitement and fear. I saved as much as I could and feared something might happen.

Every day, there were more cases of someone robbing girls. In Mullingar and other cities, it even happened that the police robbed girls. They booked themselves as clients, arrived in a company car, confiscated their money and phones "as evidence," and left. So, the girls weren't just targeted by angry criminals but also by law enforcement officers. The biggest fear paralysed me in the apartment in Tallagh. Yes, in that apartment where I last met Mr. Ben. I spent the last few days there alone. Alla escaped to live her free life, and I experienced mixed feelings of panic and fear. I shared my feelings with Bernard, and he watched over me from afar, which was charming and nice. Jane was my operator, and of course, I confided in her. She behaved absolutely humanly, which I wouldn't have expected from such a harpy. She only sent me clients who had been with me in the past. One client even came from Belfast by train to say goodbye. He was a very nice man and reminded me a bit of Bernard. He always paid for an hour, but we had such a good conversation that he stayed a little longer. My last days of personal hell were coming to an end, and I don't think I believed that it was actually happening. I had been waiting for it for so long, and now it was finally here. I packed my things, left condoms, tissues, and all other aid someone might need in the drawer, and that evening, I fell asleep as a free woman. Bernard picked me up in the morning, we went to breakfast together, and then he was supposed to take me to the bus stop to get to my brother's house. I was supposed to spend my last days in Ireland with Oliver and then leave the country. After a wonderful breakfast, Bernard took me to Oliver's place, not wanting to let me go. We stopped at a gas station, and I found many things no one needed. It was the first time I bought a man a bouquet of freshly cut flowers. I'm incredibly original, so I also bought crystals, which Bernard trusted and a lot of chocolate. It's amazing what you can get from an Irish gas station. I'll never be able to repay him enough for what he did for me, but it was just a small gift to show him my gratitude. When he drove me to my brother's house, we talked in the car, mainly about the future of both of us and about the past. We were memorising everything we went through together and we both loved to remember especially one story: A few months ago when he collected me from Ennis hotel and was taking me to a different place to stay, we stopped in Ennis town on our way. I took him to the local church, where I was praying and after that

276

we went for a lovely breakfast. In the town we met a homeless man, I considered he was a Muslim. That guy was hungry and we could sense he really needed some help. I was listening to my intuition and got him food. I went to three different shops, to get him fruit, vegetable and sandwich. I made sure the sandwich had no pork in it. When we brought the food to the fella, he was grateful and happy. It made me happy he appreciated the help and my gut feeling was correct. Bernard always admires how I made sure he didn't get anything with pork in it. We also had some different experiences, for example visiting the Rock of Cashel together, which is incredibly beautiful place and you can feel the history everywhere. It was too hard to say goodbye. We both knew it was "See you," not "Goodbye."

After a few wonderful days spent with my brother, walking on the beach, having BBQs, and one visit to the hospital because that idiot stepped on a jellyfish, it was time to go home. I informed my mom about my arrival but made her swear not to tell to my daughter. I wanted it to be a surprise, and it worked. After my arrival, I set up toys behind the door, one of which was from Alla, who decided that she had to buy something for my little one. I called my princess and asked her if the package had arrived while I was hiding behind the corner of the house. After she found one toy in front of the main door, I quickly set up another surprise, and in the end, she found me standing there with the phone in my hand. She looked at me incredulously, cried, and hugged me as if she wanted to crush my ribs, which I might deserve. It was amazing to hold her again finally; I trembled with happiness. The whole world ceased to exist, and there were just her and me. I can't tell my family the truth. I know that in their eyes, I'll always be the one who abandoned her daughter, but in my little angel's eyes, I'm the one who loves her unconditionally, the one who returned, and in her eyes, I'm a damn proud mom who would go through hell for her child and would even dethrone Lucifer himself if necessary just to be with her

The soul thrives on freedom,
just like the body thrives on oxygen...

Almost immediately after my arrival, we started with the reconstruction. My mom is a tough woman and taught me how to plaster, lay floors, install a toilet, and many other things. So, if I ever decide to become a labourer, I already know the basics. I don't want to brag, but my workmanship is comparable to any professional trade person. So far, the ceiling hasn't collapsed on me, so I'd call it a success. Sometimes, the past still haunts me; the sound of my mom's mobile phone alert reminds me of the hotel phone ringing when they called me from the reception. I'm scared, and I'm terrible at building relationships with men with whom I don't put too much trust after all this. However, I wake up daily with a smile, grateful for every new day of freedom. I walk with my dog in the forest daily, where I read. I have my child every day next to me and misbehaves as much as she can. I'm working on my future and drawing energy from my family, whom drive me crazy sometimes, and from nature. Bernard and I call each other almost every day, and our friendship grows stronger daily. We can spend hours on the phone together and still have plenty to discuss. Sometimes, I feel like if someone were listening to us, we'd both end up in a mental hospital. Compared to his crazy ideas and sense of humour, I look normal, and that's what I adore about him. Alla and I support each other, and we're glad we have each other. It's exceptional to have friends you can rely on in any life situation, and I feel blessed. Life would be incredibly dull without such people around me. These two humans were some of the best things I never planned. We have a connection that can't be explained, and they helped me change everything. I carry with me demons that I still fight, but I'm not alone in this, and I'm free. It's an incredible feeling when your prayers are answered. I'm sad that now that I'm back home, my dad isn't here. He used to wake me up in the middle of the night to go to the garden and watch fireflies and bats, so sometimes I wake up alone and watch the creatures of the night while hoping he's there with me. I'm a girl from a mountain town. I grew up surrounded by nature, which makes me happy on my journey through life. It always gave me the strength to keep going and charged me with energy. I love sitting in my favourite café and admiring the view of the majestic mountains. It would take your breath away. I can't imagine being in a more beautiful place because this piece of land, made by God with love and care, I proudly call my home. Lately, I haven't been going to church as often as I used to, and I know it's not good, but I know God is with me. I could sit and blame him for everything that happened to me, be bitter and angry. I have chosen to be grateful for the tough lesson I was subjected to; it gave me a lot and took a lot from me. In all that pain, I found my strength, and now, being able to sit on a bench in front of the church, sipping coffee and watching my little one play in the park is one of the most beautiful things I could wish for. I still remember the days when I prayed for everything I have now, and finally, I can say that I am thrilled! I have reached a point in my life where I have finally found myself. I am content with myself and work on my personal development every day despite all the adversity I have been through. I rejoice in the little things, love life, ignore the slowly forming spiderwebs in my crotch, and disregard men! Simply put, I focus only on the good and positive, and you should do the same. It's the gateway to happiness!

"And if you're curious about how things turned out for the characters in this book, they all lived happily ever after!' Well, just kidding — this is based on a true story, so the rest of their lives was a real rollercoaster ride!"

Printed in Poland
by Amazon Fulfillment
Poland Sp. z o.o., Wrocław

39158351R10168